snapped!

A MEMOIR

DEBORAH VINES

snapped! © 2019 Deborah Vines

www.deborahvines.net

Events and conversations were created from the best of my memory. In order to protect individuals' privacy, I have changed the names of people as well as some identifying characteristics and details such as physical properties, occupations, and places of residence. Please also bear in mind that parts of the manuscript are rather risqué.

debvines@gmail.com

dav4ny@optonline.net

First edition 2019

Interior and Cover Design © 2019 by Maya Román

www.vitawoolfbooks.com

ISBN 978-1-0906-3437-5

This book is dedicated to the amazing baristas in Starbucks who kept me sated, sane, and fueled with lattes during the thousands of hours I spent laughing/crying/angsting as I poured my heart out in words.

CONTENTS

snapped!

PART I—THE REACQUAINTANCE

SPANKED—BY "PEOPLE YOU MAY KNOW"

I shook my head and looked up at my husband, feeling a little less than thrilled with how things were progressing in my creative life. "Well...another day, another doughnut."

Andy plopped a bowl down on my desk. "Here. Have some oatmeal, instead."

"Thanks, hon," I said, feeling grateful that my life partner was not only a nurturing soul, but one of my greatest advocates. I also appreciated his sense of humor, despite his penchant for punning (badly).

My husband petted my cat, Mamie, who was lying comatose next to my computer, and wandered off to his home office down the hall for an early AM conference call with his staff.

I checked the weather and the news online, then scanned through my email, hoping against hope that one incoming message would change the course of my life—or at least shake things up a bit. It would go something like this:

THEM: *We LOVED your play (we are SALIVATING!) and want to fast-track it to Broadway. Would you be available next week to meet with our creative team?*

ME: *I'm already on the train!*

(If only.) Along with the usual e-notes from friends, work-related updates, and solicitations from left-leaning groups and "green" non-profits, all that showed up was a request to connect with another writer/editor on a well-known professional online networking site. Figuring I should stay open to opportunity, reminding myself of the adage that "you never know," I hit the *accept* button, which routed me to a roster of more potential connections. Second row down, under the heading *People You May Know*, I spotted a familiar name (sans photograph) and clicked on the link that brought me to the man's home page. Once there, I scrolled through the bio and quickly realized this was the same Carl Franks I met in Los Angeles years ago. But ours wasn't a business relationship—not in the remotest sense. Carl was the first man who ever spanked me (recreationally).

After I fired off a note to say hello, I got a response back within the hour.

CARL: *It's so good to hear from you! What's new? I guess you saw I'm in Syracuse, where I'm exec creative director for this ad agency. I was in Colorado for three years after LA and then Pittsburgh pretty much doing the same thing. Looking forward to catching up. By the way, the email address below is the best way to communicate with me.*

His user name, ALap4OTKS, told me it was not his work email, since OTKS is an acronym for "over-the-knee spankings." It also told me that he was still very much into the game of "disciplining" consenting women. (Rock on, Carl.)

JANUARY 25

CONTENTED WITH REHABS

After my husband and I came back from Starbucks where we downed our customary three-pumps, no-water, no-foam, extra-hot soy Chai lattes to jumpstart the day, I wrote Carl back and encapsulated the past several years as best as I could—including that Andy and I were in the process of rehabbing our newly purchased summer home, a 180-year-old Victorian in Vermont. Fixing up old houses, I told him, had become our hobby, as well as part of our retirement strategy when we bought our year-round place in New York after my novelist friend, Angie, suggested we all settle around Piermont, a village in the Hudson River Valley that's home to a number of artists and entertainment professionals. (Angie never moved here).

Andy found the 3,100-square-foot NY house in the late 1990s when

I was on one of my treks out to Los Angeles to record a demo CD for the musical I'd written. By that time, I explained to Carl, I was ready to leave eastern Connecticut to get closer to NYC and the theater and film scene. The town Andrew and I were living in also felt way too incestuous, with everyone knowing everyone else's business (not that I had anything to hide—at least not at that point).

ME: *Thankfully, my husband was more than willing to pack up and go, since he too still has a bit of the wanderlust in him, and he's pretty accommodating, But he also likes to work with his hands. You know, get down and dirty. Believe it or not, I've become an expert at tearing down and putting up walls and sanding and installing hardwood flooring. (Put a sledge hammer or a nail gun in my hands and I'm ready to rally!) We still have a lot of work to do on this one, and we've just started on the place up north. Gluttons for punishment, I guess:) But I have to say, it's fun and quite rewarding as the results are pretty immediate.*

CARL: *You guys are apparently doing very well. I'm happy for you.*

He also wanted to know how I ended up back east.

ME: *I came out to showcase my musical. It went really well, broke box office records at the 200-seat theater in town and was subsequently picked up by a local college as part of their Creative Arts Series. We had someone interested in investing in it, but...you're not going to believe this...the poor man died of a heart attack before anything could happen. I met Andy shortly after.*

CARL: *How long have you been with your husband? Any kids?*

ME: *No kids of my own. But I have a stepdaughter, Courtney, who's turned out to be a kid any mother could love (after some rocky years dealing with emotional and physical issues). Anyway, I've been with Andrew for 17 years, married for almost 14. I guess I could say I'm content.*

In addition, I told Carl that this was my first marriage and when I tied the knot I was in my forties. What I did not tell him was that when Andy and I met, I did not fall head over heels in love. I was still very much smitten with (translation: in lust with) my soon-to-be-divorced boyfriend of nine months who had recently dumped me over dinner. And even though I did not feel physically attracted to Andy and was well aware the chemistry was off, I gave in to his pursuits. Maybe it was because I felt a kinship with him; we both were from similar upper-middle-class backgrounds, had master's degrees, and shared many of the same interests, including writing, music, and theater. But perhaps what really solidified our bond was that he, too, was on the rebound, having split up with his wife after she'd taken off with one of their friends. In fact, when we started dating, Andy and I spent many nights commiserating, tears running down both of our cheeks, talking about relationships.

After about two months, my future husband asked me to move in with him. I agreed, in part because I was unsure of what I was going to do next in my life. I also did not want to go back to Los Angeles, as it never really felt like home to me, even after living there for sixteen years. I was also lonely as hell. But mainly, Andrew seemed to be a good man, and he had qualities that I felt were important at this stage of my life—qualities that were missing in some of my prior relationships: I could be 100% authentic with him, and he was emotionally available, unlike my ex-boyfriend. I thought this was a step in a much better, and smarter, direction. He also offered a sense of security, which I craved, since the life of an artist/writer is not always a stable one.

After I wrapped up the email with Carl, us both promising to stay in touch, I shut down my computer and went into Andrew's office to say hi.

"Hello, Debby Vines," my husband said, patting his thigh. I sat down on Andy's lap, put my arms around his neck, and gave him a loud, sloppy kiss on his face. "I love you, Andrew Shine," I said and stuck my forefinger in his ear, wiggling it around playfully. "That's for calling me 'Debby!'"

"Stop!" he said, squirming.

"Oh, come on. You know you love it," I said.

"Busted." My husband smiled, and I slid off his lap and went into the bathroom to shower. Before I was finished, he took my towel off its hook and placed it over the glass door within easy reach—just as he'd done for years.

FEBRUARY 2

SPANKING—IT'S IN YOUR DNA

My "new old friend" was now emailing me on a daily basis, anxious to know more about my life over the past decade and a half. I updated Carl on my professional endeavors, which involved writing and editing collateral for a high-tech firm, and gave him the lowdown on my creative projects, all of which seemed to have stalled midair. Carl empathized; he'd finished a novel, but it had not yet seen the light of day as it needed some significant rewrites.

He then asked me if I ever thought about spanking. I told him that I did sometimes, but only on those occasions when it was referenced in a movie or on TV.

CARL: *I think about it daily. I still visit sites and watch videos. There are tons of them out there now. When was the last time you got spanked?*

ME: *Wow. It's been a while.*

After he prodded me for the details, I somewhat reluctantly recounted my trip to LA twelve years ago and the scenario I played out with Darren, an active participant in "the scene" and current paramour of Brenda, my friend who originally introduced me to spanking—and to Carl.

ME: *Darren was fun, but he spanked really hard. I went home a bit marked.*

CARL: *Darren's notorious for that. Huge hands. What did you tell your husband after he saw your bottom? How did you get around that?*

ME: *I didn't get around it. Even though I told Andy what I'd done and was all hot to trot when I got back, he started thinking about it—you know, me lying across a man's lap, bottoms up, and got furious. I couldn't convince him it was just play and had nothing to do with sex. He didn't buy it, and I guess I can't blame him. So, I pretty much shut the door on it all. However, he later tried to do it himself, but he was too afraid of hurting me. He just couldn't do it.*

CARL: *That's because it's not in his genes. You either have the spanking gene or you don't. It doesn't sound like you do, either. Otherwise you would have found a way to continue. At least that's my opinion.*

On the way over to the train station to pick up my husband who had to go into his NYC office for his bi-monthly staff meeting, I couldn't help but wonder about that—whether or not I did have that gene—which sent my mind racing back to my "first time." It was shortly before I met Andy, and I was heading out to Los Angeles to see friends and lick my emotional wounds after the painful breakup with my divorcing boyfriend.

Arriving at Brenda's house about an hour after picking up my rental car at LAX, I found myself greeted by someone I didn't quite recognize; my friend had obviously gone through some kind of metamorphosis. She was bristling with energy and dressed in a miniskirt, versus her usual long and flowing dresses. Her legs were also tanned and surprisingly toned. And she couldn't stop smiling.

"What the heck is going on with you?" I asked, as she led me to the dining room table. "Is it a guy? It has to be a guy."

"Sit," Brenda said as she poured us each a glass of wine.

"So, come on. Don't keep me in suspense, here. Are you in love?"

"No," she said. "Spanking. I've always had a fantasy, and I decided to do something about it."

"Spanking? I don't get it." I remember feeling a bit naïve at that point.

"I am completely and totally on fire," she said.

"That's quite obvious. I mean, look at you!"

Brenda provided the details, explaining that she went on a search and discovered two LA-based organizations devoted entirely to the fine art of spanking and discipline.

"Two organizations?" I asked. "It's that popular?"

"Apparently." My friend then told me about her mentor. "Carl's well known in the scene for introducing women to spanking. He's great. You really should try it. It's a total rush, and I know he'd love meeting you."

"Uh, well, gee," was about all I could muster at that point.

Over the next few days, anxious to get me onboard, Brenda plied me with crudely printed black-and-white magazines that described in practical detail what happens to "naughty girls." One was called *Devoted to Discipline* and was touted as "the forum by and for adult spankers interested in REAL old-fashioned behavior modification." The publication contained articles and letters, fiction, and hand-drawn pictures as well as photographs.

The second magazine had pretty much the same material, except it was all female-to-female scenarios. In both, the people in the graphics doing the spanking were fully clothed, while the people being spanked were bare-bottomed, with skirts up, panties down. It appeared to me that it was pretty much all about role playing, which appealed to the actor in me. It also seemed rather innocuous—kind of fun, in fact.

Once I relented, Brenda called Carl and explained the situation: she had a visitor in town who wanted to have "an experience." They conferred, and we collectively settled on 3:00 PM the following day.

"Don't worry," my friend said. "I told him that you only want to be spanked. He won't do anything you don't want him to. Those are the rules."

I didn't think to ask what else this activity might entail.

"And he'll be gentle," Brenda said, reassuring me. "He always is with first timers."

About two hours prior to Carl's arrival, I began slugging down huge quantities of Pepto Bismol to soothe a nervous stomach and hopefully rid myself of the diarrhea that kicked in around noon. My heart was palpitating wildly, the adrenaline coursing through my body. I was dizzy with excitement; it felt similar to what I'd experience before I did a cold reading in acting class or when I was waiting to go on stage. It also felt a little bit like falling in love.

On the dot, Carl showed up. I liked him immediately. He had a pleasant face, gentle blue eyes, and floppy grayish-blonde hair. Some would have called him boyishly handsome; he also had a deep, resonant, authoritative voice.

After a polite "hello" and a little bit of chitchat, Carl took a straight-backed chair from Brenda's breakfast nook and placed it in middle of the living room. The drapes had been drawn shut to deflect nosy neighbors.

My mentor quickly launched into his role of disciplinarian.

"Come over here, young lady," he said pointing at me. "Now!"

With years of theatrical performances under my belt, I easily adopted the role of "the recalcitrant child" as Carl yanked me across his lap.

Brenda, who remained close by to watch over me, started to giggle as he hitched my ankle-length sundress up over my butt and pulled my panties down around my knees. The fun had begun, and my virginal backside was no more. Carl's spanks were firm and well-placed. His palm stung my bottom as he paddled me twenty times, making me count every smack.

He finally took a break and tenderly kneaded my bare, burning flesh. "You are a naughty girl, aren't you, Deborah?"

"No!" I said and swatted him on the leg, suddenly wanting more.

"Deborah, Deborah," Carl said, admonishing me. "You must learn to behave."

My mentor began spanking me again, and I kicked out my feet. Like the consummate disciplinarian, he immediately pinned them down with one of his legs. But it was my cursing that got me corner time, which I found I hated with a passion.

"Nose up against the wall and don't move," he said, as he zeroed in on Brenda, which took my friend completely by surprise, since she was not expecting to play. "Over my knee, miss." His voice was stern, commanding. Brenda squealed with delight as Carl took her by the arm and pulled her over his lap for a serious spanking. He delivered the goods, and I heard the snapping sound of palm meeting flesh. "No. No. No! It hurts!" Brenda's voice was now small and childlike as she fully embraced the part of the submissive ward.

I couldn't help but turn my head, my curiosity having gotten the better of me. Not a smart move, since Carl apparently had his eyes on me as well as Brenda's bare, well-shaped bottom. But it was a calculated one, and I was silently pleased that he'd noticed. Within moments, Brenda had her face in the corner, with her skirt up around her waist, her panties down around her ankles—a punishment that in theory was designed to humiliate and embarrass.

Suddenly, I was back over Carl's knee, and from that point on the focus remained on me and me alone. And oh boy, was I loving it: the simulated drama, the unmitigated attention.

At the end of the session, the three of us positioned ourselves on the couch, with me lying over Carl's lap, face down, my dress up around my waist. My mentor talked casually about his job in the advertising business, while Brenda applied ice to my bare bottom to ward off bruising—a common occurrence among people like me who have pale skin. And, although this tableau we'd created must have looked like a scene from some cheesy B movie starring three WASPy-looking people (who had lost their marbles), I felt cared for, and I felt exhilarated. I had also completely forgotten about my heartbreak and my ex-boyfriend back east. I was totally in the moment.

Once Carl had left, just thinking about what happened in my friend's living room got me extremely turned on, even though I had no sexual longings for the man who'd just spanked me.

"Same thing happens with me," Brenda said.

"How curious."

FEBRUARY 7

AN AWAKENING OF THE LOWER CHAKRA

Mid-afternoon, I got an email from Carl. It was the third one today and had a document attached.

CARL: *I think you'll enjoy this. It's a story written by a friend of mine. It's cool. Female-to-female. Also, you should set up an account with Yahoo so we can instant message as well.*

With eagerness, and a bit of trepidation, I did as he asked and provided him with my new user name. Pushing all else aside, I focused on the story, which was about a young, bratty English miss and her stern housekeeper who caught the girl out on the town, dressed like a tart, in her husband's absence. The woman took the girl in hand, dragged her home, and disciplined her for her misdeeds. The story was set in the Victorian era and could easily have taken place at Andy's and my summer home in Vermont.

By the end of the piece, the housekeeper had not only spanked the girl with a hand brush until her bottom was raw but had inserted a butt plug into the girl's bottom that she was ordered to keep in place overnight.

The story hit the spot—the spot right between my thighs. In fact, it felt like my lower chakra had suddenly been reawakened after years of being in the deep freeze. And this surprised me, since anal discipline had never been part of my repertoire, nor was it something I sought out or craved.

Putting these thoughts aside, I reported back to Carl via IM and told him I'd read the story.

CARL: *Did you masturbate when you read it?*

ME: *Shut up!*

HIM: *Watch your mouth...*

ME: *Okay, yes, I did.*

CARL: *How many times did you cum?*

ME: *Ugh. I hate that word.*

CARL: *Tell me.*

ME: *A few. Okay???!!!*

CARL: *Be careful with that attitude, miss.*

Something twisted in my gut when he reprimanded me—a quick shot of adrenaline, and I found myself feeling even more titillated and wishing Andy was around so I could jump his bones. And this was curious, indeed, since I usually had to force myself to indulge; that or I tried to avoid sex altogether, which only exacerbated Andy's physical and, as a result, emotional neediness. Our sex life was one of the few things my husband and I fought about, although I did my best to smooth things out, usually promising that we'd "have a romp next weekend" (which I'd try to push off until the weekend after the next, and so on). Although we adored each other and greatly enjoyed being together, we both suffered from my lack of sexual desire. He felt rejected, and I found myself missing the powerful chemistry I had with my ex-boyfriend. In truth, in the beginning of our relationship, after Andy and I would make love, I'd sometimes go into the bathroom and silently weep in mourning.

"Wow," I said aloud, thinking that I might have stumbled upon the magic elixir that would enable me to give Andy more of what he wanted while finding some satisfaction myself.

FEBRUARY 8

ACROSS THE POND—BACK INTO THE DEEP

"Hi, hon," I said into the phone. "How's everything in London?" Andrew, who was a marketing exec for the same company I freelanced for, told me he was crazy busy, running from one meeting to the next. He also made it very clear he missed me.

"I miss you, too," I said. "Hurry home!"

I heard the plink of an incoming instant message and looked up at my computer screen.

CARL: *Are you there Deborah?*

ME: *Yes.*

CARL: *Where's my story you promised to write? You owe me one.*

"Andy, call me when you can," I said into the phone. "Love you." My husband said he'd ring me tomorrow, and I quickly diverted my attention to my IM and sent off a response.

ME: *Sorry. Got home late last night. Didn't have time.*

CARL: *Get to work, miss. Now. And I want it hot and steamy and fe-male-to-female.*

I didn't want to let him down and felt obligated to return a story that trumped Mrs. Livingstone. I pumped the piece out in about a half an hour:

You know what the '80s were like. It was a decade of sex, drugs, and bad disco music. It was also a time when men were fucking women like dogs and when men were also fucking men and women were fucking women. And I'm glad to say, I was part of the zeitgeist.

The third time I had sex with a woman did involve some anal play. Sissy, who I met at Fox Studios while working for a producer on a temp job, was planning on moving back to N.Y. She needed a place to stay for a month or two before making the transition, and we had an empty bedroom. At the time I was living with George, who scored music for a no-low-budget film-maker. Sissy had just come out of the closet and was very keen to experiment with another woman. And as usual, booze and cocaine were the precipitating factors for what happened this one particular night. After splitting half a gram of coke, we opened our second bottle of wine. We were alone in the house, since George was off doing some weird thing (he was a kinkster in his own right, but a lovely chap).

Once Sissy saw that I was sufficiently loosened up, she asked me to come into her bedroom. She said she wanted to show me something. I said, okay, thinking it was a book or something. It didn't even occur to me she had sex on her mind. She led me to her bedroom; then, once inside, she closed the door with a gentle push and locked it. Click. My stomach heaved.

She looked at me and asked, "Are you okay?"

"Uh, yes. I think I am," I replied.

I waited for her to say something, to do something. And she did. She started to pull my tee shirt off over my head. I let her. At that point I didn't care, and I liked the attention. And of course, being an adventurous soul, I decided to let things play out and see where it all went. She then asked me to take off my jeans.

"You're kidding," I said.

"No, I'm not." She had a half smile on her face, and I did as she'd requested.

"Okay. Panties next."

Once my undies were off, Sissy gave me a little shove and pushed me down onto the bed. I sat upright.

"Bra off, too," she said. Sissy quickly reached around me and undid the clasp. My breasts sprung free, and I was completely naked. I was pretty well potted by now, otherwise I'm not sure I would have been so willing. She stood there smiling. "I like what I see," she said. "Now, please, spread your legs."

I felt a warm rush between my thighs.

"Please," she asked again. "Spread your legs."

I did as I was told.

"I like your cunnie," she said. "It glistens. Now turn over."

My head was reeling; my body on high alert, my clit pulsating.

Once I was on my stomach, Sissy gave me a little smack on my bottom.

"Now, start masturbating," she said. "Slowly."

And I did. She then told me she had a surprise for me.

"Don't flinch," she said, "but keep touching yourself. Not fast, please, but slowly."

Again, I did as I was told. My face was turned toward the head of the bed. I could not see what she was doing, but I heard the snap of a rubber glove and then the plastic-sounding snick of a jar being opened. I knew it was Vaseline.

"Keep stimulating yourself," she said. "I am going to touch you now. Please trust me."

For whatever reason, I did. I then felt her hands on my bottom. She began to gently spread my cheeks. I started to masturbate faster.

"No!" she said. "Please, slowly. Like this."

She inserted a finger into my anus and began rotating it round and round, very slowly and lovingly, then in and out. "That's it. Good girl," Sissy said. "Easy does it."

I felt like I was ready to explode.

"Please, slow down," she said.

She rammed another finger in my bottom.

"You have a beautiful rosebud," she said. "A beautiful ass."

I arched my back. She slapped me hard; once on my right buttock and once on my left. For such a petite woman, she packed quite a wallop. I raised my butt up.

"You like that don't you?" she said.

I didn't answer.

She spanked my right cheek harder and then the left. "Answer me, please," she said.

"Yes. I like it."

"Good, then you'll like this even more." In two seconds flat, she had pulled out her fingers and inserted something long and cold into my butt.

"Oh my God!" I had to stifle a scream—a scream of pleasure. I felt both humiliated and excited beyond belief.

Sissy began pushing the object in and out slowly. "Keep masturbating, but to my rhythm," she said. She began fucking my ass faster and harder. "To my rhythm, damn it," she exclaimed.

I began to rub myself faster and harder as she increased her pace, the object pumping up and down, my hips gyrating in both pleasure and pain as my hungry ass swallowed up this foreign object. She spanked me once more, hard, on both cheeks. It was not her hand, this time. I think it was the back of a brush. I remember wondering, oddly enough, how in hell she was so adept at doing two things at once: fucking me in the ass and spanking me. As soon as that twenty-first (yes, I counted) slap landed on my bottom, I came like a monsoon.

After I caught my breath, she sat me up, touched me sweetly on my face and said, "Now it's my turn."

Carl IMd me within the hour.

CARL: *So damn hot. Thank you!*

ME: *I can't believe you made me do that! I can't believe you made me write that story!*

CARL: *I didn't make you do anything, Deborah.*

(He was right. He didn't.)

FEBRUARY 10

AGHAST, BUT ONLY FOR A MOMENT

I kissed my husband on the cheek after he climbed into the car.

"How was the flight?" I asked.

"Not too bad," Andy looked over at me. "You seem distracted."

"No. Not really," I said, telling a little white lie. "Do you have the energy to go out tonight? There's no food in the house."

"Sure."

After dinner in Piermont, during which Andy and I chatted casually about his trip and the repairs that needed to be made on the houses, I drove us home, as I always did. And as usual, I told him that I would get him back safely, since I tended to hold my liquor better than he.

My husband fell into bed by ten and was asleep within minutes, so I went over to my desk at the far end of the bedroom to check my email. As I was waiting for my computer to fire up, I listened to the sound of Andy's C-pap machine as he breathed rhythmically in and out. The device, I often said, helped save our marriage, since it muted my husband's snores, enabling me to get a decent night's rest in my own bed, versus the couch or guest room. But more importantly, it kept Andy, who was diagnosed with sleep apnea, from having a heart attack. And at this juncture I simply could not bear the thought of losing my life partner—and, really, my best friend.

Once I was logged in, I instinctively checked my junk mail and spotted one of Carl's e-missives, in which he recounted yet another one of his many experiences disciplining women.

15

CARL: *This one lady I played with had an issue with foul language. She had to be punished. So, this one afternoon, I met her at her house. After I told her to remove her clothing, I had her hold a thick bar of soap between her teeth, with her hands behind her head. She hated it and began to stomp her feet like a bratty little girl. Bad idea. I pulled her over my knee, then spread her hot, red cheeks and lubricated her tight, winking hole generously with my forefinger, knuckle by knuckle until I had it deep inside. I could now feel her contracting muscles reluctantly welcoming my finger. In and out. Slowly. I could feel her relax. So, I began to introduce the second finger. Stretching her. Filling her deep. She began breathing through her nose. I could see her sex leaking onto her thighs and coating them with slick wetness. My fingers were now like a piston plunging deep, in and out, faster and faster. Her hips joined in the rhythm, and she arched her back to accept the thick rude intruders.*

Once I was satisfied that she'd be able to take more, I reached into my pocket for a long, thick finger of ginger root. I spread her cheeks wide. She was vulnerable, wet, curious. She felt the root entering her. It' was a bit thicker than my fingers. She inhaled, sharply. The spanking had taken refuge in another part of her mind. I knew for certain that all she could think of was what was being put into her bottom. I pressed firmly, and the root slid deep inside her. A side effect that she did not know is that ginger root heats up and will begin to burn. Bad. She began to feel the pain and started to shake her bottom. Her red cheeks wobbled and squirmed. Now the heat was unbearable. She begged for me to take it out. Her supplication was ignored, and I scolded her for her foul language. Her mouth was frothing with soap, and her bottom was on fire inside and out. When I saw she'd had enough, I slowly and methodically took out the ginger root. I watched the tears Niagara down her cheeks and removed the soap. She'd learned her lesson. For now.

His words had potency. I reread his story, feeling the heat radiate throughout my body. I momentarily thought about waking up my husband for a quick roll in the hay, but I knew he was dead tired from the flight. Instead, I slipped into bed beside him and quietly pleasured myself.

FEBRUARY 11

A SWITCH GETS FLIPPED

It was like a switch had suddenly been flipped. My head was now filled with thoughts of spanking and discipline 24/7, and today I dedicated myself to learning more about BDSM and submissive/dominant relationships. I visited various Internet sites and familiarized myself with scene terminology. I found out what it meant to "top" someone and how it was the dominant's responsibility to ensure the safety, psychological well-being, and after-care of the submissive or "bottom." I studied up on the different types of bondage and the various methods of discipline. I viewed videos of lazy maids with bad attitudes—some completely nude, pitched over table tops or chairs—being paddled by erudite mistresses in long dresses with high lace collars. I watched clips of English school girls, skirts up, panties down, bottoms in the air, being flogged and caned by their teachers. And although I flinched at every blow, I could not stop watching.

FEBRUARY 12

FULL THROTTLE

Desperate to ramp it up, I shot Carl a text, asking him if he would be my disciplinarian—my long-distance "dom." I was terrified he'd reject me as I knew this was something I had to have. But instead he told me that "it would be a pleasure." It was an interesting choice of words. He also made one thing very clear:

CARL: *What we did in LA was child's play. This is a serious game, Deborah. And I am a serious disciplinarian.*

He then stated very explicitly that from this point on I was to address him as "sir." I was ecstatic.

FEBRUARY 14

LOVE AND DISCIPLINE ON V-DAY

My husband and I went out to Flanagan's, a funky bar/restaurant along the Hudson River, for dinner. (No need to spend oodles of money on a day neither of us took too seriously.) And although we professed our affection for each other, my mind was cluttered with thoughts of being disciplined by my new dom.

When Andrew got up to go to the bathroom, I checked my cell phone for missives from Carl. Nothing. But of course that made sense, since he couldn't email from home without arousing the suspicions of his wife, who was now back in town. I felt momentarily deflated but was certain that during regular office hours tomorrow I'd be flooded with emails or instant messages reprimanding me for my misdeeds, which I made sure were many by later sending Carl a few e-notes that were loaded with curse words.

FEBRUARY 15

MANY BENNIES

My dom now preferred to communicate mainly via Yahoo instant messenger. However, I was not so sure I liked that; I wanted to have a record of our emails in which he would scold me, as I often went back and reread them to get myself turned on. And that had to be a good thing since my husband was now benefiting from my increased sexual desire.

This new dominant/submissive relationship with Carl was also providing a much-needed distraction. I found that I didn't care so much anymore that my creative projects were in limbo. And that was good, too, since I'd stopped driving my husband crazy with my weekly laments about not being successful enough. So those were two huge benefits. But there was a downside, which I shared with Carl.

ME: *I'm having a bit of a hard time with the guilt. If my husband knew what I was doing with you, even though it's just play (right?) and it's online, I know he'd feel threatened. Even though he shouldn't. Do you battle with that? The guilt?*

CARL: *I've been spanking women since I was 11. And disciplining them is second nature to me; any guilt went out the window a long time ago. However, I can understand how you feel. But remember, you need this.*

ME: *I know. I know I do.*

Ironically, a friend later sent me an article written by an ex-journalist. The author said that real intimacy and a truly deep connection between two people could only be achieved when the partners were able to be completely honest with each other. But, he wrote, that takes a significant amount of emotional maturity and courage.

I sent the article to Andrew, hoping it would open up a discussion of sorts, but he didn't mention that he'd received it—or if he'd even bothered to read it—although I'd flagged the email as "important." I guess it simply wasn't that critical in Andrew's mind.

I just wished I could tell my husband what I was doing. I wanted to. Very much so.

FEBRUARY 16

CAN YOU LEND A HELPING HAND?

Seemingly overnight, I found that my hunger had escalated—big time—and I began to wonder if this was not unlike what eventually happened to drug addicts. They lust for a more heightened experience after each fix; they want more and more of the drug and become driven by their cravings, often to the point of their own demise. And now, like the addict, I ached for more intensity—I had to have a real-life, real-time experience. So, I sent a frantic SOS to my dom, spelling out my pressing dilemma.

ME: *I feel like I'm going out of my skin!!!!*

CARL: *First of all, settle down. Let's take a methodical approach. We need to find you someone in your area.*

ME: *I can't! My husband would kill me. You know what happened when I came back from LA What do I do? I can't bear it!!!!!*

CARL: *What about a woman? Maybe he'd be okay with that.*

ME: *A woman?*

CARL: *Yes. Find a woman who can do this; I think if you got an intense and effective spanking, you would find some relief.*

ME: *Really?*

CARL: *What I would suggest is this: Find someone online and email her. Tell her your situation: that you are looking for a disciplinarian in NYC and need a good old-fashioned, over-the-knee, bare-bottom spanking. Tell her that you need to be disciplined because you have a foul mouth and need to be punished for other misbehaviors. You need to discuss thresholds, boundaries, and expectations. I'm sure she'll lay out her parameters as well. Then, when you see her response, you'll know in your gut whether or not it's a match.*

I told him it made perfect sense but asked if he could participate long-distance over the phone, since I felt I needed that male influence.

CARL: *As far as I'm concerned in the mix, you'd have to clear it with her what her rules are in that regard. She may accept it or reject it. We won't know until you ask.*

LOOKING FOR MRS. GOOD SPANK

I logged on to the Internet and clicked over to the Google search page. My nerves were jangled, but I screwed up my courage as I launched into this uncharted, alien territory. I suddenly found myself worrying that some Big Brother type would track my every move, report it back to the Morality Squad, and have me arrested or locked up in a rehab center for perverts. Or what if I pulled down a cyber virus? What would I tell the Geek Squad when I schlepped my laptop into Best Buy for repair? That I was online looking for Spanx intimate apparel and misspelled the word and was routed to this infected site?

Figuring I'd cross that bridge if and when I came to it, I decided to get real specific to avoid having to troll through the numerous spanking sites and keyed in *NYC female disciplinarian*. I was surprised when only a few links popped up, having thought that this would be a popular search item and I'd be routed to all sorts of options. I tried a few links and found that they were now obsolete, but soon came across one that was still live and looked promising: Ms. Henrietta Maplethorpe, Professional Disciplinarian and Spankologist, New York City.

On Ms. Maplethorpe's homepage, there was a photo of her sitting in a straight-back chair, holding a wooden ruler. Her hair was in a ponytail, tied up in a big black bow; she wore a calf-length black skirt, white blouse, and sensible heels—the quintessential, uberstrict school marm, *an expert in delivering old-fashioned spankings, canings, and discipline.* It was hard to tell, however, if she was pretty or old or young, since her face was averted away from the camera, most likely to ensure anonymity. But to me it didn't matter so much, as I'd be looking at a wall or the floor most of the time during the session.

I read on: *Ms. Maplethorpe addresses the transgressions of her wards in the comfort and privacy of her Upper East Side NYC apartment. Discretion is 100% assured and expected from clients as well.* I hurriedly checked out the photos of her sessions, most of which showed Ms. Maplethorpe (always fully clothed) spanking grown men, who were either bare-bottomed or naked, with paddles and other implements. In most of the shots, the guys were either draped over her lap or an oblong, cushioned leather bench, which I'd recently learned was called a spanking horse.

Hoping to find pictures of female clients, I scrolled further and finally came across one of a young miss with her nose in the corner; her panties were down around her knees and her bottom was a bright red. Ms. Maplethorpe, who was holding the offending implement (a wooden bath brush), wore jeans and a tee shirt; her hair was loose. I clicked over to the "disclaimer" page where the domme made it very clear that she would not engage in any sexual activity—none *whatsoever*. I felt relieved and decided right away that Ms. Maplethorpe seemed like a good choice. I also got a sense that I'd feel safe with her. I was jazzed and immediately IMd my friend and disciplinarian to tell him about my recent find and had him log on to her website to take a look.

CARL: *Well, good girl. I think we've found a candidate.*

ME: *Yippeeeeee!*

CARL: *From the looks of those pictures, Deborah, I suspect she is quite capable of taking you in hand and administering a proper spanking to your naughty bottom. She looks attractive, in shape, and is obviously qualified to dole out punishment when called for. What was your response when you found her?*

ME: *What do you think?*

CARL: *Is that attitude I detect?*

ME: *No. Not at all. Sorry if it came across that way.*

CARL: *So, I guess you'd better behave. She has quite an arsenal of implements to use on a tender, white, unspanked bottom.*

ME: *Yes.*

CARL: *Yes, what?*

ME: *Sigh. Yes, sir.*

CARL: *Good girl. And make that uppercase.*

ME: *Yes, Sir.*

I composed an email, a letter of introduction, as soon as I signed off from Carl:

Dear Ms. Maplethorpe, I would like to have your help with a somewhat unique situation. I am in dire need of disciplinary actions, including spanking, for various reasons. I have a male disciplinarian, but he is geo-

graphically unavailable. He told me to find a female in my area who could do what he "physically" cannot. He would, however, like to communicate with you via email to discuss proper punishment—and participate over the phone (my cell on speaker) during our sessions.

I read your website with interest and saw that you were recommended by several people. For the record, I am 5'9", 135 pounds, in good shape, but probably don't look my age (for what it's worth). You can find out more about me on my website.

I provided the link to my site, hoping that she'd see I was a normal human being (the irony was not lost on me here). I hit the send button and felt a surge of anxiety. What if she didn't respond? Then what? I was convinced my body needed this, as did my mind. And, despite my apprehensiveness, I was extremely excited—as was Carl, because it surely fed his own addiction.

FEBRUARY 18

LOOKING FORWARD, LOOKING FOR ANDREW

Late afternoon, I received the email I'd been so anxiously waiting for.

Dear Deborah, I'm willing to discuss the possibility of my disciplining you in your dom's absence. I don't usually take instructions from others in my sessions, but now that you mention it, it sounds like it might be fun. Moreover, we seem to have a lot in common. I'm also a produced playwright and screenwriter (not under this name, of course). I've done my share of acting too, but it's not a skill I'd do any bragging about.

I do require a thorough screening interview by phone before deciding if I'll take on a new client. When would you be available for that?

Looking forward to chatting soon. All the best, Henrietta Maplethorpe

She provided her phone number at the end of the email. I called her immediately and left a message on her answering machine. My body tingled, my stomach lurched.

A bit later, my husband and I went out to Home Depot, which we did a lot, ever since we started rehabbing the New York house. I often mentioned to Andrew how solid our marriage must be since couples that undertake protracted rehabs often end up divorcing—and that's frequently in less than a year's time. Our NY project had been going on for more than twelve years.

At HD, Andrew and I played in the aisles like children, as we always did; he pinched me on the butt, and I went after his chest hair, this time getting lucky enough to grab a handful. I squealed with laughter, then wandered away to look at what was new in the kitchen and bath section. Andy rambled off to pick up various items from his "to get" list.

When I was fully sated from checking out fixtures and cabinets, I went to look for my husband. But I could not find him and was hit by a surge of anxiety that seemed to come out of nowhere. So where was Andy? Where was my husband? My rock of stability? He was nowhere to be found. I dug in my purse for my cell phone to call him and clicked on his number. No reception. The tinny sensation of dread began to spread through my body as I bolted from aisle to aisle. What if he'd had a heart attack and was being rolled out on a stretcher? What if aliens were working in Home Depot and had sucked him up into their mother ship to obtain more understanding of middle-aged men with hairy ears, chests, and butts, and not much head hair? What if he took off with the cute little cashier? But that's the last thing Andrew would do; the alien scenario would be far more likely. After all, this was a man who'd tell me over and over how much he loved me; how much he was still in love with me. So why was I panicking? Why couldn't I control my imagination?

Finally, after doing an aisle-to-aisle search, I spotted him looking at electrical outlet boxes.

"There you are!"

Andy smiled, and I breathed a sigh of relief.

On our way out, we ran into the woman who'd helped us choose and configure our kitchen cabinets a few years back. She was an energetic brown-eyed blond and, sadly, a two-time cancer survivor. She was also very unhappy at home and had told us on more than one occasion that she was thinking of leaving her husband.

"He just doesn't get it," she'd say.

On a gut level, I knew she'd never leave the marriage. Just like I knew I'd never leave my husband; nor would he ever leave me.

FEBRUARY 19

WELCOME TO THE DARK SIDE

After watching a movie on TV with Andrew, I headed upstairs to my office while my husband loaded up the dishwasher. The light was flashing on my answering machine. I pushed the button, abuzz with anticipation. "Deborah. This is Ms. Maplethorpe. Please call me at your earliest convenience. I'll be awake for another hour or so if you want to call tonight. But when you call, you must announce yourself, otherwise I won't pick up the phone." She was completely no-nonsense and stern, which was good. She also sounded mature, perhaps forty-years old or more.

I called her right away. We chatted gaily and talked about dates. March 8 was her first available time slot, which told me she was a busy gal. She also informed me that she charged $350 per session and required a deposit via Pay Pal.

"I look forward to meeting you," I said.

There was a lengthy silence on the other end of the line. And then I heard her take in a sharp breath. "Welcome to the dark side," she said, her voice suddenly cold, dry.

I felt the blood drain from my face.

FEBRUARY 20

SPREAD THE CHEER

Carl needed to be apprised of this latest news.

ME: *It's a go with Ms. Maplethorpe!*

CARL: *I'm very happy for you. Did she top you on the phone? Reprimand you?*

ME: *No. We just talked about who we are, what we each do in real life. That kind of thing.*

CARL: *I'm surprised. But I'm sure she will give you exactly what you need when you see her.*

ME: *Hope so. Now I have to tell my husband. Wish me luck.*

FEBRUARY 21

PLEASURE FOR TWO

Andrew and I went to one of our favorite restaurants in the NYC theater district, arriving a bit after 8:00 PM so we could avoid the Broadway-bound crowd that piles in a few hours before curtain time. We landed on the short side of the L-shaped bar, settling in at our customary spot. After a glass of wine and a game of Scrabble on Andy's iPad (us playing against the machine), I felt sufficiently relaxed enough to broach the subject. "Andrew," I said, bringing my mouth up to his ear. "I've figured out a way to spice up our sex life."

"Okay."

"Why do you look so concerned? You should be elated."

"What is it?" he said, his eyebrows still furrowed.

"I'm going to get spanked by a woman. A professional."

Andrew paused, blinked once. "I'll be right back."

"Where are you going?"

"To the men's room to jerk off."

I laughed out loud. "Now <u>that's</u> funny."

"Better than my horrible puns, I'm sure," Andy said.

As my husband slid off the bar stool, I leaned back and smiled. I was pleased. It seemed like Andrew was too. I knew, however, I could never tell him about Carl's participation, even though my dom would not be physically in the room.

FEBRUARY 22

COLOR ME ASHAMED BUT HAPPY

Today all I cared about was feeding my addiction, so I shot Carl an email and threw him a boatload of attitude along with a few strategically placed F-bombs. Of course my disciplinarian took the bait.

CARL: *Deborah. You are being very naughty. You need someone to wash out that mouth with soap.*

ME: *I am NOT naughty!!!!!*

CARL: *You certainly are, my dear. And you are in dire need of a shellacking. You need to cut down a few switches and have Ms. Maplethorpe use them on your naked bottom. A nice crop of raised welts would cure you for a few days. Guaranteed, missy.*

ME: *I most certainly would not cut down anything that was going to be used on my bottom. Do you think I'm nuts? That's like buying a gun and giving it to the guy who's planning to break into your house. No friggin' way.*

CARL: *Okay, now let's get this straight once and for all. When and if I tell you to cut down a switch to be used on your defiant ass, girl, you will, or I swear I will tell Ms. Maplethorpe to find the thickest cane and stripe you so bad you'll have marks for weeks. Stop this attitude. Now! You are the last person who knows what is good for you. You need to start showing more respect. Now! I swear, if we ever meet, I will discipline your bottom inside and out. You will drive home with a butt plug so big it will stretch you to the limit. Your attitude is taking me to a very extreme place. And if you think that I will have any mercy about your nudity, you've already thrown that away. Not a stitch of clothing, Deborah. Yes, I will tweak those*

pink nipples. Hard. And watch you grimace, then sigh, as I release them from my thumb and forefinger. Spank your pussy. Indeed, it will be as pink as your bottom. You are going to get the full treatment, dear.
  Now, apologize immediately.

  I hated him. I hated him because I felt ashamed that his words— his reprimands and his sexual explicitness—got me so turned on. And I hated him because I needed him. I needed this. And I didn't fully understand why. But I did not care.

FEBRUARY 23

SAFE, FOR NOW

Mid-afternoon, Carl instant messaged me.

CARL: *I have not heard back from you. Did I frighten you, Deborah?*

ME: *Yes.*

CARL: *I don't know why. I can't get to you. Now, are you going to apologize for your behavior yesterday?*

ME: *Yes, Sir. I am very sorry. I am truly very sorry.*

CARL: *You do understand that I have a responsibility to you and your behavior. Now think about how you behaved and write 300 times on a tablet: "I will not be a naughty girl." When you are finished, send it to my office. And by the way, I want you to use three different colors: red, blue, green. You will alternate every letter: "I" in red; "w" in blue; "i" in green. And use crayons, little girl. Understood? I also want it in my hands within two days.*

  I went to the mall, relieved that my husband was in his NYC office, and bought a box of crayons. Feeling charged up and surprisingly cared for, I sat in Barnes and Noble to complete my task.
  Not being one to waste time, I quickly figured out a way to make the job go faster. And, of course I thought my technique was brilliant. Instead of writing from left to right and changing crayons each time I did a letter, I wrote one letter from top to bottom, down one column, in the same color: *I*. That letter I did in red. I went to the next: *w*. I did that one in blue, and so on, until I had thirty-plus lines of "I will not be a naughty girl." I repeated that on the next ten pages.
  I stopped at the post office and sent the document via Express mail, since Carl had given me a deadline. What I found perfectly amusing was that if someone, like my husband, attempted to control

26

me in this manner, I would have been out the door in a shot. I hated anyone telling me what to do—in real life that is.

At around 7:00 PM, I picked Andrew up at the train station, and we headed into Tarrytown for dinner. He filled me in on his trip to the city. I didn't fill him in on my trip to the mall and my purchase of Crayola Crayons®. But we did have some "fun" later in the bedroom. I was, after all, extremely stimulated by the day's activities.

FEBRUARY 26

BEND ME, SHAPE ME, BREAK ME

Carl popped up on IM shortly after noon.

CARL: *I got your package. You obviously found a way to expedite the exercise. Very clever.*

ME: *I hate you for making me do that.*

CARL: *I was only giving you what you deserve. At least at this juncture.*

My husband walked into my office, and I casually pulled down the lid of my laptop to obscure the instant messaging app. "Hey," I said, turning toward Andrew, feeling like I'd just been caught doing something terribly egregious.

"What's going on?" Andy asked, looking slightly dubious.

"Nothing." I tried to sound nonchalant, aware of my reddening face. "Just work stuff."

"Want to grab some lunch?"

"Sure. Give me a few minutes."

Andrew went back into his office. I quickly pushed my laptop open, anxious to resume my conversation with Carl—anxious to keep the dialogue going.

ME: *Deserve? And what do you think I might deserve, Mr. Franks, at a later juncture?*

CARL: *We both know the answer, but mine might be a bit more definitive. You need to be taken over my knee and spanked to tears. Sobbing, blubbering tears. Crying as if your heart would break. That barrier has to be broken. You have to learn that your attitude and behavior can no longer be capricious and disrespectful without consequences. A good five minutes with the bath brush will have you rethinking your drink, miss. Your bottom will feel like a foreign object by the time I stop. If I stop. You will beg for the cane after the first purposeful swat. I can truthfully say, Deborah, that it will be a very dark day if we ever meet.Will I take it easy on you because of our friendship? Absolutely not. I will administer an extreme dose of discipline for as long as I see fit. Does that answer your bratty question?*

I told him that it did.

After I paid some bills, Andrew and I grabbed a Chai at Starbucks in the mall and went off afterwards to get lunch at the Japanese restaurant. We talked about putting together a budget to reduce our monthly outlay of cash and decided that maybe it would be a good idea to cut back on our daily runs to Starbucks.

"It'll be a challenge," I said, already missing my quotidian fix.

Andy nodded in agreement. "Tell me about it."

My husband, however, did not mention the money I was going to spend for my session with the NYC domme—an amount that was comparable to a monthly car payment and about seventy Chai lattes.

"Andrew," I said as I reached across the table and placed my hand over my husband's. "If I ever hurt you, you have to let me know." I felt compelled to say this, and I was not exactly sure why. "Have I? Have I ever hurt you?"

"No," he said, his voice soft but his face unreadable.

"It would break my heart if I did."

FEBRUARY 28

THE LIST THAT DEBORAH BUILT

Carl asked me, rather instructed me, to make a list of my transgressions and said that, together, he and Ms. Maplethorpe would decide on the proper punishment. I quickly wrote one up and titled it "The List That Deborah Built." Knowing exactly what I was doing, I sent a curt, disjointed email to my long-distance dom.

ME: *Here's the friggin' list. OKAY??!!!!*

Capitalizing letters always pissed Carl off, since it was akin to "yelling." I simply could not get enough of this—this wonderful, glorious attention from an authoritative male.

CARL: *I'm counting to 10 before I respond to that email. You are out of control. I'd advise you to temper that attitude once and for all. If this keeps up, I will be sure you are stripped naked in front of Ms. Maplethorpe.*

ME: *What???!!!!!! No! Not nude!!!!!!*

CARL: *I can assure you that there will be nothing sexual during your session. That's not in the mix. What is in the mix is you getting your bottom blistered for an attitude like you just displayed.*

ME: *Okay, okay. Sir...Sorry. So did you talk to her?*

CARL: *Yes. We spoke for 25 minutes. She wants me to send her an email. It will contain what I think you need and how I think she should approach your disobedience. I'll now take a look at your own list and see where we stand. In all seriousness, Deborah, I'm warning you again, get that attitude in check. Am I making myself clear?*

ME: *Perfectly clear, sir. I mean, Sir.*

MARCH 5

A.K.A.

At around 9:00 PM, the NYC domme emailed me detailed instructions as to how I was to proceed:

MS. MAPLETHORPE: *Go to the corner of 95th and Lexington and call me at home at exactly 2:55. Not one minute before. Not one minute after. And when you get to the reception desk ask for Fontana Jones.*

(Fontana Jones?)

I contacted Carl and said that I felt like I was going on some covert operation for the CIA. I also told him I was about ready to go out of my skin with anticipation. He responded immediately, knowing all the right buttons to push.

CARL: *How embarrassing this is going is to be for you, standing in front of this strong, strict lady. Wet from the idea of being over this woman's knee, and that soon she's going to pull up your dress, insert her fingers into the waistband of your panties, and slowly yank them down to your knees. Poor little Deborah. Bare and vulnerable. And look at those tender, white cheeks. In mere seconds they will take on a red hue, and you'll be kicking and squirming, begging another woman to please stop spanking you, promising that you'll be a good girl going forward. But only this time, she isn't going to stop until you've been thoroughly punished. Lucky you.*

Damn straight I was lucky. (Although I would not be wearing a dress.)

MARCH 8

FULL KNOWLEDGE OF THE FUN UP AHEAD

Before I headed out the door, I gave my husband Ms. Maplethorpe's address and phone number to assure him that it was all on the up and up.

"I'll be safe. Don't worry," I said.

"What time will you be back?" Andy asked.

"Seven the latest," I said. "Should I pick something up for dinner on the way home?"

"Whatever you want to do is fine with me." My husband's casual demeanor further reinforced my belief that he really was okay with what I was doing.

"Okay." I said. "I'll call you later. We'll figure something out."

Once I got into Grand Central, I anxiously checked the clock at the information booth, even though I'd given myself plenty of time to get to the Upper East Side.

At the appointed destination, I waited ten minutes until it was exactly 2:55 and made the call. Ms. Maplethorpe picked up on the other end within two rings. In a steady, controlled voice, she gave me the address.

I walked two blocks east to her high-rise, entered, and went up to the reception desk, as instructed. "Deborah Vines for Fontana Jones," I said, wondering how many other aliases the domme had and if the man at the desk knew what she did for a living.

The clerk smiled and picked up the house phone to announce me, gave me Ms. Maplethorpe's apartment number, and pointed me in the direction of the elevators.

Gripping my purse tightly, I flashed on the wad of cash in the white envelope that I'd tucked securely at the bottom of my purse. "I feel like a 'jane'," I'd said to Carl earlier in an email. "You know, the female version of a john." I felt somewhat relieved, and a bit less of a degenerate, when he told me that years ago he had to pay to spank women before this practice became more acceptable and was no longer relegated to the underground.

Stepping into the elevator, I hit the button for the fifth floor. The cabin jolted once and began the trek upward. Suddenly, I had a strange sensation that I was headed, not up, but down the proverbial rabbit hole. But unlike Alice who accidentally fell to her fate, I was doing this willingly. I tamped down that thought and realized my palms were sweating and was momentarily thankful I had remembered to double-apply my deodorant. My panties, however, were not wet as Carl had predicted.

At the fifth floor, the doors slid open. I stepped out, looked for the wall marker that would guide me to Ms. Maplethorpe's apartment, and headed off down a semi-dark and quiet hallway. My heart was racing like a frightened animal, and I wondered if I was not walking into trouble. I immediately conjured up images of me being chopped into little pieces and thrown into the alleyway dumpster. "Don't be ridiculous," I whispered, reminding myself that this was a "professional" situation and Henrietta had been in business for years.

I went up to Ms. Maplethorpe's door and knocked lightly, hoping the domme would open it up and quickly take me in hand and address my transgressions, fueling my fantasy. Instead, she smiled and welcomed me inside. But she was not what I'd imagined. Instead of looking like a conservative schoolmarm, Ms. Maplethorpe seemed more like a leather-loving dominatrix—a sex goddess. She was dressed in tight black jeans and a black spandex top; her hair was long, straight, and silky. In the picture on her homepage, it looked thick and wavy, so I figured she must have been wearing a wig. She was also tiny, about six inches shorter than me and probably thirty pounds lighter. But, clearly, she was in excellent shape—a critical component, I suspected, because otherwise how could she have handled having large and/or heavy men lying prone across her lap? Or perhaps she made the hefty ones lie over the spanking horse.

Ms. Maplethorpe offered to take my coat and asked that we "transact business," meaning she wanted me to pony up the cash. This further diluted my fantasy, so more than ever I knew I needed Carl's participation.

As she went to put my coat away and stash my money, Ms. Maplethorpe told me to call my long-distance dom on my cell and activate the speaker phone. I did as instructed, and my dom picked up right away. His voice was composed yet commanding—exactly what the doctor ordered.

"I'm a wreck," I said after he asked how I was doing.

"You should be," Carl said as my female disciplinarian walked back into the modest living area. I swallowed hard.

Ms. Maplethorpe pointed down a narrow hallway. "March! And make it snappy, Deborah."

At the far end of the hall, we stepped into the "spanking room," which, although on the small side, was replete with chairs, two types of spanking horses, and an assorted display of paddles, canes, and switches.

The domme immediately took the phone from me, set it on a table, and I got the giggles. I didn't know if it was because what I was doing suddenly seemed absurd or if it was simply nervous laughter.

Probably a bit of both. But my mirth displeased Ms. Maplethorpe, so she reached up, grabbed me by the ear, and pulled me into a corner.

It also displeased Carl. "Not a good idea, Deborah," he said, his voice booming out from my cell. "There's nothing funny about this at all. Ms. Maplethorpe, get that girl's pants off right now."

"What? Why so fast?" I said.

Ms. Maplethorpe told me to drop my jeans "right now!" which I did. "Get those panties off, too!"

"Shit," I said—a move that earned me a powerful, stinging swat on my behind. "Ouch! Stop it!"

She didn't stop, of course, and I got the giggles even worse. My disciplinarians were not exactly happy with my reaction; yet when I turned to Henrietta, I could have sworn she was repressing a smile, which made me laugh even harder. But after several more very intense whacks to my bottom, I finally shut my mouth.

"I said, get those off," Ms. Maplethorpe commanded, pointing to my panties. "Immediately!"

I dropped my underwear and felt my face flush with embarrassment.

During the first half of the session, I was hand-paddled at least a hundred times, sent back to the corner, put over a spanking horse, and disciplined with a wooden spoon, which was a first for me. The pain was acute.

Finally, after a round of twenty-five, Ms. Maplethorpe paused. "Deborah's getting too bruised, Carl," she said into the phone. "We need to stop."

"Give her ten more," he instructed. "And don't hold back."

"Shit! No more!" I was loathing him at this point. "No, no, no, no, no!"

"Deborah, watch the mouth. Otherwise we'll make it twenty. Ms. Maplethorpe, ten more with a paddle," Carl said, his voice resonating with increasing impatience. "And Deborah, you are to count each one."

The tiny domme grabbed a round, flat paddle, delivered my punishment obediently, but pulled back a bit on the intensity as we began the countdown. Unfortunately, I became addled and miscounted.

"Start again. From one," my long-distance dom commanded. "Get it right Deborah, otherwise you won't be sitting down for at least a week."

I placed all my focus on counting the blows accurately, knowing that otherwise, if I had to start from the beginning again, the pain would become unbearable. Suddenly, it was over. But I had to wonder why no one ever mentioned the list—the list I made of my transgressions. Yet it didn't matter; I was in an altered state. It seemed almost like a drug-induced high, which supposedly is the result of all the endorphins that flood the brain when the body experiences extreme physical discomfort.

"Deborah," Carl asked over the speaker. "How do you feel now?"

"Hmmm?" I said, as Ms. Maplethorpe handed me my cell phone. "Oh, I feel fine." I put the phone up to my ear.

"Wow," he said. "You don't even sound like the same person."

"Yeah." I was aware my voice was pitched higher and softer than usual. "It's like wild."

"Yes, it is," he said. "I'll check in with you later to see how you're doing. Okay?"

"Sure. And thank you. For being here. On the phone."

I shut off my cell and put my panties and jeans back on, thankful that I was never told to take off my shirt or bra. Ms. Maplethorpe knew I didn't have much experience as a submissive, that I'd never done anything this intense, and had agreed that she would not strip me naked. I'd also made it very clear that I didn't want to go "from zero to sixty" in one shot. She'd said that it was better anyway to introduce various methods of discipline incrementally, over time, to condition the body.

We headed to the living room where Henrietta offered me water. By now I'd come down from my high, and we talked like two old friends; she told me about the handbook on spanking and discipline that she was writing for a small publisher and mentioned her inability to get organized.

"You probably need to be punished," I said.

She laughed appreciatively.

I looked over at her and noticed her eyes for the first time, since I'd spent most of the session looking down at the rug.

"Her eyes are strange. The pupils are diamond-shaped. Like the eyes of the devil," I told Carl later when he called me on my cell. "It freaked me out. Do you think she wears some kind of special-effect contact lenses?"

"I think you're imagining things. How's your bottom? Did you look?"

"No. I didn't want to," I said. "But I'm sure it's not a pretty sight."

When I got home, my husband didn't even ask me how it went, but

I chalked it up to Andrew's occasional moodiness.

I then remembered something a dear friend of mine said to me back in the 1990s when I first met Carl and experimented with spanking and discipline. "Why would you want to do this? You're such a loving person." I was unable to answer her question.

Later, when Andrew and I decided to forgo dinner at home and go out to Wing Night at Flanagan's, I focused on my rear end, which was sore and made sitting uncomfortable. But I was charged with sexual energy and replayed the scenario with Ms. Maplethorpe and Carl over and over in my head, not giving another thought to the domme's weird eyes. After a few hours of eating and imbibing, my husband and I went home and had sex—with the lights off. I didn't want him to see my bottom, and he promised to not look. We both knew it would upset him.

MARCH 10

BUDGETS BE DAMNED

Our determination to pinch pennies flew out the window, and Andrew and I went off to Starbucks during lunch hour for our habitual Chai lattes and a game of Scrabble on the iPad. During the particularly intense battle with the computer, my cell phone buzzed like crazy with Carl's incoming messages. I knew I was being way too attentive to my little device and unable to fully repress the excitement I felt inside. And once again, I found myself wishing I could share all this with Andrew, tell him about Carl. I sincerely wanted to—because, really, this was just a game—a game that had gotten me back in touch with my sexuality.

MARCH 19

A CRUSH IS JUST A CRUSH

I met with my business partner, Ron, to discuss our upcoming shoot for a film I wrote. He admitted in so many words that he harbored a crush. I suppose I could have said it was somewhat mutual. But that's all it was: a crush. I later had a discussion with my sister, Wanda. We both agreed that it's perfectly natural, but what matters is what you do with those feelings.

"It's a choice you make," my sister said. "You either act on them or you recognize the feelings for what they are and tuck them away in the back of your mind."

I told her that I would never sleep with a man other than my husband. "And besides, some things are better left fantasies," I said thinking about the wicked crush I once had on this particular entertainment attorney.

I also thought about what my dom had said during one of our e-conversations: that people who act on their fantasies, people who live them out, like I was doing, were truly the courageous ones. Or maybe that was his way of justifying his own behavior.

MARCH 20

A SAVINGS OF FIFTY BUCKS—KA-CHING!!!

I decided I was not going back to see Ms. Maplethorpe. It wasn't only the eye thing that bothered me; I felt I overshadowed her both in size and personality.

ME: *What do I do now, Carl?*

CARL: *I'll find you someone.*

ME: *Bless your twisted soul :)*

Within a few hours, he located another woman in NYC through one of the spanking sites. Unfortunately, she too charged for her services, but at least it was fifty dollars less. I checked out her website and told my disciplinarian that this one might be a better fit. She might be a bit on the short side, but at least she was stocky and seemed to have some heft to her. And her arms looked strong, too, so there was a good possibility she'd be able to effectively deliver the goods.

I sent the new woman the same letter I had emailed to Ms. Maplethorpe, replacing the recipient's name. I heard back from her at the end of the day. Her screening process was not quite as thorough as Henrietta Maplethorpe's, and there was no phone call of introduction. But my gut told me she'd play safe. Communicating via email, we set a date to meet.

ME: *Do I come to your place?*

MS. C: *I work out of a dungeon on 29th Street.*

ME: *A dungeon? Wow. Will there be slime dripping off the walls?*

MS. C: *I'll be sure to scrub them clean before you get there.*

I felt even better knowing she had a sense of humor.

MARCH 23

INSATIABLE

In between our e-conversations about work and creativity, I bratted out in my IMs to Carl, needing more attention and discipline. I truly had become insatiable.

APRIL 6

GIVE ME MO' (AND YO') MONAY!

My business partner came to the house with his camera and lighting equipment, and we set up in the living room to shoot a comedic crowd-funding video for our short film, in hopes of using it to raise money for the full-length version.

Ironically, in one of the skits I played a dominatrix, during which I wore black leggings, thigh-high, black vinyl boots, and a black leather jacket. But before we could shoot the scene, we needed to find some kind of a chain that I could dangle over Ron, who was dressed like a conservative business man. I asked my husband if he could help out. "Okay," Andy said, without a trace of enthusiasm. He went out to the garage and within a few minutes came back with a heavy-gauge steel chain. Along with his sullen demeanor, I found it odd that Andy didn't stay to watch us film. Ordinarily he would have, since in the past he always wanted to be involved in my projects; actually it got to the point where everything I undertook, like yoga, Andy wanted to become a part of. Finally, I had to encourage him to find his own hobbies, as I began to feel a bit suffocated. Today I fleetingly wondered if something was upsetting him, but figured it was because he'd rather be out in his workshop experimenting with wood—a pastime he'd recently adopted, much to my delight—and relief.

Ron turned the camera on and positioned himself on the couch. I stood over him, my leg hitched up on top of the coffee table. I swung the chain slowly back and forth and smiled seductively into the lens. In a subsequent shot, where I was behind the camera, I pulled in close on Ron's face. He raised an eyebrow and said, in perfect timing, "I gave...willingly."

We rolled the camera back and watched the takes. They looked good. And they were funny.

After we'd finished our filming and Ron had gone home, I told my husband that I was going to see another woman to get spanked.

"She charges less money, and we'll save at least fifty bucks."

"Whatever it takes," Andy said, his voice flat.

"Do you think it's weird what I'm doing?" I asked.

"Well, it is ritualized abuse," my husband said, forcing a half smile.

Tonight, before we climbed into bed, I jutted my rear end out and pointed to one of my buttocks, a devilish grin on my face. Andrew gave me a quick, playful spank, and I giggled. Everything seemed back on even keel.

APRIL 7

MORE CAMERAS, CONCALLS, AND CLAIROL

Carl IMd me and said he wanted me to set up the Yahoo camera feature so I could stream the session tomorrow with the new domme live to his laptop. I called him a pervert.

CARL: *No Argument there.*

ME: *But you are a nice pervert.*

I really didn't like the idea of capturing any of this on camera as it seemed like an act of betrayal on my part. But I went ahead and set up the account anyway, just to appease my disciplinarian.

When my husband went out to Home Depot, we did a test run.

"You look wonderful," Carl said. "And I like your glasses. Sexy."

"Ugh. Please. I hate the way video makes me look. I need controlled, soft lighting," I said. "Calling makeup! Hair!"

"You know, I have to tell you, when I walked into Brenda's apartment and saw the two of you standing there together, I honestly thought I'd hit the jackpot: two perfectly lovely, sophisticated, tall, blond women. And I'd get to spank them both."

"Awwww, shucks," I said, "you're making me blush." I told him that he looked great, too, and no different than when I knew him in LA all those years ago. "And you've still got your hair! Lucky you."

"It's much grayer," he said.

"Whose isn't at this stage of the game?" I said, smiling. "But that's why we have Clairol."

APRIL 8

A NEW PLACE, A NEW FACE, A BARE ASS

Andrew offered to accompany me into the city to see Ms. C, who was also known in the scene as Ms. Cynthia.

"You don't have to," I said, choosing to go solo since I was worried my husband might question why I was taking my computer with me.

I headed on out after Andy had settled in at his desk, my nerves jangled. I'd never met this person and had no idea what to expect. I was, however, reassured by the fact that Carl would be there on speaker phone. But I became totally addled when I got close to the midtown location and mixed up the address, arriving ten minutes late. I raced up to the building and pressed the buzzer next to the dented steel door. After I was let inside, I climbed up the narrow, heavily trafficked stairs, my lungs pumping wildly and my hands their usual pools of sweat, as I knew I'd be called out on my tardiness.

Once I was at the fourth floor, I took a deep breath and rang the bell to the right of the entrance. An attractive woman in her twenties, sporting chin-length auburn hair, opened the door and welcomed me inside with a bright smile, as if I was coming in to get my nails done. A reception desk was off to the right; several closed doors lined the hallway to the left. The interior was painted in red and black; the one window near the desk was adorned with black lace.

The young woman, who wore a short red skirt, black tights, and a slinky silver top, pointed down the badly carpeted hallway.

"Ms. Cynthia is in the last room on the right," she said.

As I walked down the hall, I called Carl on my cell phone. "I'm here," I said, my voice shaking slightly.

The door at the end swung open with a whoosh and Ms. Cynthia stepped out. She had a pixie-like face, but I saw that her arms were beefier than I'd thought, which would certainly help enhance the experience. However, she was obviously not a fashionista, I thought, taking in her tan shorts, black tights, and chunky brown shoes.

"You're late," she said, pulling me by the arm into the room. "Ten minutes late."

I liked her stern tone. "I'm sorry," I said, doing my best to sound contrite.

My apology was ignored. "Turn on the speaker," she said, pointing to my cell.

I did as I was told.

"Carl," Ms. Cynthia said. "Deborah was late."

"We're going to have to address this." My dom's voice sounded strong, even though he was hundreds of miles away. "Ms. C, give her a good sound spanking right away for each minute she was late."

I continued spouting off excuses, but my words fell on deaf ears. Ms. Cynthia immediately pulled me over her lap and delivered ten stinging swats.

"Okay," Carl said. "Let's get that camera working."

"Up on your feet," Ms. C said.

My stomach lurched. I definitely did not want to film this, but I fired up the computer and made a half-hearted attempt to log on to Yahoo. "Sorry, can't get reception here," I said into the cell, trying to sound disappointed. "I had a feeling it wouldn't work."

The lack of reception turned out to be a godsend, since during the session I ended up buck naked, as per Carl's instructions, due to a gush of foul language that slipped out of my mouth every time I was paddled. How mortifying that would have been to be on display to my male disciplinarian. And, certainly, my husband would not approve. Rather, he'd kill me if he knew another man had seen me in my birthday suit.

The session proceeded until Ms. C told my dom she wouldn't deliver any more punishment. "Deborah's getting too bruised," she said into the speaker phone.

"All right. Give her ten more."

"What is it with this magic fucking ten?" I said loudly. That comment got me an additional fifteen, and I was made to count each and every painful swat. This time I didn't miscount.

"Want to check it out in the mirror?" Ms. C asked as I got dressed. Apparently, some people got a charge out of inspecting the aftermath of a harsh spanking.

"No, that's okay." I honestly had no desire to examine the damage.

After money changed hands ($250 for Ms. C and $50 for the room), Cynthia and I went out for a bite to eat.

"You don't look your age," she said over a plate of salmon sushi.

"Neither do you," I said.

"I like playing with you. You're fun."

Outside the dungeon environment, Ms. C came across rather shy and unassuming, a quality reinforced by a lilting voice and slight lisp.

"Just goes to show," I said when I remarked on her demure manner, "you can never judge a book by its cover."

"You have no idea." Ms. Cynthia grinned wickedly.

I smiled and asked her about her life in the scene.

"Been doing this for twenty years as a top and a bottom. I like to punish, and I like to be punished."

"So, you switch?" I asked, aware that many people jump from one role to the other, both men and women.

"I guess I have a little of each in me," Ms. C said, smiling. "The sadist <u>and</u> the masochist."

"Maybe we all do," I commented, reflecting on the time I spanked my friend Brenda and then helped her discipline her boyfriend, Darren, also a switch.

"I recently asked a friend of mine to become my dom," Ms. C continued.

"Oh? Someone you know from the scene?"

"Yeah. He's a lawyer. He has his own practice."

"As a dom?"

"No," she said, laughing. "As a lawyer."

I then mentioned what Henrietta Maplethorpe had told me: that many people who indulge in this fetish are successful, educated, worldly professionals.

"It's true," Ms. Cynthia said, nodding.

As we were finishing up our food, Carl called me on my cell. "Hey." His voice was filled with tenderness. "I just wanted to make sure you're okay."

"I'm fine," I said. In spite of a very sore bottom, my heart was light.

"I'll be out of pocket all weekend, but let's touch base on Monday," he said.

"Sounds great." I couldn't help but smile. "And thanks."

Once I got home, I realized I'd never turned on the button that enables wireless connection on my computer. Lack of reception was not the issue. I had my limits, scruples, after all, I thought, mentally patting myself on the back.

APRIL 14

OUT OF CONTROL—IN CONTROL

I decided to go into therapy—not to explore the reasons behind my current fixation, but to address my obsessive-compulsive disorder. It wasn't severe, like it is with some people who can't get out of the house for hours due to, say, the need to make sure every electrical device is unplugged. My OCD manifested a bit differently, and I was curious to know if there was anyone else out there who did the same things, like subscribe different energies to plates. In my skewed universe, there were "good" plates and "bad" plates, so if I picked "the wrong one," I felt that something terrible would happen. I also tugged at my underpants, when the urge surfaced, while driving to ward off a potential accident. I recognized this behavior as a manifestation of my need to control the world around me, which on an intellectual level I knew was impossible.

Taking the proverbial bull by the horns, I shot an email to my friend who had a counseling practice in White Plains, NY. Within an hour, she sent me the names and numbers of two local female therapists. I mentioned my decision to my husband.

"You should go," he said.

"Do you think I'm nuts?" I asked.

"No. I just think it's a good idea."

"Oh." I let the matter drop. I didn't want to ask him if he thought it was a good idea because of the spanking. I was afraid of what he might say and wondered how I would handle it if he suddenly expressed disapproval. Would I be able to give this up? I didn't think I could.

Those thoughts aside, I ruminated on my control issues a bit more and realized it made perfect sense why I found the spanking scenario so appealing: during the scene, the submissive gives up control to the dominant, which on a psychological level is a relief for people who feel like they have to be in control all the time. But ironically, the submissive is really the one who's in the driver's seat. The submissive sets the parameters.

Or at least that's what Carl told me. "If there's something you don't want to do, you establish that up front with your dominant."

MAY 7

MATT THE DOORMAN

Andrew stayed in Piermont to have a few beers and to work on some plans for a new garage at the VT house, and I went to dinner with Gaby, who was my roommate in LA for a short time back in the late 1980s before I came back east. She was now in a love relationship with Claire, a smart, artistic, witty woman.

Tonight, after we enjoyed a satisfying meal at an Indian restaurant and a bottle of wine, I begged Gaby to go with me to Paddles, which is dubbed "the friendly S&M club." My curiosity (not to mention my burning desire) had gotten the better of me, and I was driven to check out this place that Carl had mentioned on more than one occasion. The club, according to its website, was a "playground" for a wide range of fetishes, including whipping, spanking, bondage, domination, submission, foot fetishes, cross-dressing, and more. I didn't know what the "and more" might constitute, and didn't really care, since I was only interested in the spanking and discipline.

Before we hit the sidewalk, my friend called her partner and got her permission to accompany me. Claire said it was fine, as long as Gaby didn't go inside. If Claire were with us, however, she'd gladly partake. I'd never met Claire, but something told me we'd get along great. She sounded adventurous—like me.

Tonight was supposedly dedicated to spanking fetishists versus the more heavy-duty, leather-loving S&M crowd. Once we'd arrived at 26th Street, we began scanning the buildings for the right number. We finally found the place—a large black structure next to a parking lot. The entrance, which was on the side, was devoid of any sign or marquee proclaiming its existence.

A buff-looking doorman in his thirties greeted us. Gaby immediately struck up a conversation and explained our (my) situation. "She wants to go inside, but she's scared."

Matt, the doorman, laughed.

"I'm not scared. I'm going in," I said, heading toward the door, rising to the challenge.

"You sure?" Gaby asked.

"Go boldly where no sensible person has ever gone before," I called out, over my shoulder.

I gingerly made my way down a long, steep staircase that spilled out into a dark hallway where a hostess in a booth collected my entry fee of ten dollars.

Another door led to a large room decorated in what I now understood to be the industry-standard blacks and reds. The lights were dimmed, and there was a bar to the far right—a bar that apparently only served soft drinks and juices. (Too bad since I could have used a little more reinforcement to quell my nerves.)

I hastily decided to expedite and made a mad dash through the place, going full circle on the lower level. People looked at me like I was an intruder, an imposter, so I kept my head down. As I came around the last corner, I spotted a woman shackled to a wall. She had on a tight leather bustier and dark stockings and wore a spiked collar around her neck. She was quite beautiful with long, shiny blond hair and a shapely body.

A crowd of about five middle-aged men formed a circle around her. I was afraid to look too closely, as I didn't want to appear rude (which I realized was totally illogical considering where I was), but I got the sense that whatever activity the female slave and her partner were indulging in was coming to a close, since the observers began to wander away. My heart palpitated even more furiously as I bolted back up the stairs and went outside.

"How'd it go?" Matt asked.

I told him I didn't really see much. "I thought it was just a spanking night, though" I said.

"It's whatever you want to do," the doorman said.

"She wants to get spanked." Gaby was now apparently functioning as my spokesperson.

"Really?" Matt said, cocking his head. He seemed interested in helping out.

"Sort of." I quickly assessed the situation: me, man, get spanked=guilt-stricken.

Before I could protest or lay out my concerns, Matt took me by the hand and led me back downstairs. He was very "Jersey," with gold chains draped around his muscular neck and tattoos that ran the length of his arms. Yet, despite his tough-looking exterior, he exuded gentleness.

We bypassed the hostess station (good to know people in high or, rather, low places) and Matt took me into a cubicle, which was narrow and long and painted black. The metaphorical straight-backed chair sat at the far wall.

"What do you like?" he asked. "I like role playing."

"Sure. Whatever," I said, quickly adding that I couldn't be marked. He blinked a couple of times. I couldn't tell if he was disappointed or just processing the information.

Matt cleared his throat and told me to stand in the corner. I did as he instructed, and he came up behind me, launching into an office scenario. "Clarisse, you've been bad. You made another mistake on that letter I wanted you to send out."

I immediately realized I was not a fan of this kind of role-playing.

"That's not my fucking name," I said.

Matt, however, did not pick up on my cue, ignored my foul language, and kept on going with the Clarisse scenario. I hated it and wanted to punch him in the arm. He was also a very bad actor and spoke in monotones.

"Damn it," I said, my nose to the wall.

Finally, Matt pulled me over his lap and spanked me over my jeans. After a few well-placed swats, he reached under me and began to unbutton my pants, obviously wanting to deliver a bare-bottom spanking.

"No. I can't," I said, thinking about my husband.

"Okay, but you've been very naughty, Clarisse."

"Whatever."

Matt continued to spank me over my pants for a few minutes, but it was lacking in intensity. I decided I was completely bored and pulled myself up off of his lap. "Well, thanks," I said.

"Sure," he said. "Anytime."

We went upstairs and back outside where Gaby was waiting.

"Was it good?" my friend asked.

Since the doorman was within earshot, I told her it was great.

Gaby and I said goodnight to Matt and went our separate ways. She headed off to the subway; I began my walk to Grand Central to catch the train home. There was no need to say anything to my husband. It was an insignificant dalliance.

MAY 9

A THOROUGH SHOT LIST AND SUSTAINABLE FAITH

My business partner and I began putting together the shot list for the June shoot and, in between spurts of work, I spun out my personal philosophy, one that I really wanted to believe: that a person's thoughts to a great degree determine his or her reality—whether they're deeply rooted in the subconscious or otherwise. Ron explained his position: that reality, life on planet earth, was more of a crap shoot. For some reason that depressed me.

"Are you afraid to die?" I asked, knowing I could talk to him about pretty much anything if I needed to.

"I try not to think about it," Ron said.

And then something occurred to me, which I didn't share with my business partner: Since I'd begun indulging in this little ritual with my dom, my incessant, obsessive fear of death—the ultimate loss of control—had receded into the background. Spanking and discipline, it seemed, had provided the consummate distraction. And oddly, I was feeling more alive than I had in years. (Contentedness be damned.)

MAY 10

RARE FORM, LIMITS PUSHED

Feeling relieved that I'd once again gotten out of broadcasting my session with Ms. Cynthia by claiming my computer was malfunctioning, I showed up for my appointment in rare form, ready to push the limits: mine, Ms. C's, and Carl's. I walked in and immediately began to curse and throw attitude. When my domme ordered me to strip naked, I begrudgingly ripped off my top, pants, and underwear and flung my clothing across the room.

"I said to place the items across the chair—nicely," Ms. C said, turning toward my cell that lay on the bureau at the end of the room.

"Carl, she's very unruly today."

"Whatever," I said, snarling.

"Get over here now." My domme reached out, grabbed me, and yanked me across her solid thighs.

Throughout the next twenty minutes, I continued to pitch tantrums like an unmanageable child to ensure I got what I needed—and wanted. Ms. C spanked me, her muscular biceps ensuring a satisfying blow with every move. And with each whack I cried out.

I was then ordered to put my nose in the corner and, after stomping my feet like a three-year old, Ms. Cynthia made me bend over, my hands on the wall, my nakedness on display, for a sound, semi-brutal flogging with a switch. But I couldn't control myself, or rather I chose not to, and after I let loose with another long string of F-bombs, Ms. C lost her patience. "Get over there," she said, pointing. "On your stomach."

My bottom smarting, I obediently lied down on the leather bench, which was covered with fresh towels.

"Hands out in front," Ms. C said. "And keep still."

"Use the bath brush and give it to her hard," Carl commanded, his rich, authoritative voice flowing through my cell's speaker.

"She needs to understand, once and for all, that this is not a game."

"Oh, God," I said, remembering that the bath brush was one of the more brutal implements, capable of reducing, as Carl had mentioned months ago, the most masochistic of women to tears.

Ms. C began to paddle my behind, and I yelped like a wounded animal, reacting to the sting of wood on flesh. The pain was now almost to the point of being unbearable, yet I wanted more. I kicked violently, my legs pounding up and down, and reflexively put my hands behind me to protect my bottom.

"Hands in front," Ms. Cynthia said.

"Fuck you!"

"That's it." Ms. C retrieved a longish piece of rope from her bag and, in a few deft moves, tied my hands in front of me. "She's out of control, Carl."

"Get out the gloves," my long-distance dom said, his voice crackling through the speaker.

My body now prickling with dread and anticipation, I watched as Ms. Cynthia snapped on a pair of rubber gloves and dipped her fingers into a jar of Vaseline.

"No!" I screamed. "No fucking way."

"Watch that mouth, Deborah," Carl said firmly.

Before I could take another breath, I felt a finger, and then two, enter my bottom. Oddly, I didn't find it unpleasant and was intrigued by my reaction.

"Apologize for your foul language," Carl said. "Ms. C, three fingers. We have to let Deborah know she cannot get away with this kind of behavior."

"No fucking way," I said as Ms. C carried out my dom's instructions.

"Deborah," Carl said, sounding more than just a bit exasperated. "Will you ever learn? Give her thirty with the bath brush, Ms. C, and make her count every single last one."

"Thirty?" I cried out, fully aware that this was going to hurt—a lot.

And it did. The first blow stung like hell, and I knew my butt would soon morph into a gruesome display of reds and purples.

"Start counting," Carl bellowed.

I began to count the spanks, my voice tiny and weak like a child's.

"Carl," Ms. C said, after delivering fifteen swats with the bath brush, "her skin is broken. She's bleeding. We have to stop."

"No. Fifteen more."

I could sense Ms. C's hesitation. But she did as she was told, and by the time we'd finished, both she and I were spent.

"Do you want to look at your bottom?" Carl asked. I guess he got off on this, too, and would most likely have me describe the spoils of the BDSM session.

"Not particularly," I said, glancing over at the full-length mirror that lined the far wall.

"Are you sure?"

"Yes," I said, feeling sore, but sated and calm.

"Pick up the phone, Deborah," Carl demanded.

I retrieved my cell, turned the speaker off, and held the phone up to my ear. Ms. C nodded and left the room to give us privacy.

"How are you feeling? Are you okay?" Carl asked.

"Yes," I said softly. "Thanks."

"I'll check in with you later if I don't get caught up in meetings. Otherwise we can catch up tomorrow."

"Sounds good. Talk to you soon," I said, figuratively glowing on the inside, but literally burning on the outside.

"I hope you got exactly what you wanted."

On our way out of the building, Ms. C made a point to tell me that she had fun, but delivering the anal punishment was a first for her. "I actually enjoyed it," she said. (I guess I did too.)

MAY 11

MARKED

The hostess at the Japanese restaurant in the mall led my husband and me to our booth. Without thinking, I slid across the seat.

"Ouch," I said. "My butt is a bit sore."

Andrew nodded, his eyes cast downward.

"I'm a bit marked."

"I know," Andy said, quietly. "I saw it when you went into the shower."

"Ritualized abuse. Ha, ha" I said, trying to inject some levity.

My husband did not seem so amused.

I quickly changed the subject.

MAY 15

A ROSALYN BY ANY OTHER NAME

I'd decided I couldn't shell out money to get spanked anymore. It wasn't so much about the cost, as Andy didn't seem to mind; it was how it made me feel to have to pay for it: sordid.

CARL: *There has to be someone out there who would be more than happy to paddle you into a state of bliss. Give me a couple of hours.*

It took him less than an hour to find a willing female spanker. Free of charge.

CARL: *Her name is Rosalyn. She said she would be delighted to help out.*

I was delighted, too.

Carl sent me the link to Rosalyn's information page (on two spanking sites), where I checked out her photos. In one, her head was pitched slightly to the right. Her lips were painted a fire-engine red and her eyelids a bright blue. She had chin-length hair, which was gray, slightly curly, and a bit on the thin side. I would have guessed that she was in her fifties. She wore a matronly looking dress but sported what appeared to be a faux fur cape, which made the animal-rights activist in me happy.

But something seemed off in her picture, and I couldn't quite put my finger on it.

MAY 16

BEND ME, BREAK ME

This obsession, this need to be disciplined, was now consuming every fiber of my being, my every waking thought, and I found myself wanting to be taken to the edge—taken <u>over</u> the edge, to the point where I would relinquish complete control of my psyche, my body, and my soul. And I wished to hell it could be Carl who would take me there.

ME: *Are you there?*

CARL: *Yes, what's up?*

ME: *I want to be broken. I want to give myself up completely. I want to be brought to tears. And cry like I'll never be able to stop.*

CARL: *Oh boy.*

ME: *What's wrong?*

CARL: *There's a part of me that fears this: once you get the proper discipline, you will be thrown deeper down the abyss of surrender. Your hunger for pain, humiliation, and embarrassment will never be satiated. It will only make you more ravenous. Be very careful; this is a very strong drug.*

ME: *Do you really feel you could make me cry?*

CARL: *Yes, dear. If we ever got together, I could most certainly bring you to tears. Easier than you could ever imagine.*

ME: *I really wish I could see you.*

CARL: *Me too.*

ME: *It's probably better, though, that you are so far away.*

CARL: *For you, yes. But for now, you need someone who can satisfy your needs. Give Rosalyn a chance.*

Apparently, I'd have to try and find satisfaction with another stranger. Another woman.

MAY 21

A PUBLIC SPANKING

Andy said he wanted to go with me into the city and was somewhat relieved that Rosalyn was meeting me at a public place. I was too. But I really wouldn't have wanted it any other way; at least not without a thorough screening.

On the way in on the train, my husband and I sat close and held hands. His mood seemed to have shifted, and I felt pleased that he continued to allow me my indulgences and reminded myself, for the umpteenth time, that this did benefit him.

We arrived at Grand Central Station an hour or so before I was to meet Rosalyn. "Let's grab a drink."

I took my husband by the arm and led him up the marble stairway to one of the station's restaurants.

Once we were settled in at the bar, Andrew ordered a beer, and I ended up knocking back two martinis. I mentioned how nervous I was; my husband just shrugged and gave me a half-hearted smile. After we paid up, we took the S train to Times Square. Andy went off to wait for me at our favorite bar on 46th Street; I walked several blocks to the west and headed toward the allotted meeting place: a bistro across the street from Paddles.

The bar area inside was long and narrow and manned by a female Russian bartender. No one was there who remotely resembled Rosalyn, so I plopped myself down on a barstool and ordered water to remedy a severe case of dry mouth. About fifteen minutes later, my "playmate" arrived, spotted me immediately, and slid onto the stool next to me.

"The traffic going through the tunnel was a bitch," Rosalyn said, apologizing for being late. Her voice was smoky and deep—masculine. She wore a white blouse with pearls, a dark skirt, and heels. She was also sweating profusely, which created an odd effect on her heavily powdered face. It made her look plastic, wax-like. I smiled pleasantly, working very hard not to register any dismay.

After we each had ordered a glass of wine, Rosalyn launched into her story about making the changeover from a man to a transgenderist. "I've been taking hormones for several years," she said, "which is why I've been able to grow breasts." Leaning closer, Rosalyn informed me that she still had her man parts "by choice." Her arms, legs, chest, and face, however, were pretty much hairless, and for a moment I felt a pang of envy and thought about getting laser treatments to get rid of those pesky chin hairs that kept sprouting up.

"Whew, it's hot," my new friend said and took out a Kleenex to wipe at her forehead. She seemed just as nervous as me.

After another glass of wine, I felt certain that I was sufficiently lubed and my inhibitions low enough to embark on this adventure with my play pal. I also knew instinctively that I could trust Rosalyn and that I wouldn't be harmed. Over the years, my deep intuitive nature always seemed to pay off. My husband did not fully understand my abilities, yet at times he would rely on me to make decisions based on my gut feelings about people—contractors in particular.

Rosalyn picked up the bill for our drinks in spite of my protests, and we headed across the street to the S&M club. A memorial party was in full swing, commemorating the former, recently deceased manager of a notorious underground BDSM joint that sprang up in the 1960s. The place was wall-to-wall with all sorts of enthusiasts, young and old, and I would have bet my last dollar Ms. C was there among them.

My new playmate led the way through the crowd and brought me upstairs to an open room that was more of a platform without walls. A portly man dressed in a maid's outfit was bent over a spanking horse, his broad, flat ass sticking up in the air. A tough-looking woman with massive, tattooed arms was flogging him slowly, methodically, with a tasseled whip. She appeared extremely bored. The man, who was wearing thigh-high, white fishnet stockings, winced and tittered with each lashing, and I had to repress the urge to laugh.

Rosalyn led me to the far side of the room and pulled a straight-backed chair toward the center. She sat down, flung me over her lap, and began spanking me over my pants. At one point, I looked up at her and saw that she had dropped her blouse, exposing small, slightly engorged breasts that jutted out above a tight black corset.

Oh God, no, I thought. I was not expecting this at all.

My disciplinarian continued to spank me, mumbling phrases like "naughty girl" and "bad little Deborah." Soon, after one particularly mild swat on my bottom, I bit her arm to provoke her, since she was just not spanking me hard enough. Rosalyn laughed, unbuttoned my jeans, and pulled them down, exposing my bare bottom. I squirmed and wriggled about on her lap, but within a few minutes I lost my enthusiasm, like I did with Matt the doorman. It was just not satisfying, and I was feeling a bit repelled by the boob action.

Not wanting to hurt Rosalyn's feelings, I made up an excuse. "I need to get back to my husband.

As I pulled myself up off her lap and fastened my pants, I spotted a young man standing a few feet away and realized he must have been watching the entire time. His eyes were dark and angry, but he was quite obviously hungry for some fun.

Rosalyn buttoned up her blouse and patted her sweaty face with a handkerchief. We headed back downstairs and snaked our way through the crowded room. Suddenly, I became keenly aware of a presence behind me and spun around. It was the guy from upstairs.

"Do you want to spank me?" I said, taunting him.

"Yes." His eyes burned with desire.

I strongly sensed that this kid was a sadist-in-the-making, but I didn't care. "Are you sure?" I smiled and gave him my version of a wink.

"Yes, very badly," he said, revealing a German accent.

Sticking out my bottom, I let him deliver a couple of sloppy swats. I quickly straightened up and, along with Rosalyn, bolted off through the sea of people, leaving the little Nazi behind.

Once out on the street, my play pal, who still had the gentleman in her, both figuratively and literally, hailed me a cab. I hopped in, told Rosalyn I had a good time and that I'd be in touch. I knew I wouldn't, however. Not that I didn't like her as a person. I did. The male/female thing was just a little too radical for me.

But I made a huge mistake: I told my husband on the train ride home that Rosalyn was half male.

"It's really not a big deal," I said. "And I'm not going to see her again."

Andy clamped his mouth tightly shut and shook his head.

"I'm sorry," I said.

He fumed silently all the way up the line.

MAY 22

SUNDAY FURY

My husband was not the only one who was upset: I was supposed to contact Carl after my session with Rosalyn, but I got distracted talking with the cabbie on the way back to Joe Allen's. And then I was with Andy, who I eventually managed to placate by telling him I had no clue Rosalyn was a tranny until we met.

As soon as I logged on to my computer, after rolling out of bed close to noon, Carl popped up on IM.

CARL: *I was in a complete state of panic when I didn't hear from you last night. And then this morning: Nada. Zip. Zilch. No email from you. Nothing. I set this up with Rosalyn. I don't know this person, and if anything had happened to you, I would feel extraordinarily responsible. I would not be able to live with myself. I care very deeply for you, Deborah. But when I tell you to do something, you do it. I have an amazing memory; and if we ever meet, this will be addressed.*

I apologized for my misdeeds; we smoothed things over, and he wished me a good day. But I was secretly pleased that he seemed to care so deeply—and a bit turned on.

Later, following an impulse, I called the first person on the list of therapists given to me a month ago. Katarina happened to be there and picked up the phone. She had a pleasant, appealing voice, and I could easily have imagined her doing voiceover commercials. Katarina told me she'd be willing to take me on as a client, although she'd be retiring in a year.

"Hopefully, I don't need more than a year to get fixed," I said, joking.

Katarina laughed. "When do you want to come in?"

"As soon as you have an opening."

"I have a cancellation tomorrow at 2:00."

"Great. I'll be there."

She rattled off the address.

MAY 23

FIRST DAY OF A NEW SCHOOL OF THOUGHT

It was my first therapy session in decades, which made me feel a bit apprehensive, but it was a far cry from what I would experience before I'd go in for a spanking and discipline session. This seemed more like the first day of school.

After I dropped my husband off at Starbucks where he planned to work remotely from his laptop, I parked on the street near Katarina's building, a stately white Victorian that had been converted into offices. At the front door, I punched in the code she'd given me and was buzzed into the building.

Once upstairs, I plopped down on the bench outside my new therapist's office and checked my cell for messages from Carl. Within a few minutes, the door opened and I was greeted by a mature woman who dressed like Rosalyn, with pearls and a conservative skirt and blouse, and I had to stifle a chuckle. I highly doubted, however, that she wore a corset.

After we settled in, Katarina asked me why I sought out therapy.

"Well in part for my OCD and largely to figure out what's keeping me from success—the kind of success I want."

"Tell me about the obsessive-compulsive tendencies."

"Boy. Where do I start?" I said. "It's really second nature by now."

"Would you describe it as debilitating?"

"No. Not really. Just an annoyance."

Katarina asked me when it began, and I told her about the time I was twelve and walking home from school, taking my usual short-cut through the woods. "As I approached this very large pine tree, I had this bizarre thought pop into my head: if I walked around the tree 'X' amount of times, until it felt right, my mother would buy me a bra, which I desperately wanted. When I got home, my mother handed me a bag. And guess what was in it?"

"No," she said, her eyes widening.

"I not only got a bra, but I felt I could now control events around me. And I officially became a dyed-in-the-wool, obsessive-compulsive quasi-neurotic. But then," I explained, "it eventually morphed into something different, and I would perform these little rituals to keep something bad from happening." I paused. "So far, so good. Knock on wood."

Katarina smiled and asked about my marriage and my husband. I gave her the lowdown, telling her that I never felt physically attracted to Andy.

"Do you like the way your husband smells?"

"I can't believe you said that. When I first met him, no."

"That can be a hard one to overcome."

"But," I told my new therapist, "I really don't notice it anymore."

There were other things, however—in particular, my husband's peculiar habit of putting IEs on the ends of words, which drove me crazy. "He says things like duckies and goosies. I tell him that three-year olds don't get laid."

Katarina seemed amused but suggested there might be a more constructive way of communicating my feelings.

"I thought I was being clever and not hurtful," I said. "But this is all pretty insignificant stuff. All couples have their issues. Right?"

And then it occurred to me. I really should discuss the spanking, since it was intertwined with my relationship with my husband, and it was definitely an obsession. "Katarina, you might think it's a little strange," I said, stopping to take a sip of water. "Have you heard of BDSM?"

"Body dysmorphic disorder."

"No. Actually, it stands for bondage, discipline, sadomasochism."

"Oh." She seemed rather surprised. "I didn't know that."

(I guess the subject was not part of her graduate course work.)

Taking a somewhat clinical approach, I filled her in on the spanking and explained that it's a part of BDSM. I also told her about the two women I saw in NYC—and Carl.

"One of the reasons I think I do this," I said, "and trust me, this is just conjecture—is because I'm looking for the love and attention I never felt I got from my father, who traveled a lot and was never really emotionally available. And the reason I'm pretty sure it's in part a father issue is because I don't think I'd have responded to the women if Carl were not participating."

Rambling on, I recounted the first time I heard that my Dad loved me. "I was going back to college after having dropped out in my freshman year. I called his office to ask him something, and his secretary answered the phone. She said she was very happy for me that I was going back to school and asked me if I had any idea how much my father loved me. I said nothing. I didn't have a clue."

Katarina tilted her head, as she digested what I'd told her. "Okay. I would have to agree with you. There might be a deep connection between fatherly love and the spanking and your attachment to Carl."

"There's more," I said. "Last summer my brother told me I was irrelevant when we were growing up, mainly due to the age difference between me and him and my older sister. He's seven years older. My sister is six years older. And a week before he told me that, my sister said I wasn't wanted, that I was 'a mistake.' Maybe that's why

I have this insatiable need for attention from an authority figure. Also, I <u>was</u> kind of ignored by my mother and father—even though I know there was love there, unexpressed of course—but I guess it was the parenting style back then. And I have definite abandonment issues." I suddenly flashed back on the incident in Home Depot and the anxiety I felt when I couldn't find my husband.

Something else occurred to me. "Andy doesn't have an authoritative bone in his body. I pretty much wear the pants. He'll basically do anything I want him to do. And he lets me do whatever I want. So, I wonder if that's part of it too. Maybe I need that...Oh hell, I don't know. It's all so confusing."

Katarina scribbled something down on her yellow pad. I didn't ask what.

"But the main thing is, and this is kind of weird, and I don't understand it: I get incredibly turned on by the thought of being spanked and disciplined. And it really does help my sex life at home as I'm able to transfer those feelings to my husband."

"But you don't feel attracted to Carl?"

"Correct," I said. "I have no sexual feelings for him whatsoever."

"Hmmm" I could tell Katarina was doing her best to take all this in. The fifty minutes went by quickly.

"Shall we set another appointment?" she asked.

"That bad, huh?"

Katrina laughed, and I told her that, yes, I'd like to come back, that I was glad I was doing this. In fact, something told me it would pay off—that maybe I sought out therapy for a reason of which I was not yet aware. Once again, it was that old gut instinct.

JUNE 12

READY, ACTION, MORE

We managed to shoot our short film in three days. It provided a wonderful distraction from my other distraction. However, as soon as we wrapped, it was back to business as usual. But my need to have a physical experience with my dom had become almost unbearable. My body ached for it.

JUNE 17

HOW CAN I HELP?

As I walked by Andrew's office, I overheard him on the telephone with one of his colleagues from work.

"What can I do for you," he said, in a robotic tone. "How can I help you?"

I stood in the doorway and waited until he hung up. "Andy, you really need to stop trying to save everyone," I said.

My husband looked at me solemnly and said nothing in response.

Later, when I went in to take my shower after exercising in the living room, Andy neglected to bring me my towel—for the first time since he'd started this little ritual.

"Andy? Did you forget?" I called out as the water cascaded down my back. Within a minute or so, my husband came into the bathroom and placed my towel over the shower door.

"Thank you!"

Andy nodded slightly, his mouth downturned, and went back into his office.

JUNE 24

THAT OLD MONSTER JEALOUSY

After spending the week working on the NY property, with me weeding the gardens and Andy rewiring parts of the house, the two of us plus my cat, Mamie, headed off to VT. After my husband wrapped up a few conference calls on the way through Connecticut, we stopped at our usual spot to get a Chai in Massachusetts and later got lunch in southern Vermont at our favorite spot, a farm stand/restaurant that sells organic produce.

My husband and I chatted a lot along the way about the houses, about Andy's work, and his daughter's current challenges with her husband. We also took the time to stop at an antique place an hour or so away from our summer place. Andy looked for tools; I looked for crystal jars with silver tops and century-old dolls with china faces. It was a trek we both always enjoyed.

Finally, we were back at our beloved house and spent a half hour unpacking and settling back in. As always, I felt happy to be here, but I was not happy with my dom. Before, any time I'd fire up my computer and Carl was on IM, he'd immediately ping me. But not today, so I had to deduce he was instant messaging with someone else.

"Come on!" I said a bit too loudly, feeling thoroughly frustrated and a bit abandoned. And I was experiencing more than a little bit of jealousy.

"Who are you talking to?" Andrew asked as he stepped into the first-floor office.

"No one. Just waiting for an email about work," I said over my shoulder from my desk. "No big deal."

"You sure?" my husband asked, sensing my agitation.

"Yeah. Really, it's fine," I said, realizing how in tune Andrew and I were with each other's feelings and moods.

"Okay. Whatever," he said as he headed back into the kitchen, which was across the hall from our office.

JULY 2

FEAR—IT'S A KEEPER

The bar at the bottom of the hill was crowded with both summer people and the locals. Andrew, who had overcome a certain degree of social awkwardness since we'd been together, seemed eager to engage in conversation and, strangely enough, exuded a level of confidence I'd never really seen before—which made him more attractive in my eyes.

We spotted some new friends, a couple who had a home on a lake a few miles away and a soybean farm down south. James was a highly successful entrepreneur with his fingers in multiple cross-industry ventures. His wife, Louisa, was sweet and down to earth. I sidled up to her, and we got to talking about relationships. Andrew, sensing this was going to disintegrate into "girl talk," excused himself and ambled off to other end of the bar to chat up some of the locals.

"Marriage is hard," Louisa remarked, "especially when your husband is high profile and successful." She cocked her head toward James, who had a boyish and playful manner about him. "Women are always coming on to him."

"Andrew is not high profile, thankfully," I said to her jokingly.

Louisa then confessed to being sixty-seven and to having had a series of surgeries to keep herself young and attractive.

"Nothing wrong with wanting to look good," I said. "It's like having a haircut. Plastic surgery might cost more, but what's the difference? It's just a drag that women feel so much more pressure than men to remain young and attractive."

Louisa nodded, knowingly.

"And sometimes you have to work to keep a marriage alive," I added. "You know, find ways to spice things up."

She appeared to take in what I'd just said, but I didn't think it was wise to offer up any more information about my current foray into this other world. After all, I didn't want to come across as a freak.

Craig, a quirky, but deeply soulful man, suddenly appeared beside me; Andrew was now sitting one stool over.

"How are you doing?" Craig asked.

"Good," I replied.

"Fear keeps us stuck in relationships."

I shot Craig a puzzled look. I knew he was prone to speaking in non-sequiturs, but this time his comment struck a chord within me. Was he talking about Andrew? Was he talking about me? Or maybe I was being paranoid and he was simply talking about himself. I didn't know. But what I did know was that, stuck or not, I didn't like being alone. Never have. Never will. And besides, I really did enjoy my time with Andy and appreciated all we'd done and created together—maybe now more than ever before.

"I guess you're right," I said, not really wanting to continue the conversation. I reached over to my husband and asked him how the Scrabble game was going on the iPad.

"Kicking ass," Andrew said, refocusing on the game.

I turned to back James and Louisa, who were ready to leave with their takeout dinner.

"How long are you staying up here?" James asked, knowing that I traveled back and forth to NY.

"About a week," I said. "Then off I go again."

I always quipped with our VT friends that, for me, going back to New York was like going to rehab, since I often spent my evenings at the house by myself watching a movie and drinking water. "Got to give the system a rest. Clean out the pipes, so to speak," I'd say.

It did, however, cross my mind that Andrew might think I was going home for reasons other than seeing friends and keeping appointments. I was not.

Tonight, thanks to the always-generous bartender and my tendency to forget to go to the bathroom before leaving, I had to stop and pee along the roadside on the walk up the hill. Andrew and I got the giggles, even though he seemed slightly mortified.

"Okay. So, it's not dignified," I said, pointing to a bank of bushes. "But I either go in there or I go in my pants."

When we got back to the house, we ended up wrestling in the living room and having sex on the hand-crafted wool rug like a couple of drunken teenagers. But before I went off to sleep, while Andrew was in the bathroom brushing his teeth, I made sure to check my cell phone for emails from Carl. We seemed to be back on track, and I was now getting the attention from my dom that I truly felt I needed.

JULY 4

KABOOM—WITHOUT THE BANG

"Damn it," I said, when I couldn't get an online connection. I spun around in my desk chair. Andy was rumbling about in the kitchen, gathering up the recycling. "Andy? Can you help me with this? I think it's the cable."

My husband walked up behind me. "What can I do for you?" I looked up at him. He had a far-off look in his eyes.

"Jesus, Andy. You sound just like you're talking to someone from work. I'm your wife; not your colleague." My email suddenly sprung alive. "Never mind. It's all right. It's working now."

"Okay," he said quietly and went back into the kitchen.

After dark, Andrew and I settled in on the screened-in porch to watch the fireworks that were being set off across the lake. It was the customary annual duel between two families who had houses on the same cove. The sky lit up with reds, blues, and whites.

"Wow," I said. "That was a good one."

Andrew nodded.

I reached over and touched his arm lightly. "You seem sad, Andy."

"No. Just a bit tired."

"Okay," I said, accepting his explanation. "Maybe we can turn in early."

JULY 7

ANOTHER DISTRACTION FROM THE DISTRACTION

Two years ago, I bought a stuffed Halloween witch at a shop that sells antiques along with arts and crafts, and I'd been trying to find the place ever since. It was as if it had disappeared. No matter how many times Andrew and I drove around the lake that lay to the south of us, no matter how many small towns we went through, I couldn't find it. I had no idea why it mattered so much to me. But it did. And today I was on a mission.

"This is crazy," I said, glancing over at my husband in the passenger seat. "It doesn't make any sense. It's like the shop fell off the map."

We ended up driving for an hour in search of the shop.

"I think you need to let it go," my husband said.

"I know. It's obsessive, but it bugs me," I said, happy that I'd been able to get my mind off Carl and discipline. The relief was short lived.

JULY 10

OFFICIALLY ADDICTED TO CARL

I had not heard back from Carl since I'd emailed him two days ago, and I felt the burning tingle of anxiety spreading down my arms and up my back. I couldn't seem to control my feelings of abandonment, and it was getting worse. I was unable to stop thinking about him. I wanted to scream. I was getting angrier and more upset by the minute, and it felt really bad.

On my drive back to New York, I resolved to break my addiction to him—this extreme emotional dependency. I had to; for the sake of my own sanity. I also knew on some level it was not fair to Andy.

But how? Suddenly, the light bulb went off in my head: I would find another male disciplinarian, someone in New York City—even if it was just an online relationship. "That's exactly what I'll do," I said to myself.

When I got home, I decided I would join a spanking site, one of several dedicated to consummate practitioners who were looking to find playmates. And even though I'd been indulging in this fetish for a while, I still felt nervous and somewhat intimidated, not to mention guilty. But this seemed, in perhaps my delusional state of mind, the only way to extract myself from Carl's grip. Breathing deeply, wiping my damp palms on my pants, I scrolled through several of the bios, which described what each guy liked and if he had a particular fetish, and found two possible candidates.

The first man's profile said he was into domestic discipline and "enjoyed" caning women, which I found intriguing but a bit distasteful. I labeled him "Satan." The second one, who sported a white beard and had a bit of a gut, said he was a "gentle dom." I dubbed him "Santa." I wrote a brief note to them both, asking if they would be interested in disciplining a "naughty miss."

JULY 11

FURIOUSLY DISAPPOINTED—BUT MOVIN' ON

When I got up, I immediately IMd Carl.

ME: *I think I have found two possible doms in NYC. Waiting to hear back.*

CARL: *That's great!*

That's "<u>great</u>?" *What the heck,* I thought, realizing that what I really wanted was to make my dom jealous; but no such luck, since he encouraged people to play with multiple partners to avoid emotional attachments, which was exactly what had happened to me.

CARL: *Let me know how it goes.*

ME: *Sure will. Talk to you later!*

I wanted to tell him to go fuck himself. But I didn't. Instead, I sent each of the two doms a second message and bratted out big time—a sort of screening process to see how they would respond, which would help me determine who was the best fit.

JULY 12

REVENGE

"Satan" contacted me first. He came across angry and cruel, and I quickly struck him from the list. "Santa" responded pretty quickly as well, and I decided I would follow through, since he sounded nice and was eager to pursue a dominant/submissive relationship.

Anyone could be replaced. <u>Anyone.</u>

JULY 14

SCREW THE GUILT

I began exchanging emails with Santa—furiously, just like I did with Carl. To my delight, my new dom seemed smart, funny, and engaging. He told me a bit about his past playmates and said that he tended to have long-term relationships with his submissives.

SANTA: *I don't believe in spreading myself too thin. I like to really get to know the woman I play with.*

I told him I had to agree with his approach, but I did not mention my tendency to become emotionally attached.

Santa informed me that he too was married and that he had three children from his former marriage and a stepchild with his current wife, who he had no plans of leaving. I told him the same applied to me where Andy was concerned, which was the ultimate truth.

ME: *Just curious, though, how do you handle the guilt, since I'd say it's safe to assume your wife has no clue what you do?*

He immediately sent back an email.

SANTA: *Screw guilt. What she doesn't know won't hurt her.*

ME: *I wish I could get there. But maybe men are better at that: compartmentalizing.*

After I had dinner by myself in front of the TV, I called Andrew. But he was not picking up. I tried again in a half an hour and then two hours later. At 11:45 PM I still hadn't heard back from him, so I called RJs, the local bar in Garnersville, where we have our summer house. "Hi," I said into the phone. "It's Deborah, Andrew's wife. Was Andy there tonight? I can't find him, and I'm worried something's happened."

According to the bartender, who was also a friend of ours, my husband had left about fifteen minutes ago. I wanted to ask if Andy was alone, but I didn't want to come across like a distrustful spouse—or a stalking one.

"Thanks. At least I can rest assured he wasn't attacked by a bear. Just a few beers," I said, making a rather lame attempt at humor.

After I hung up, I called Andrew's cell again. No answer. Now I was really concerned, so I shot my stepdaughter a text. Thankfully, she was still awake.

ME: *Have you heard from your Dad? He's M.I.A.*

COURTNEY: *Not since a few days ago.*

ME: *I can't find him. I've been calling him all night long. This is not like him to not call me back. I know he was at the bar.*

COURTNEY: *Where are you?*

ME: *Back in New York. Andy's in VT.*

COURTNEY: *I'm sure he's ok. Maybe he went home and fell asleep on the couch.*

ME: *Maybe that's it.*

I hung up feeling disconcerted. Andy was always responsive and always at my beck and call. The only other time something like this happened was when we were first together, and he went over to

Europe on a business trip. He had gone out with a bunch of his colleagues, and I could not get a hold of him until the next morning. His excuse was that he got drunk on Jägermeister at some bar and passed out in his hotel room. I believed him. First of all, he cannot hold his liquor well, and there was no reason to think he was not being truthful.

JULY 15

PROMISES, PROMISES

"Where were you last night, Andy?" I said into the phone, my tone casual, neutral. I didn't want to sound accusatory as I generally try to give people, including my husband, the benefit of the doubt.

"I was home. I fell asleep early and woke up at 3:00 AM. I didn't want to call and wake you up."

"Oh geez. I don't care what time it is. You know how I worry," I said. "I want to know you're okay."

My husband promised he would do his best "to remember."

"What's to remember, Andy? Just call me back when I call you, so I don't worry myself sick."

JULY 17

BACK TO THERAPY

"Maybe I should take up golf instead of this BDSM stuff," I said to my therapist, forcing a smile. "But Andrew would be really pissed then. He hates golf."

"Do you think what you're doing is upsetting him?"

"I'm not playing with anyone at the moment. The women, I mean. Andy doesn't know about the online stuff. I know it'd freak him out."

I put down my water glass and told Katrina about my attempts to break my addiction to Carl by reaching out to someone else and realized it was not as successful as I'd hoped.

My therapist uncrossed her legs. "What's that look on your face?" she asked.

"I really feel like I need to see him."

"Carl?"

"Yes."

"Are you falling in love?"

I sighed. "No. Not at all, but it's hard to explain. It's very different than romantic love. I would never, ever sleep with him. I wouldn't

63

want to. And yet on some level I need him, for all the reasons we talked about before. But it's definitely more like an emotional addiction. Who knows? Or perhaps it's my need for excitement."

"Your husband doesn't bring that to you, then? A sense of excitement?"

"I don't think it has anything to do with him; it's me. This thing, this discipline game, it also elicits the same kind of feeling I used to get before I'd perform—an adrenaline rush. So maybe that's some of it as well. Maybe it satisfies my need for a sort of excitement that's lacking in my life right now." I thought about what I'd said months ago to Carl when we first started communicating: that I was "content."

"Have you considered going back to acting?"

"I don't really want to. I hate the rejection. I hate being judged. And besides, I think it's too late."

I then mentioned something I'd read online in my attempts to understand what the hell I was doing—and why. "One psychologist said that submission—and this is like, in relation to the scenario between the disciplinarian and the sub—gives a person a break from all the responsibilities and stresses you can feel in life. Another one said it's is an attempt to find safety through dependency. That might also explain something since I never felt safe as a child."

"Really? Why?"

I told Katrina about this baby sitter, an older woman who was the mother of my mom's best friend, that used to terrify me with stories of sadistic caretakers who did things like submerge their wards in tubs of boiling water so hot their skin would peel off. "She also used to spin out these horrific tales of an apocalyptic world where the entire earth was on fire after a nuclear war," I said. "And I started having these recurring nightmares where everything on the planet had been destroyed. All the animals and people, except for me, were dead—burned alive from the radiation, and I would wander around in the wreckage, alone, cold, and petrified. She always said that the third world war was coming, and it was coming soon."

"She obviously had some serious issues there. Very sadistic."

"And this went on for ten years until my parents finally figured out what the deal was when they spoke to another couple who used this woman to babysit their son. She did the same thing to the boy. But I guess he eventually said something."

"_Ten_ years this went on?"

"Yeah, my parents thought that when she left, I was crying because I loved her and didn't want her to go. I did love her, but I didn't understand that what she was doing was not normal, that it was cruel."

"Why didn't <u>you</u> say something to your parents?"

"I didn't know how to communicate. I call it the Vines 'fine'."

"What's that?"

"In my family everyone and everything was always 'fine'. Even when it wasn't," I explained. "We never talked about anything. And when I would cry, no one asked me what was wrong. Or if there even <u>was</u> anything wrong. I cried all the time when I was a child. I also cried my way through high school."

"It sounds like you were neglected," she said. "You know, neglect, emotional abandonment, unless it's dealt with can translate into severe anxiety and obsession-compulsive behaviors."

I paused a moment. "I guess I am kind of messed up."

"I wouldn't say that. We all have challenges."

I shifted in my chair and took the dialogue in a different direction. "I don't know if anyone, including me, really fully understands why people get involved in this BDSM stuff. I feel like I'm grasping at straws." By the look on my therapist's face, I could tell she was just as clueless.

"But you know," I said, "I think it's just replacing one obsession for another." I explained to her about how my obsessive fear of death had been significantly mitigated since I started playing. "In a sick way, it's a huge relief."

JULY 18

THE ADULT SPANKING MANUAL

My first and former domme, using yet another pseudonym, recently published her instructional manual on the fine art of spanking, which I decided to bring up to Vermont to my husband, thinking it might help shed some light on the subject, at least in a clinical sense.

"You really need to read the book," I said to Andy as we sat out on the porch, watching the wild turkeys rooting around for seeds that had spilled out from the birdfeeder. "It really is well written. And it's funny."

Andrew didn't seem all that interested, but I went ahead and put it on his bedside table later that afternoon—just in case. What I really wanted was for him to understand that in my scenarios spanking did not involve sex. In Ms. Maplethorpe's world it didn't either. With couples who both practiced, it certainly could, but that was an entirely different story. I really hoped Andy would get it.

JULY 19

WHAT A DIFFERENCE A DOM MAKES

At around 6:30 PM, my husband and I made our usual trek down the hill to RJ's, where we were now considered regulars. Walking with our hands entwined, I remarked how fortunate we were to have all that we do, including each other. Oddly, I found myself saying that a lot lately.

Throughout the night, my cell phone buzzed with emails from Santa. But I'd begun to notice something: It felt different with him. I could not get him to slip into the role that Carl once inhabited as my disciplinarian, no matter how much I bratted out and misbehaved. I found myself wanting Carl even more.

JULY 20

A NOT SO HAPPY BIRTHDAY

It was my husband's birthday, so I offered to take him out to dinner at the local inn. Andrew had his favorite: mussels. I had mine: crab cakes. Our conversation was superficial, impersonal. We talked about the antique hutch that sat in the middle of the restaurant and how good business seemed to be for the owners, but not much else. Andrew checked his phone regularly, as I did mine. Something was not quite right between us, but I chose not to address it. It was, after all, a night of celebration.

When we'd finished eating, my husband and I headed off to RJs for a nightcap. We found a seat at the far end of the bar, where I struck up a conversation with a twenty-something blond man who was well on his way to becoming a successful businessman.

"I wish I had that kind of confidence when I was young," I told him. "When I was your age, self-esteem had not yet been invented—especially for women."

The young man laughed. My husband, however, who was sitting to my right, seemed sullen and moody.

"What's wrong?" I asked him later at home.

"I don't know why you have to do that," he said.

"Do what?"

"Never mind."

"You mean the guy at the bar? For God's sake, Andrew, he's twenty-two. Compared to us, he's a baby."

"Whatever."

"You know how I like talking to people," I said. "I don't understand why it's such a big deal. I'm not going to run off with anyone."

JULY 22

A JUGGLING ACT

"Make sure Mamie gets her pill every other day," I said to Andy as I packed my bags for my trip back to New York. "And be sure to give her the good cat food. Not that icky stuff we bought at the hardware store."

"Okay. No problem."

The drive back to New York was long, but the emails coming in from both Santa and Carl, who had recently become more attentive, kept me preoccupied and distracted. It was an interesting juggling act.

JULY 24

M.I.A. AGAIN

"Andrew, where are you? Can you call me please? I'm worried." Once again, it was midnight and my husband had not called me back. I'd left a message late afternoon and again at around 10:00 PM. I was now concerned that all was not well up there in the north woods. Or maybe I was just being paranoid. I knew my husband would never do anything untoward, anything that would hurt or compromise our marriage. He, after all, adored me.

JULY 25

A CALL TO ACTION

As soon as I hung up from Andy, who said that he once again fell asleep on the couch, my phone rang.

"Hello?"

My friend Adele wanted to know if I could come out for an impromptu board meeting in western NY for her non-profit arts organization. "You still want to participate, right?"

"Of course," I said. "I'll do anything I can to help."

After our call, I pushed a gush of guilt aside, fired up my computer, and shot my dom an IM.

ME: *Are you there?*

CARL: *What's going on?*

ME: *I'll be driving out to western New York for a board meeting. Syracuse is not too far off the beaten path. I could take a detour :-)*

CARL: *No way! How cool is that?*

ME: *Completely. But yikes...The thought of it makes me a nervous wreck.*

CARL: *It should. I will deliver everything I said I would.*

We decided where we would meet, and Carl spun out a rich scenario of how I'd be disciplined, how I would be punished. He also asked me to pick up some items, including a wooden bath brush, which he planned to use to spank me, and some latex gloves, the kind they use in doctors' offices. Apparently, anal discipline was on the agenda.

ME: *No fucking way! You do it. I'm not going to get gloves!*

CARL: *Watch that mouth, miss, and you do what I say, or I swear I will beat your ass to a pulp.*

ME: *Please don't ever use that word "beat."*

He apologized, but for one brief moment, an uncomfortable feeling passed through me, and I could not help but question my sanity.

My long-distance dom gave me further instructions: He wanted me to get some lubricant and a butt plug—all of which could be purchased online. Being a good little submissive, I did as I was told and had the items sent express mail. My excitement masked anything else I might have been feeling.

JULY 26

A NECESSARY EVIL

I was sitting cross-legged on the examination table, fully clothed, and had my nose in my cell phone obsessively checking for emails and texts. After lightly knocking on the door, my GP, a tall, handsome, dark-haired man, came inside. Dr. Simmons smiled congenially. "You're looking well."

"Doing my best," I said, my heart pounding heavily in my chest.

"So, what can I do for you?" My doctor quickly scanned the information on the top page of the file containing my medical history.

"I need to refill my Xanax prescription." I quickly uncrossed my legs and let them dangle off the table. "It's a necessary evil right now."

"Are you going out to LA?" he asked, knowing that I usually get a refill when I fly.

"No. It's stress. Good stress, though," I said thinking about all the adrenaline that floods my body on a daily basis due to this fetish of mine. But I realized that that stress is stress, no matter how you look at it, and I had to wonder if I was doing damage to my body—irreversible damage.

"Hmmm," Dr. Simmons mumbled. "Let me recheck your blood pressure." Apparently, it had registered above normal when the nurse took it earlier.

"Oh brother," I said, afraid of what the numbers might reveal.

Simmons gave me a look, wrapped the cuff around my arm, and pumped the black rubber bulb. I turned and watched the numbers on the display.

"One-thirty over 100," Dr. Simmons said, shaking his head of thick hair.

"Yikes." I was normally 110 over 80, sometimes even less.

"Can you tell me what's going on?" he asked, a look of concern passing over his face.

"Oh, you know, it's just life stuff." What could I possibly say? That I was going to drive over two hundred miles to get spanked, disciplined, and humiliated? That BDSM was now an important part of my life, and I needed it to enjoy sex with my husband who had no clue about my sub/dom relationship with Carl? And that within twenty-four hours, this man who I haven't seen in almost two decades would be thrashing my bottom until it was sore and bruised and maybe worse?

Thankfully, my doctor didn't push me for answers and wrote out the prescription. Relief was now on the way in the form of an oblong pink pill.

JULY 29

OFF TO SEE THE WIZARD

The drive along route 17/86 in upstate New York is generally a pleasant one, but this time I was too highly charged to fully appreciate the natural beauty as I zipped along the tree-studded highway. It normally took me about seven hours to get to my friend's house, but today it would take much longer due to the detour I planned to make.

About an hour after I'd gotten on the road, I took a phone call from my husband who was visiting his folks. "Hey," I said into my cell. "How are you?" I did my best to sound present and not seriously distracted. "How's D.C.?" I could feel my palms begin to dampen and my heart race.

"Good. Mom and Dad are doing okay. But Dad's slipping. His short-term memory is going."

"Oh, no. Not what I wanted to hear. I'm glad you went down." I'd always loved Andy's parents right from the day I met them. I particularly liked his father's dry sense of humor and his mother's no-nonsense approach to life.

I then asked how his daughter, Courtney, and her husband, Rod, were doing.

"Good. They were happy I stopped to see them."

"Of course they were," I said.

We chatted a bit more, and I updated him on my location and promised to call when I got to Adele's.

I clicked my phone off and grappled with a surge of remorse that made me ache inside when I thought about where I was headed. The walls of denial were beginning to crumble, and guilt was starting to rear its ugly head. I had always, up until five or six months ago, been completely honest with my husband—at least in matters that, well, mattered. Not those insignificant, nonthreatening things that occurred now and then, such as when a guy would come on to me when I was out with my girlfriends. I might have flirted back a bit, but nothing else happened, nor would I let it, so why even mention anything? What I was about to do, however, Andy would never understand. And I was certain if he knew, it would ruin my marriage, like it almost did Carl's several years ago.

"My wife must have suspected something," he'd told me last month. "She went rooting through my computer and found several emails from a woman I'd been playing with for years. The emails were very emotional. This woman thought she was in love with me. And like I told you, that's why I encourage my subs to play with other doms. Anyway, I spent thirty-six hours talking nonstop to my wife, trying to explain that this wasn't an affair. But she couldn't comprehend it. People outside the scene never will."

I was certain he was right about that. And, in spite of the conflict that raged inside of me, I also knew I couldn't stop myself from proceeding; I desperately needed the fix. I also understood, perhaps for the first time on a deep emotional level, that this fetish was no longer a desire or a want—it had become critical to my emotional survival.

As I pressed on the accelerator, I spotted a family of deer standing too close to the road. "Damn it. Get off the highway," I said aloud, unable to bear the thought of any harm coming to an animal. "Go home," I mumbled, wondering if I shouldn't heed my own words, but the thought was fleeting.

My brain went into spin mode as I zipped toward the Syracuse exit. What was about to take place, I once again rationalized, had nothing to do with sex—or love. And although I would be stripped naked, there would be absolutely no intercourse involved. But he would for sure throw me across his lap and spank me; he would make me crawl across the floor on my hands and knees, and he would paddle me until I was crying like I'd never stop. He would also discipline me anally. And when he felt I'd been properly punished, he would comfort me.

I popped half a Xanax and replayed the scenario over and over in my head. But as I took the turn off route 17/86 to go north, I began to feel sick to my stomach—especially since Carl had mentioned that he would often try to bring his subs to climax by manually stimulating them. For good reason, I'd shut that out of my head. And besides, he knew I would not allow it, because, for me, I would consider that a sexual act—an act of duplicity—but not anything else that might happen.

After driving twenty or so miles, I pulled over to the side of the road, took in a few deep breaths to stave off the nausea, and dialed my dom's number. He picked up immediately.

"Carl, it's me."

"Where are you?"

"I'm...I don't know where I am. Somewhere south of Syracuse. This is messed up."

"What's going on?" he asked.

"I don't know if I can do this. I want to. With all my heart and soul, I want to."

"Okay," he said, waiting for further explanation.

"I just—"

"Why don't you meet me for coffee, and we can talk about it."

"Because I'm afraid of what would happen," I said.

"Yes, you know exactly what would happen, young lady."

My body responded to his words, his stern tone a surefire trigger. But I didn't know what else to say.

"Deborah, are you all right?"

"No. I don't know." I realized I had stopped breathing and pulled in a lungful of air.

"I'm not going to hurt you. You know that. And you know exactly what I'm going to do. We discussed it. And you can tell me to stop anytime if you feel uncomfortable." His tone was gentle, reassuring.

"I really want to see you," I said into my cell, fighting a growing sense of panic that if I didn't see him, I might lose him for good.

"Then why don't you?" It was a perfectly logical question.

"Because—"

"Remember, you need this, Deborah." His comment mirrored my thoughts of a half an hour ago.

"I know I do." We remained in silence for a moment.

"I'll text you when I get there."

I clicked off the phone, got back on the road, and headed north.

Shortly before I got to our meeting place, a motel just beyond the Syracuse city limits, I called Andrew. He answered right away.

"Hey," I said. "I know we just spoke, but I wanted to hear your voice. How's it going?"

"Good." He then paused. "What's going on?"

"Nothing. I miss you."

"Me, too," Andy said.

"Do you still love me?" I tried to disguise the nagging doubt in my voice.

"Yes," he said. "Do you still love me?"

"Of course. Why wouldn't I?"

I ended the conversation feeling very unsettled and popped the other half of the Xanax.

After checking in at the motel where a wedding party had taken up most of the rooms, I anxiously waited for Carl. My thoughts were jumbled, but the adrenaline that now coursed through my body from the anticipation of what lay ahead was enough to overshadow any other emotion that I might otherwise have harbored. After I had neatly laid out the accoutrements that I'd purchased from the online Pleasure Chest store on the bed, I began pacing back and forth. I could barely sit still, even though I'd ingested 0.5 mgs of my antianxiety drug.

Within fifteen minutes my dom was knocking on the door. I let him in; we both broke into big smiles, hugged briefly, and remarked at how great it was to see each other after all this time—just like two long-lost friends from college.

And then a wave of guilt flooded through my body, and I felt like I was going to throw up. "I can't. I'm sorry. I just can't."

I could see the look of disappointment on Carl's face. He reached out and touched me lightly on my arm. "There's nothing to feel badly about. It's just play. We both need this."

Tongue tied, I stood there shaking my head. "I really have to go," I said, my voice barely a whisper.

"Wow. Okay, then," Carl said. "I understand."

He handed me a hundred-dollar bill to reimburse me for the cost of the room. "Thank you," I said, appreciatively.

As I stood by the door to say a final goodbye, Carl leaned in to me and kissed me on the cheek. "I love you," he said softly. I was taken aback by his words, stunned, really, since I had been convinced he was pulling away. But I also knew that he did not mean he loved me in the same way a husband loved his wife, but in the way that a father loved a child—or rather, the way a dominant "loved" his submissive.

"I'll walk you out to the car," he said.

"No, that's okay. I'll just go."

"Okay. I have to use the bathroom, anyway," he said, smiling slightly. "Take care. Drive safe."

"I will."

When Carl closed the door behind him, I felt a pang of something I could not quite identify. I did not want to leave and seeing him did nothing to quell my obsession with him as my dominant or my need for his attention.

By seven o'clock I'd arrived at Adele's house. After a solid dinner of Indian food, my friend and I stayed up late, talking and drinking wine. I told her what I was doing and what had happened with Carl and what he'd said to me.

Adele frowned. "What's going on with you and this guy?"

"Nothing. Honestly."

"Are you in love with him?"

"God, no! It has nothing to do with love," I said and flashed on what Ms. Maplethorpe had said on her website: *Discipline is love.*

"But I am emotionally attached to him." I tried to explain to Adele how it helped me with my sex life, but I could tell she was not really buying it. I also told her about this new dom, Santa, and how I felt it might well help reduce my dependence on Carl. It was almost as if I was discussing my rationale behind buying a more ergonomic office chair.

I knew by the look on her face that she thought I'd truly lost my mind. "Not that it's any of my business, but I think you need to be really careful with this, Deborah."

"Why?"

"Don't you think on some level Andy knows what you are doing?"

"But I'm not doing anything. I haven't done anything. I mean to compromise my marriage. I'd never do that. Nor would I ever leave Andy. Really, this is just a game," I said, repeating Carl's words.

"Whatever you think you're doing or not doing, I'm sure he's sensing your distraction," she says.

"Seriously?"

She nodded vehemently. "I think you really need to stop this. It's an emotional affair."

"But I don't 'love 'Carl. This is different." I could tell I wasn't going to get anywhere with this and dropped the subject.

Around eleven o'clock Adele and I headed upstairs. I considered my friend's warning, but at this point I was not able to walk away from this obsession. What I was able to do was to focus on breaking my addiction to Carl. That, I felt, would at least get me centered, which was a good thing, just in case Andy truly was sensing something. Although I was obsessive-compulsive, which is a bear to manage, I was also very strong willed, and once I would make my mind up to do something, it was done. I had quit smoking overnight after a two-pack-a-day habit for twenty-five years. I also had quit a twenty-two-year stint with bulimia on my own, with no help from anyone. And I knew I could release myself from my long-distance dom. I had to.

Once I was nestled in the guestroom bed, I checked my cell phone and found an email from Carl saying that although he was disappointed we didn't play, it was wonderful to see me. There was also an email from Santa. It was a long missive in which he told me about his penchant for cooking and the meal he'd made for his friends over the weekend. He then asked me what I like to do most in a sub/dom situation. I sent off an email right away.

ME: *I like to be spanked. And disciplined. Pretty cut and dried.*

SANTA: *Then that's what Deborah will get. I'm sure you deserve a good paddling, dear. Over my lap. Panties down.*

It seemed like we were on the right track, but when he asked me if I shaved myself down there, or if I trimmed my pubic hair. I was a bit taken aback; this was not exactly where I wanted to go. He then spun out a rich scenario during which he disciplined one of his past playmates with a hair brush, spanking her until she came from the pain. I didn't even know that was possible. What I did know was that my body reacted to his words. Maybe this new guy was just what the doctor ordered to help me break my addiction to Carl.

JULY 30

AN EASY SWITCH

At around 10:00 AM, Carl called me to ask how I was doing.

"Everything is fine," I said, wanting to get off the phone and check for emails from my new dom. "I'm really sorry I couldn't follow through."

"It's all right. I understand. Maybe another time. Anyway, I just wanted to check in."

"Thanks," I said into my cell. "I have to go. My friend's waiting for me."

"Oh," he said, sounding a bit let down that I wanted to sign off so quickly. "I'll touch base with you this week. Be a good girl."

Whereas before my stomach would have flipped when he told me to be a good girl, I now had no reaction. The tables, I realized, had now been turned, and I was quite stymied at how fickle I seemed to be, but pleased at how seemingly easy it was to transition from one dom to another. But, I realized, the explanation was pretty simple: The drug was the same. It was just a different pusher (so much for emotional attachment).

I got dressed, wandered downstairs, and found Adele in her office. We decided to go to the coffee shop down the street from her house to have a late breakfast.

On the way over in Adele's car, I obsessively checked my cell for the tenth time and found a message from Santa. I felt an initial surge of excitement as I opened it up. But instead of meting out discipline in response to a very bratty email I'd sent when I woke up, he told me another story.

SANTA: *I had a client in NYC who I did a favor for; he owned an S&M club and as payment he told me to come down on Friday night; that he would have a present for me. So, when I got there, he brought me down to a room in the basement. He led me inside, and there was this beautiful redhead strapped to a pool table, lying naked, spread-eagled, with restraining cuffs around her legs and wrists. Her pussy was shaved, and she was blindfolded. My friend said to me, "She likes to be fucked by strangers. In her cunt and in her mouth. Have at it." So, I did.*

"Good God," I said, jamming my cell phone in my purse, feeling a mix of disgust and titillation.

"What the hell is going on?" Adele asked.

"It's this new guy. The new dom."

"I really think you need to cut this out, Deborah. You might get hurt."

"I can't," I said.

"Okay. Whatever." My friend sighed deeply.

Later that night, at Santa's urging, I agreed to meet him on Sunday if I was able to get home at a reasonable hour. And what harm could it do, anyway? It was just dinner. I also made it very clear, once again, that I was only interested in spanking and discipline. Sex was definitely not on the menu.

JULY 31

SUNDAY, SUNDAY—CAN'T TRUST THAT DAY

On the drive back from western New York, I texted Santa, my car flying along at eighty MPH.

SANTA: *Where are you now?*

ME: *Midkde of mowhwere. PRoghaobybg gioing way 2 fas=t. Hrd to txt an drivfe.*

I had made sure my typing was almost illegible, but he didn't comment. And that pissed me off as I wanted to be reprimanded, so I continued to push at him, telling him I was being "quite naughty." He certainly knew that it was illegal to text while driving. But he wouldn't scold me.

"Come on! Say something!" I yelled at my cell. This man was simply not playing the game right—the way I wanted to play the game.

I got back to my house around 5:00 PM in plenty of time to meet my new friend and potential playmate. After dropping off my bags, I drove north about twenty miles to a Mexican restaurant he had chosen. On the way, Santa texted me and told me that he'd be in a black Mercedes convertible. He also gave me the model type. Subtext: I drive an expensive car. I'm successful.

When I pulled into the restaurant parking lot, I spotted Santa immediately and pulled up in front of his Mercedes. He broke into a smile and waved. He looked older to me than his online picture and was heavier than I thought—which in retrospect was not much of a surprise since he apparently owned 2,500 recipe books and loved to cook and (obviously) eat.

I hopped out of my parked car to greet him. "Hi." I smiled broadly in attempts to cover up my growing feeling of disappointment. I could already sense the lack of chemistry, which practitioners of BDSM say is important in a successful sub/dom relationship.

"Nice to meet you, Deborah." His voice was also on the high side, which I found unappealing. It was not authoritative and deep like Carl's.

"You too," I said, doing my best to sound chipper. "And what a stunningly beautiful day."

We continued on with polite chatter as we wound our way up the flagstone path. When we entered the restaurant, we were immediately greeted by a rotund hostess with mounds of black hair piled on top of her head. She led us to a booth and slapped down two menus. I slid into one side; Santa struggled into the other, grimacing as if he had a bad back or leg. It quickly became clear that he was not an effusive man, so I had to take the lead and draw out conversation.

"Where do your children live?" I asked.

He filled me in with some of the details, then nodded at the menu. "Let's order something," he said, waving at one of several middle-aged waitresses.

The woman looked irritated and sauntered slowly over to the table. "Yes? Can I help you?"

"We'd like to order some food." Santa looked over at me. "What would you like, Deborah?"

"Salsa and chips will be fine. I'm not really hungry. And a Margarita," I said, thinking about my nervous stomach. I wanted to tell the waitress to double up on the tequila, but silly as it was, I didn't want to give Santa the impression I was a heavy drinker.

My new acquaintance ordered two colas (no booze for Santa Claus), BBQ beef burritos with extra sour cream, a side of rice and beans, and a double helping of guacamole. I did my best to avoid looking at his bulging gut, which was pressing against the edge of the table. Our conversation went on in a pleasant vein, but I couldn't get beyond his eyes. They were cold and dark, like the eyes of a snake.

After finishing up our food, we split the bill and went out to our cars. I was ready to go home, but Santa seemed intent on showing me his GPS system. "Come. Sit with me for a minute," he said.

"Okay." Acquiescing, I slipped into the passenger seat and smiled courteously as he filled me in on the technical details—details that I could have cared less about.

He looked at me, a grin forming on his face, and asked if we shouldn't go somewhere for a little discipline session. "I think you need to be spanked, Deborah."

I felt a slight charge, felt myself getting turned on, but told him that, unfortunately, I needed to meet a friend in a half an hour—a complete and total lie.

When I got back to my house, I emailed Carl to tell him that I didn't want anything to do with Santa; that it was simply not a good fit.

After I shut down my computer, I called my husband to say "hi" and let him know that I'd be driving up to VT tomorrow.

"I can't wait to get back," I said.

As we hung up, I felt a rush of emotion and my eyes welled up. I could not put a finger on why.

AUGUST 1

FEELINGS NO MORE

CARL: *What happened with Santa?*

ME: *The eye thing again. Don't trust him.*

CARL: *I think you're being overly dramatic.*

ME: *Just a gut instinct.*

CARL: *Did he spank you?*

ME: *No. He wanted to. But I couldn't do it.*

Even though I'd decided to jettison Santa, I realized that the deep feelings of attachment I had for Carl had oddly waned. So maybe this meant that I could continue to play with him in a much healthier—and saner—manner. That, I thought, would be perfect.

AUGUST 4

A FAMILY GATHERING

My brother, Ed, and his wife, Sharon, arrived up at our summer house. The weather continued to be pleasantly warm, versus last year when it remained rainy and cold for almost the entire month of August.

For dinner, the four of us went to the local restaurant and muscled our way into the bar. My brother and my husband sat next to each other and talked about house stuff: wiring, plumbing, rebuilding foundations—guy talk.

Sharon and I ordered glasses of Chardonnay from Gwen, the thirty-something bartendress with long, sandy blond hair, and went into our usual verbal dance, indulging in a heart-to-heart talk, during which I espoused the benefits of therapy. "You oughta try it."

"Meh," Sharon said, without an ounce of enthusiasm. "Too late for that."

I smiled. "Okay. No sale there, I guess."

Suddenly, I felt a desperate urge to tell my sister-in-law about my fetish, but I decided against it. I didn't think she would approve. Or understand.

I glanced over at my husband, who was staring at Gwen. His eyes burned with intensity, and it was not a look I recognized.

"Andrew?" I said, leaning over toward him. "What's going on?"

"Nothing," he said, shrugging his shoulders. Andy asked for the check, offering to pay for the four of us. My brother accepted graciously and after he and his wife had finished their drinks, they headed off back to the house.

Andrew and I figured we'd hang out for a while longer and chat with Trudy, a spritely, highly revved woman we met last summer when she was waitressing at one of the inns near town. She mentioned that she'd just finished up dinner with her mother- and father-in-law, which I found odd, since she'd been separated from her husband for almost ten years. "Yeah, it's weird, but we like each other," said Trudy, who has big bushy hair, a flat nose and face, and a tendency to talk nonstop and in non-sequiturs like our friend Craig.

True to form, she told us that she'd purchased some chickens and that a rooster had mistakenly gotten into the mix. "Every morning he wakes me up," she said. "He's driving me crazy."

"Cock-a-fucking doodle doo," I said.

Trudy went off on another tangent and told us about her life in the Far East where she had lived with her diplomat husband. For some reason I could not envision her as a diplomat's wife, not that there was a preset mold for such a role.

"Oh my God." Trudy suddenly zeroed in on the doorway at the far side of the bar.

I followed her gaze and spotted a man settling in at a high-top table under the wide screen TV. He reminded me of a young Roman Polanski.

"I really like him," Trudy said.

"So, go talk to him."

"Nah. We went out once. It didn't turn out so hot. He's kind of a jerk. But who knows, maybe there's hope."

"There's always that," I said, trying to make sense of her comment as a stray thought suddenly flashed through my head: maybe Trudy was a pathological liar.

Later, when Andrew and I were on our way back to the house, I mentioned my inkling about our friend.

Andrew shrugged. "Perhaps," he said, tonelessly.

We got home around 11:00 PM, and after a little TV and a quick nightcap with Ed and Sharon, Andrew and I headed upstairs.

Once we were in bed, I flung my leg over my husband's side; he massaged my foot, while I scratched and kneaded his back—another little ritual we'd indulged in from the very beginning of our relationship. When I was well sated, I turned off the beside lamp and leaned over to pet Mamie, my beloved cat, who was sleeping peacefully on her own special pillow next to mine. Andy, however, did not seem peaceful at all, and for the next half hour tossed and turned, despite my earlier efforts to give him a relaxing back rub.

AUGUST 8

GROUNDED, CENTERED, AND SAFE

My sister, Wanda, and her husband, Curt, arrived with their dog, a day after my brother and his wife had left for Philadelphia. The house was once again filled with "people energy," and I was loving it. We ate dinner together at the dining room table, with the doors to the screened-in porch opened wide.

After the food was cleared and the dishes were cleaned and put away, we played Scrabble, with the boys against the girls. My sister and I won by a landslide. The men grumped; we laughed. And although we all seemed to enjoy the game, I noticed that my husband seemed somewhat distracted, a bit distant. But, again, I tossed it off as his occasional moodiness.

AUGUST 10

BE STILL THY BEATING HEART

I was now back in New York for a sonogram at the local hospital. My heart had been beating irregularly lately to the point where at times it felt like it was going to burst out of my chest, and I had to wonder if it didn't have to do with my indulgence of seven-plus months and the fact that I kept myself in a constant state of arousal.

AUGUST 12

A SIGH OF RELIEF

It turned out my heart was okay (phew), so within a few days I was on the road heading off to Vermont. I made several stops along the way to respond to Carl's emails. I didn't really understand why or how this could have happened, but I was clearly "under his influence" once again, and I momentarily hated myself for my weakness. In AA they'd consider this a relapse; this was obviously not an easy addiction to break. And since I'd had such a negative reaction to Santa, I had to feed my need somewhere, somehow. Carl was the simplest solution. I really didn't want to meet anyone new.

AUGUST 15

PINGING LIKE A MAD MAN

Carl was pinging me like mad today on IM, and I did my best to hide what I was doing from Andrew, who sat at his desk next to mine, by angling my computer screen away from his sight line. This had been my tactic all summer long, and I had to assume I'd been successful in my efforts, otherwise Andy certainly would have said something. Or so I thought.

AUGUST 21

A SUNDAY REUNION FOR THOSE WITH ALL SORTS OF CHALLENGES

My husband chose to stay in Vermont while I headed down to New York for a reunion dinner with some of my old college friends, including Pran, an ex-hippie type who now worked on Wall Street, spending most of his days in a suit and tie. We all met at a midtown NYC restaurant, which was easily able to accommodate our group of seven. I had not seen several of my classmates since the 1970s, and after the conversation opened up, I found out that everyone had more than their fair share of challenges: One woman had just been let go from her job of twenty years; Pran had lost his wife in June to heart disease, while two of the men were battling cancer. I found myself feeling very fortunate: I had a good marriage to a man who cherished me and was gainfully employed. I had a wonderful family, two beautiful homes, my health, some money in the bank, relatively steady freelance work, and an adoring, but elderly, cat. (Knock wood. Tug on pants. Select the right plate.)

"Why didn't Andy come?" my friend Robin with the bright blue eyes asked.

"He had to stay up in Vermont." She didn't question why, and I didn't tell her that Andy had not given me much of a reason for not coming other than he "didn't feel like it."

During after-dinner drinks and a discussion with one of the guys about his failed marriage, once again that disturbing thought popped up: maybe my husband thought I was having an affair, with all this travel back and forth, to and from NY, and my obsessive checking of my cell phone. So, was this why he was zeroing in on Gwen the bartendress? To get back at me? And if that was the case, did he see her when I was home in New York? Is that why I sometimes was unable to contact him late at night? But, I reasoned, once again, that he couldn't possibly be having an affair. This was, after all, my steadfast husband who would do anything in the world for me.

AUGUST 22

ROPED IN

I met with Ms. C at a coffee shop near Grand Central, where she gave me an update on her recent activity in the scene. "I'm giving a bondage workshop in New Jersey at a BDSM convention the weekend after next. It's going to be huge. They've got all sorts of events: cocktail parties, meet-ups, all that."

"Huhn," I said.

"You should come. There's going to be a ton of people there from all over the country."

"Are you trying to rope me in?" I joked.

Ms. C smiled appreciatively.

"Maybe I'll check it out," I said, but something told me I probably wouldn't be attending.

My former domme also mentioned that she no longer charged for her services and if I wanted to play some time, we could split the cost of the room. She said she'd really like that. It didn't particularly appeal to me, as I knew a woman-to-woman scene would not give me the rush I desired—and craved.

AUGUST 25

A SAD DAY

I was glad to be back in Vermont. But today, my sister and her husband, who usually stayed with us for several weeks, had to leave to go home to North Carolina. My eyes filled up as I watched their car move up the graveled driveway and out of sight. There was a hole in my heart; Andrew's too, as we both would miss their company—and their dog as well.

AUGUST 26

A DAMN GOOD SANDWICH AND
AN UNUSUALLY QUIET LUNCH

It was a workday for both me and my husband, so we took a lunch break and went to see "the girls," which was how we referred to the two women who owned the inn at the bottom of the hill from our summer house. Although the restaurant tended to be a bit on the pricey side, catering to a high-end clientele, it had one of the best vegetarian sandwiches ever. "It's all about the bread," I'd often say, fully intending the double entendre.

During our walk down the hill, Andy did not hold my hand, which triggered something in me—a sort of bitchiness that really was not normally a part of my character. He had gotten new sneakers and was walking awkwardly—like a child, almost. And I started to match his gate.

"Stop it," he said. "Why are you making fun of me?"

I told him I really wasn't, that I was just playing, and quit immediately. I felt badly that I had hurt his feelings but recognized that I must be harboring some anger toward him—but I didn't understand why. Perhaps I was angry at myself; or maybe I was trying to push him away. But, why, after all these years? Did my attachment to Carl trigger something? Did I not respect my husband fully, as a man, as a person, because he'd always caved in to my desires and wants?

Was he not strong enough for me? Were we really mismatched? Did I not love him enough? Was physical chemistry between two people really that important, especially when it usually wanes over the years anyway?

I felt compelled to tell Andrew about Ms. Cynthia and her heavy involvement in some edgy BDSM practices, including electrical play and suspension, where people were bound and gagged, often blindfolded, and hoisted up into the air with various rigs. I also made sure that Andy understood this was not—and never would be—my thing. My husband said nothing in response.

Over lunch, Andrew was quiet and introspective, and I sensed I should not have shared the information about Ms. C. But there was something else going on, and that uneasy feeling I experienced a week or so ago rose to the surface. Or maybe he was mad at me for teasing him about his sneakers. I really didn't know and did not press the issue. When the waitress brought our food, Andy took a bite of his sandwich and set it down. He had a look on his face that seemed to be a mix of melancholy and irritation.

"What are you thinking, Andrew?" I asked.

He shrugged. Normally he would have told me. In fact, we'd often ask each other what we were each thinking and always shared whatever was on our minds. But not today.

My husband half-heartedly pulled out a piece of paper and a pencil and began drawing a schematic of the garage he wanted to build for the summer house. We talked about the design, but not much else. Our time together seemed strained.

As we walked back up the hill after lunch, our lungs working overtime, I had an epiphany: Andy had been making some serious effort as of late to lose weight to, in his words, get rid of his belly fat. And that, according to the love psychologists, is one of the signs that your partner is having an affair—or at least thinking about it. Another sign: spending more time than usual texting, which Andrew had been doing a lot of over the past few weeks. Granted, I'd been doing that since February, but I was not having an affair; at least not in the traditional sense of the word. I suddenly felt nauseous.

AUGUST 29

WHO ARE YOU?

I stepped out onto the porch that wrapped around our summer house, holding a fistful of peanuts. "Come and get it," I said, whistling for our resident chipmunk, who both Andy and I had developed a special bond with over the past few summers.

The chipmunk usually responded right away, but today he was nowhere to be found.

"Where's the Chipster?" I said to my husband who walked up behind me.

"Don't know. Maybe he's off building a bunker for all the peanuts we've given him."

"I just hope the little fur pig shares with his friends," I said, stooping down to place the nuts on the ground.

I stood up and turned toward Andrew, who was looking off toward the woods. Suddenly, something stirred inside me, and I was besieged by an impulse to take my husband's face in my hands. It felt bristly, cold to the touch. "Who are you?" I asked, pulling him toward me, my tone serious. Oddly, this was not the first time this summer I'd done this, but I realized it must be sourced in some intuitive feeling.

I looked into Andrew's eyes, and I didn't like what I saw; they appeared locked, shuttered. I dropped my hands from his face and forced a smile.

SEPTEMBER 6

BEHOLD THE BARTENDRESS

Andrew and I settled in at the bar at RJ's with the iPad. I leaned into his shoulder as we fired up a Scrabble game against Al(bert), the name we'd given the electronic tablet. I welcomed the physical closeness of my husband. He allowed my presence, but I noticed his attention was elsewhere, and it was not on me or the game we were playing. It was on Gwen, the bartendress—again.

SEPTEMBER 8

AN EMAIL, A TEXT, A BROKEN NECK

An email showed up in my inbox from Courtney, Andrew's daughter, who was plagued by tremendous abandonment issues due to the fact that her father walked out on her and her mother overnight without warning when she was a child. She told me that I was the only person who had not let her down. I mentioned the note she'd sent me to Andrew, but regretted I'd said anything. My husband, after all, perhaps due to guilt, had spent most of his adult life helping Courtney, managing her fragile emotional state, and oftentimes patching her life back together. I was very careful along the way to not enable her and advised Andy to follow suit. Support her, yes, but don't enable her, I'd say.

Later in the afternoon, Andrew got a text from Trudy.

"What's going on?" I asked.

"She wants the three of us to get together." Andrew said. "At the Flying Duck."

"Sounds good to me." Despite the deep-seated issues I knew Trudy harbored, I got a kick out of her.

Andrew and I headed out around 6:45 PM, grabbed two seats at the upstairs bar, and saved one for Trudy, who showed up a half an hour later.

Our friend ordered a glass of wine and unloaded a barrage of information that personally I would have kept to myself. It turned out her marriage had broken up because her husband was heavy duty into S&M, which seemed awfully coincidental to me, and I began to wonder if Andrew had said something to her in my absence. he also told us that she suffered from bulimia, another coincidence since I'd battled with it, and that she was ADHD—which in her case manifested in a weak filtering system, so her comment of a few weeks ago made sense. "Wow," she'd said to me when we were all sitting together at RJ's one night. "That's a beautiful picture of you on Facebook. It must have been taken a long time ago."

(I repressed the urge to clock her and laughed instead.)

After a dinner of flatbread pizza and one more drink each, Andrew settled the bar tab with his American Express, and we got up and made our way toward the exit.

"You should join my woman's group," Trudy said to me as we picked our way down the steep spiral steps to the ground floor.

"Sounds great," I said, but I didn't really feel compelled to press her for more information.

The three of us decided to stop off at RJ's so I could tell my favorite bartender a joke that I'd finally mastered after a few practice rounds at The Flying Duck. The bartender, unfortunately, had gone home.

But we each ordered another drink, and Trudy brought up her chickens again and told us about the names she'd given them. She also mentioned that she'd gotten rid of her rooster.

"Oh, did you give him away?" I asked.

"No," she said, and provided detailed information on how to eliminate the problematic male. "You yank its head through the small end of a traffic cone."

"You snap its neck? Oh my God! No way!" I was mortified but got the giggles, a defense mechanism that would sometimes kick in when someone told me something I found perfectly disturbing.

"That poor rooster. Isn't that kind of cruel?" I said to Andrew on the way home in the car.

"I suppose it's quick," he said.

Looking thoughtful, Andrew turned to me and remarked that Trudy reminded him of me.

"You've got to be kidding." I could not quite see the similarities; certainly not physically. "How do you mean?"

"You're both funny," Andy said and added, "Oh, by the way, I'm taking care of Trudy's cats and chickens while she's away in Rhode Island."

"Ahhhh. Okay." Something tugged at my gut; something about him offering his help felt wrong to me, even though he'd asked me if I wanted to come along and meet her cats. But I kept my thoughts to myself.

When we got back to the house, I parked the car, and we ambled up the porch steps. After fumbling a bit with the keys, I unlocked the front door and stepped inside, with Andrew on my heel. I suddenly spun around and pulled my husband to me. We began frantically kissing.

"We'd better get upstairs fast," I said, breaking away.

Andy and I raced up to the bedroom, dove onto the bed, and ripped off our clothes.

SEPTEMBER 9

WHAT ABOUT ME?

My husband got up early to do some work around the house while I stayed in bed a bit longer. At around 9:30 AM, he came back into the bedroom.

"Hey! Andy got off last night," I said jokingly. "What about me? When do I get my treat?"

My husband licked his lips lasciviously, which always made me laugh, came over and touched me on my leg. "Ready?" he asked.

I squealed with delight but begged off. "It's okay. Next time."

Within the hour, I wandered downstairs and settled in at my desk to check email, the weather report, and the news. Andrew came into the office from the kitchen and stood behind me, holding a cup of tea.

"What's up, hon?" I asked, turning around.

Andy looked serious, his mood having completely shifted from earlier this morning. "I'm done."

"With what? The recycling?" I asked. "We can do it tomorrow."

"Saving people. I've spent thirty years of my life saving people." His remark was completely out of left field. Courtney, coincidentally, was thirty years old.

"Does this have something to do with—" I never got to finish my question; ask him if this had anything to do with the comment his daughter had made about everyone letting her down but me.

"I'm done," Andrew repeated.

"Okay," I said, warily.

Andy turned on his heel and went out to the back porch. I had to wonder if, when he said "people," it included me as well as his daughter. Did he feel like he saved me too when I moved in with him, emotionally scarred from my break-up and unemployed, even though I had started to work almost immediately?

But that was years ago. Years.

But if he was including me in the mix, it was quite a switch from a few days ago when he told me that he was still in love with me, that we were so good for each other, and that I had helped him grow immensely over the years. That comment, too, seemed to come out of the blue.

I tucked those thoughts away in the back of my mind, since my childhood summer friend and her husband were staying at one of the local inns, and we'd agreed to meet them for brunch.

On our walk downtown, Andrew got a text and lagged behind to respond. When he caught up with me, I gave him a quizzical look.

"It's this guy from work," he said. "I don't know why he keeps bothering me."

I intuitively knew that he was not telling me the truth, but once again, I let it drop.

SEPTEMBER 12

SPILLING BLOOD

I had to head back to New York for therapy, my biannual blood work, and my first playwriting workshop of the season. Andrew was in the mood for a Chai, so we drove in tandem down to the Starbucks a few towns south and met in the parking lot.

By the time I got there, I decided I didn't want to take the Honda sedan, since I felt safer in the SUV. Andrew was fine either way, so we switched my luggage and the cooler over. He also gave me his Simon and Garfunkel CD, a gallant act since I knew he liked it just as much as I did and listened to it often.

My husband and I went inside and sat at the coffee bar. My cell phone buzzed, and I clicked to the inbox and spotted a message from Carl.

"Who's that? Who are you talking to?" Andrew asked. He sounded suspicious.

"It's my friend with the novel." At one point over the summer, I'd mentioned Carl's book to Andy, since my dom had sent it to me to read. "I'm trying to get through his book, but it needs a lot of editing. Maybe you'd like to read it, too."

Carl's email had nothing to do with his novel; instead he wanted to know how I was and if I'd been behaving "like a good girl." After I fired off a quick response, I leaned into Andrew, welcoming the feel of his body.

Once we'd finished up our Chai lattes, my husband and I walked out to the parking lot. This time we held hands, just like we'd done for years. I climbed into the SUV, and we kissed on the lips. It was a sweet, semi-lingering kiss.

"I love you, Andy," I said.

"I love you, too."

PART II—THE BETRAYAL

BURNT AFTER CALLING

I picked up the phone to call Andrew. I had emailed yesterday evening telling him I'd arrived safely home, but he didn't respond until almost two o'clock this morning. And Andy was not a night person. In fact, getting him to stay up past midnight had always been a big deal, and often, if we were out past a certain hour, I'd have to poke him to keep him from nodding off. He also didn't mention anything in his email about having fallen asleep on the couch, so I knew something was amiss.

Andrew answered on the third ring.

"Hey," I said. "What the heck were you doing up so late last night?"

"Watching *Burn After Reading.*"

"*Burn After Reading*? We just watched that a month ago," I said. "And I thought we had the DVD here in New York."

"Oh, well," he stammered. "I usually pick up some cheap movies when I'm at Wal-Mart. It was on sale."

"Wal-Mart?" I said, a bit surprised since we both hated going into that store and felt it was an assault on our senses, aesthetically speaking and otherwise. "You were by yourself?"

"No. Mamie was with me."

"You must have brought her downstairs, then," I said, feeling a prickle of anxiety. Our arthritic cat almost always stayed upstairs, preferring to lounge about on her special pillow on the bed or in the window seat.

"Uh, yeah."

I took in a sharp breath; I intuitively knew exactly what happened and with whom—and it was not Gwen the bartendress. "Andrew, was Trudy over last night?"

He paused. "Yes."

My entire body went numb. "Andrew, did you sleep with her?"

Another pause. "Yes."

"Did you use protection?" (Why I would even think of that at a moment like this, I have no clue.)

"No."

"Andrew," I said, my hands suddenly turning to ice, "I'm going to hang up now and call you back because I'm really upset."

I didn't yell, nor did I scream. Of course, I wanted to tell him he was an unmitigated asshole, along with some other choice phrases, but I remembered what my sister had told me years ago: Once it's out of your mouth, you can never take it back.

Fifteen minutes after I had calmed myself down, taking in deep gulps of air to repress my urge to puke, I called my husband back. We entered into a semi-civilized discussion. He repeated again that he had spent the past thirty years of his life saving people. He also said that he never got a chance to "play around;" that he was always the responsible one and had spent his entire adult life married.

"That's not my fault, Andrew," I said, reminding myself that I was, in fact, his fourth wife, although our relationship of seventeen years was his longest one by far (mine too).

"Well, it's my turn now." I couldn't quite believe what he said next. "And she was lonely."

"Jesus H. Christ, Andy! Some of my friends are lonely too, but I don't sleep with them!" I said, thinking he had truly snapped.

I heard him pause. "Spanking always leads to sex," he said, which pissed me off even more.

"Where the hell did that come from?" I said, even though I knew it came from Trudy. Clearly, she'd been filling my husband's head with what I considered bullshit.

"It does," Andy countered.

"That is not true! I gave you a damn handbook, which explicitly states that the parameters are set by the players. How many times have I told you this?"

"Every time you went out to LA or into the city, how was I supposed to know you weren't sleeping with all these people?"

"<u>What</u> people?" I had to fight the impulse to hurl something across the room, like my laptop. "Andrew, I have never, ever screwed anyone outside of our marriage." And I hadn't.

But I just couldn't help myself and repeated what a friend from Boston said who had moved to the town next to Garnersville. "You know what they say about the local people up there? They may be colorful, but don't, whatever you do, let them in your house. You'll regret it."

On that note, we said a perfunctory goodbye and hung up. I realized I was in a state of shock and didn't know what else to say—or do.

After spilling my guts to my sister, my brother, my brother's wife, and my other friends who I considered my emotional rescue squad, I called Adele who offered some words of wisdom about my husband. "He wasn't strong enough to withstand what was happening, whatever the fracturing was," she told me. "He had a tenuous hold on himself. He may come back, and it may be a phenomenally stronger marriage, but he will have to go through an epiphany."

"Maybe someone ought to take a baseball bat to his head," I said. "Maybe that will trigger an epiphany."

I hung up the land line and wept a bucket load of tears.

SEPTEMBER 15

THE BOTTOM OF THE LIST

Thankfully I had an appointment with my therapist, but fixing my OCD was now at the bottom of my list. So what if I had to tug at my underpants while driving down the highway to ward off an accident? So what if I had to pick a particular plate from the stack to keep the world from further disintegrating into madness?

Katarina let me into her office, offered me some water. "You look like you could use some."

"Got anything stronger?" I asked.

"Okay, what's going on?" she said, looking concerned.

I sat down on her couch and filled her in on the latest and greatest in the saga of "What the Hell Is My Husband Thinking?" and his fling with Trudy. I knew I looked shell-shocked, and I was.

My therapist was as well. "I never would have expected this."

"Never in a million years would I have expected this, either." I said. "And he's not going to stop sleeping with her. He said my spanking activities gave him a 'hall pass'. Like, why shouldn't he get to do what he wants, if I can go off and do all this wacky stuff?"

I began to hyperventilate.

"Drink water," Katrina said. "It'll help."

"Is it all my fault?"

"No. It's never just one person. If he was upset or sensed you were doing something, he should have spoken up."

As the anger rose up in me again, I made a snap decision. "Screw it. I'm going to go see Santa. I'm taking my own goddamn hall pass."

But I didn't really want it—not at all. It was a knee-jerk reaction; it would be an act of revenge, a tit for tat. I also knew how ridiculously insane and irrational it was to think it might do any good, since, first of all, I would never tell Andy. And secondly, what good would it really do me? And how in heaven's name did I think it could possibly repair the damage that had apparently been done to the marriage? I knew I was not thinking clearly. I guess I was desperate for something to distract me from this very new—and mind-blowing—reality.

Oddly, my therapist did not discourage me from going to see the white-haired, bearded dom with the big belly.

SEPTEMBER 17

WILL THE REAL SANTA PLEASE STAND UP?

Santa, who said he'd love to see me, rented a room for two hours in a dungeon in midtown NYC starting at 6:00 PM. I apprised Carl of this latest development, and he seemed pleased. This time his response didn't bother me. But, as I expected, he made me promise to fill him in on all the details. "Once a pervert, always a pervert," he'd said. I didn't tell him a thing about what had happened with my husband.

On the train going in, I found myself becoming more and more anxious and began to question my motives and, more to the point, my mental state. But thankfully I had my trusty Xanax and took half a pill. I also had a conversation with myself:

It's going to be fine. He seems like a nice man. I mean, what am I worried about? Okay, so his eyes are weird. Big deal. And I told him many times that I was not looking for a sexual relationship. He said we were on the same page about that. And it's a public place, so it's safe. So, what's my problem? Why do I feel like I want to barf? Settle down. Take another half a Xanax. Okay. I will. And why am I doing this, again? Oh, that's right: fuck you, Andy. Fuck you, fuck you, fuck you!

I got to the place a few minutes ahead of schedule and found Santa waiting outside. He spotted me immediately and smiled.

"Hi," I said. "I'm a nervous wreck." Even with the Xanax, which gets into the bloodstream almost immediately, I was a wreck.

"Nothing to worry about," he said.

"Easy for you to say," I mumbled, wondering again what the hell I was doing here.

During the ride up in the elevator we were both mostly silent. I could not get any sense of what he might be feeling—or thinking.

On the third floor at the reception area, we were met by a dark-haired man with thick glasses. His manner was warm and friendly, and he welcomed Santa, calling him by his real name, smiling broadly as if they were old pals. It seemed that Santa was a regular here. So, I wondered, was he lying when he told me that he's a one-person player and that his former sub moved away a year ago? He'd also told me they'd had a sexual relationship, since her marriage was devoid of any intimate contact.

Shit, I thought, reflecting on the e-conversation. Maybe that wasn't such a good sign, although every sub/dom situation was different, depending on what had been negotiated up front.

The man at the desk pointed down the hall and told us that we had the room at the end.

"Could you please get us a straight-backed chair?" Santa asked.

I felt momentarily relieved, since this kind of chair was at the heart and soul of a spanking scenario. So maybe it would be okay.

The man retrieved a chair from another room, and we followed him to the back of the building. After he'd placed it on the far side of the restraining table, he slid past us and left, closing the door behind him. It clicked shut loudly, and I quickly checked to see if it had a lock on it. It didn't, and I reminded myself again that this was a public place, hence a safe place—a place of business.

I looked around me. The walls, which were painted with the emblematic black and red, were covered with hooks holding all sorts of BDSM paraphernalia: leather whips, chains, face masks, paddles, and straps.

"Good Lord," I said, under my breath. I felt like a complete innocent and probably was, compared to many of the people who played in this room.

I inhaled deeply, aware of my racing heart and sweaty hands.

"Can we turn on the air-conditioning?" I asked, noticing Santa's crooked smile.

"Of course." He switched on the unit and sat on the straight-backed chair. "Now come here."

I went over to him obediently.

"Take down your jeans."

"Oh Jesus," I said, but did as I was told, leaving my undies on.

He took my arm, pulled me over his lap and delivered a few spanks. They were light, but well placed. I wanted him to do it harder and stay within the program of spanking and discipline, but he didn't seem to be all that interested in sticking to the parameters—even after I spewed out a few four-letter words.

Santa hooked his finger in my underpants and hitched them over my butt. And although I was not expecting this, he reached between my legs and began touching me, stimulating me. And I let him.

"Look at you. Look at how wet you are," Santa said.

Embarrassed, humiliated, I slid off his lap.

"Deborah, I didn't tell you to move."

"Sorry."

He shook his head and commanded me to remove my underpants and lie on my back on top of the spanking horse. Again, I did as he asked, feeling my face as well as that place between my thighs heat up.

"Spread your legs," he said. "Wider."

Santa began to arouse me again, and after a minute or so, instructed me to do it myself, to touch myself, masturbate. I obeyed. He quickly rammed his fingers inside me, first two, then three, then what felt like all five, pumping them in and out. I came within minutes. By this point, I felt as if I had left my body and was looking down on someone I barely knew—or understood.

Next, my new dom demanded that I go sit on the table and moved over in front of the straight-backed chair. He began to remove his trousers.

Oh, Jesus. Here it comes, I thought. This was not what I wanted, nor what I had expected. I sat down on the floor. "I can't give you a blow job."

"Who said anything about a blow job?" he said, stripping down to his underpants, back-peddling.

I waited, wondering what was next on his agenda.

"Come over here and massage my legs, my sexy sub," Santa said, his small black eyes narrowing beneath fatty folds of flesh.

I wanted to run from the room but didn't. Instead, I did what he'd requested and began rubbing his legs, which were muscular but crusty and swollen with age. I felt like I wanted to throw up.

"I have an old war injury," he said. "Shot in the leg."

"I'm sorry about that." I felt no sympathy whatsoever.

After I had worked on his calves for ten minutes, Santa told me to get up on the table and lie on my back. He cuffed my hands and spread my legs wide open, cuffing them as well; the sickness I felt inside began to subside as my body responded. He quickly began lapping up my wetness, and I came almost immediately. Suddenly, in a surprisingly deft move, he rolled himself up on top of the table, placing himself in the sixty-nine position, obviously choosing to ignore my earlier plea. He continued giving me head, but there was no way in hell I was going to reciprocate. I pulled hard on the cuffs, springing myself free.

"I can't do this," I said. "Sorry. I just can't."

He stopped, said nothing, and slipped off the table. A part of me felt guilty for not fulfilling his needs. Another part wanted to tell him to go fuck himself—or someone else. Just not me.

The man with the crusty legs pulled his trousers back on and sat patiently on the straight-backed chair while I dressed myself. It was awkward, uncomfortable, so I began to chatter about some inane, insipid thing, like how clean the place was and how I was not aware that the cuffs had safety devices built into them, enabling the submissive to break loose if things got too intense.

I offered to pay for half of the room. Santa accepted the money, thanked me, and on our way out, handed the wad of cash to the man at the door. Outside on the street, we said a cordial goodbye. He headed west. I went off to the east and walked north toward Grand Central, feeling extraordinarily betrayed.

On the train ride home, I sat quietly, thinking how ironic it was that I would choose to nickname this man Santa. Santa, the real Santa that is, symbolized everything that was good and gentle and kind. And Santa Claus certainly was not deceptive. But this fake Santa was—he lied to me from the beginning. I was very clear about my intentions, about my expectations, and he lied about his.

As soon as I got home, I fired off an email to Santa.

ME: *Hi. Thank you for today.*

(I figured I could at least thank the son-of-a-bitch for giving me a couple of orgasms.)

ME: *I enjoyed our emails over the summer and getting to know you. But, truthfully, it seems that you are looking for more of a sexual dom/sub situation.*

(Seems?)

ME: *I simply don't feel comfortable with that. I am sure you understand.*

I wished him well and sent off the note. He emailed me back within the hour.

SANTA: *You are a lovely, delightful woman. I enjoyed getting to know you, too, and of course I understand. I wish you all the best in your creative endeavors and otherwise. Fondly.*

He signed off with his real name, since he had no idea I called him Santa. I went into my email files and deleted every single bit of communication that ever passed between us. Carl's emails were next and, once again as I did years ago, I slammed the door shut on spanking and discipline. Just like that.

After logging off from my computer, I wandered into the bathroom to ready myself for bed. Once I'd brushed my teeth and taken my PM vitamins, I turned on the nightlight by the sink and retrieved another one from my desk drawer to plug into the wall on my husband's side of the bed.

I now found the darkness unsettling. I needed the light. (Desperately.)

SEPTEMBER 19

PARANOIA—A HEIGHTENED STATE OF AWARENESS?

"Get a lawyer," my brother advised. I didn't want to do that, since that would mean I didn't trust Andrew. I realized the insanity of my thinking, yet I <u>wanted</u> to trust him, I really did. But I got the name of divorce attorney anyway.

"In the meantime," my friend Alexis warned, "you have to protect yourself. Take the money out of your savings account and squirrel it away."

I didn't feel right about that either, but I did separate the savings into two accounts—one for house repairs and the other for school taxes, which were due soon. I called the bank's automated system to make the transfer and punched in one of the account numbers. My chest tightened. There was only a few hundred dollars left! I immediately fired off an email to Andrew and asked him if he drained our savings account.

He called me within ten minutes on my desk phone.

"I would never do anything like that," he said.

By this time, however, I'd realized I had checked the wrong account and felt badly I would think he was guilty of such a thing.

I also later told my husband what I did: that I separated the tax money from the regular savings.

SEPTEMBER 20

HONESTY UP AGAINST THE WALL

I sent Andrew a piece of writing I'd completed where I recounted the time a friend of mine stole an ashtray for me from a restaurant/bar. I felt so guilty, the next day I mailed two dollars to "management" to cover the cost. For some reason, I needed Andrew to know that I would never intentionally screw him over.

But I had to question why I was being so nice about all that had happened—meaning Andrew's infidelity. The reason was obvious: I felt a tremendous amount of guilt around my emotional attachment to Carl, the intimate nature of our long-distance relationship, and the fact that I had even gone into that hotel room in Syracuse. Yet, once again, I tried to remind myself that I never had any intentions of leaving my marriage, nor of getting "sexually" involved with anyone other than Andy. I only wanted to spice things up.

The words "denial," "delusional," and "karma kickback" flashed through my mind. I felt as though I'd really fucked up good this time and prayed that somehow this would all blow over. Couples, after all, have weathered far worse things in their marriages.

SEPTEMBER 23

CURTAINS IN VERMONT

I wasn't going up to Vermont to beg Andy to come back to me (I had way too much pride for that); nor was I going up to terrorize Trudy, although the idea was appealing. I was going up to get my cat who I missed desperately; in particular; the way she'd always wait for me at the top of the stairs after hearing me come through the front door. I was also going up to oversee the installation of some custom curtains I'd ordered during the summer. And, yes, there was a part of me that hoped Andy would come to his senses when he saw me.

Before I left, my husband sent me an email asking me to bring up some warm clothes for him. He ended it with, *Enjoy the drive. The leaves have started to turn.* Enjoy the drive? Was he out of his mind? He was sleeping with another woman, and I was supposed to enjoy the fucking drive?! Did he have any idea how devastated I was? This was truly beyond the pale and fell under the same umbrella as his "she was lonely" comment, and I wondered if I shouldn't bag the whole trip.

Nonetheless, operating on a scrap of optimism, I grabbed some heavy shirts for my husband, packed a small suitcase for myself, and double-checked my confirmation number at the inn near our summer house where Andrew and I used to stay before we bought our place. My feelings were conflicted: on the one hand, I desperately wanted to see him; my other hand wanted to wring his neck. But mainly, I could not believe any of this was happening.

As I headed for 287 East, my stomach began to churn, a common occurrence as of late. At the toll booth on the Tappan Zee Bridge, I pulled up to one of the lanes that accepted cash, since we never got around to purchasing an EZ pass.

A gentleman with bright green eyes, who I recognized from former trips across the bridge, greeted me with a wide grin. "There she is!" he said.

His exuberance took me aback, but I put forth my best, most sincere smile. "Oh, hi," I said, handing him my five dollars. "May I please have a receipt?"

"You can have anything you want!" he chirped.

"Can I have my husband back?" I said. The man gave me a puzzled look, but I simply wished him well and stepped down on the gas pedal.

All the way through Connecticut and Massachusetts, I reviewed everything that had happened between Andy and me, trying not to beat myself up; it did, after all, take two to tango, as my therapist had said. Unfortunately, I'd now lost my tango partner, and I was dancing alone.

Once I was on Route 91, I pulled off the exit that would take me to the organic farm/café. I'd been there before without Andy on my solo treks, but now the situation was different, and it felt strange—wrong. I got my usual tuna sandwich on multigrain, with the hot peppers on one half only. That part was for me. The blander half I saved for Andrew.

The trip up through Vermont was uneventful, but my chest was tight, and I felt sick to my stomach. I tried to counter these heavy feelings of sadness and anxiety by blasting music from one of my favorite bands. The songs used to get me pumped, and I would sing out loud when driving in the car by myself, bouncing up and down to the beat like a teenager. Today I didn't sing along, nor did I sway to the rhythm.

As I drove onto the route that led to our summer house, I felt the hole in my heart widen. In the past, my excitement would build the closer I got to Crystal Lake—a spot that was sacred to my brother and sister and me, as it had been to my now deceased parents who discovered the place in the 1940s. Andrew had also fallen in love with the area and its natural beauty—the towering pines, the fresh air, the star-laden night skies, and the pure, clear waters of the lake—when I introduced him to it years ago

I passed through Garnersville, which, along with RJ's, had a country store, small stone library, post office, and gas station that also sold deli food, beer and wine, and various sundries.

My heart began to beat faster as I drove up the hill to my house and went through the old wrought-iron arch that marked the entrance to our road. I knew I was not smiling like I normally would when I spotted the two resident crows—or the welcoming committee, as Andy called them—on the grassy hillside.

An eighth of a mile up the paved road I took a left and bumped my way down our driveway. After parking the car, I collected a few things and went inside, pulling open the screen door a little too forcefully.

"Hi," I said to my husband as he stepped out of his office. "I have your things in the car. Some shirts." My voice was surprisingly steady, even though I was shaking inside.

I handed Andrew the bag containing the half sandwich, which I supposed on some twisted level was an appeal of sorts, a peace offering, a bribe perhaps, or simply to let him know I cared. He put his food on a plate, and we went out to the screened-in porch that overlooked the lake. After we'd sat down, Andy showed me a bird house he had put together from wood scraps. My husband seemed, like me, low key, sad.

"Do you want to play Scrabble?" I asked, looking at the iPad on the table.

"All right," he said.

We started a new game—once again the two of us playing against the machine. I easily came up with words, solutions, but was completely frozen in my ability to express all the feelings that were whipping around inside me. Perhaps I was afraid to say anything because I was afraid of what I might hear.

Within the hour, the curtain lady arrived along with a man, who I quickly deduced was her husband. I envied their togetherness; they seemed so happy.

"Your wife has good taste," the curtain lady said to Andy as she pulled the drapes out from a storage box.

I wanted to say, Yeah, Andrew, see? Good taste, classy broad, not some wood-chopping rooster killer.

The curtain people finished the installation and left our house. The drapes were elegant, well-made, and added a sense of warmth to the living room and the kitchen; they not only blended nicely with the furniture and walls, they covered up the old, cracked windows. I knew I'd made a good choice, since the curtains would last for a long time to come. I wished I felt that certain about my marriage.

I informed Andrew that I'd booked a room at the inn. My husband didn't ask why I was not staying at the house, and I did not mention that I didn't think I could bear staying here, knowing that he'd had sex in one of the rooms with someone other than me. Hopefully it was not in our bedroom.

"Will you stay with me?" I asked my husband, tentatively.

To my surprise, Andy said he would. I questioned my good sense, or lack thereof, but he was still my husband, and I was doing my best to understand him, to understand what had happened to us, why I did what I did, and why he wouldn't cut it off with Trudy. And I missed him terribly.

When I went upstairs to say hello to my cat, Andrew followed behind me to pack an overnight bag.

"How come you're sleeping in here?" I asked, pointing to the middle guest room where I spotted his clothes and an unmade bed.

"Too much emotion in the other one," Andy said, looking off down the hallway toward the master bedroom.

I felt a modicum of relief; at least they didn't do it in our bedroom.

"Do you really want to go to the party?" I asked my husband. Before the mess that was now us, we had been invited to a friend and his wife's house for his annual chowder fete.

"I think it's the right thing to do. They'd be really disappointed." My husband then told me that no one up here knew what had happened. Perhaps, I reckoned, it was because he wasn't sure about where we, as a couple, were headed. I took that as a good sign, or at least a hopeful one. "Okay," I said. "Business as usual then." Suddenly, I had a disturbing thought. "Will Trudy be there?"

"Absolutely not," Andrew said.

"Good. Otherwise I'd have to kill her," I remarked, half joking.

Andrew didn't smile.

After I gave Mamie a few scratches behind the ears and filled up her bowl with dry cat food, my husband and I climbed into my car and drove off to the party, which was on a winding country road. We pulled up in front of the one-story ranch house, where people were milling about, drinking from cans of beer and plastic cups filled with wine. We parked and walked inside the house and into the kitchen to say hello to the host and grab a drink.

Feeling ill from the unexpressed emotion and words not yet spoken, I opted for one of the imported ales that Andrew brought, since I knew beer could soothe an upset stomach. The gathering was pleasant and attended by many of the familiar faces from RJ's, but what I really wanted was to talk with my husband—alone.

Once we'd spent an hour or so chatting with various party-goers, acting like all was status quo, Andy and I told the host that we needed to go. The man appeared a bit hurt, but I knew I could not possibly stay any longer. It took too much energy to put up this happy front. I gave the host a quick kiss on the cheek, thanked his wife, and walked with Andy out to the car. This time, my husband and I did not hold hands.

Within ten minutes, we got to the inn, which was bustling with Friday-night activity, but we managed to find a spot to park. After dumping our bags off in the room, Andy and I went downstairs to the attached restaurant and got lucky when two seats opened up at the bar. Andrew ordered beer; I asked for a bottle of wine. We also decided to get a small pizza.

My husband, who was wearing the beret I had picked out for him, looked handsome to me—more so than ever, which deepened my sadness. I maintained a calm demeanor, however, when we began a discussion about what happened, and he repeated many of the things he said when I first found out about his indiscretion.

I touched his arm lightly and implored him to please get to know himself before he entered into another relationship. "I'm telling you this as a friend, Andrew," I said, knowing that my levelheaded response was directly related to my ridiculously stubborn sense of pride.

"Well received," he said. "Sage advice."

I fell silent, and Andrew asked me what I was thinking. I didn't respond.

"Seriously, what are you thinking?" he said again.

Taking in a breath, I turned to him. "What kind of a person sleeps with their friend's husband?"

Andrew's head dropped to his chest, and he went out like a light—which is what he'd often do when we'd be lying in bed at night and I'd broach a sensitive subject. But here? Falling asleep sitting upright at a bar filled with people? With his fist around a beer? This was a first. I tugged at my husband's shirt sleeve. "Andrew, wake up. Go to bed. I'll be up in a while."

His eyes fluttered opened. He nodded once and obediently headed up to our room. I stayed at the bar and drank a little more wine, but I didn't finish the bottle. At around nine o'clock, I paid the bill and walked up the stairs to the second floor. As I stepped into the room, I saw that the light was on, but Andrew was fast asleep, his C-pap machine going full blast. I stood there listening to the sound of the device as my husband breathed in and out, the sheet pulled up over his head.

"Andrew?" I said.

Nothing. No response. I said his name a bit louder. Silence. It was like he deliberately wanted to shut me out.

I became infuriated and had to repress my urge to beat him with a pillow. "Screw it." I grabbed my bag and scribbled a note on the inn's stationary telling my husband to call me when he woke up. *I will come get you*, it said. I left it by his travel bag.

On my way out, I stopped at the front desk. "Do you have any matches?"

"We don't do that anymore," the female clerk commented.

"Oh, dear. There are no lights on at the house. I know I'll pay hell trying to get the key into the lock. It's pitch dark there."

"You're not staying? Is everything okay?"

"Husband problems," I said, matter-of-factly.

"Boy, do I know that one," the woman said, handing me a miniature flashlight on a chain. "What the heck. Take three." She pulled two more from the drawer.

I pocketed the flashlights, thanked her profusely, and drove back to my once-cherished home. When I got inside, I went upstairs, brushed my teeth, took a Xanax, and snuggled up next to Mamie. The house felt cold and empty—as did I.

SEPTEMBER 24

A SLAP IN THE FACE, A CAT IN THE CAR

At eight o'clock in the morning, I was awakened by the sound of tires crunching down the driveway. I got up out of bed and looked outside. "Jesus, you've got to be kidding me." Trudy's station wagon was heading toward the house.

I quickly retreated into the bedroom. I heard a car door slam and moments later keys jangling and the sound of the back door squeaking open. I went downstairs to confront Andrew, and through the kitchen window spotted Trudy's car rolling back up the drive.

"Why didn't you call me? I left you a note," I said to my husband, not quite believing he had the audacity to call this woman to pick him up. It felt like a harsh slap in my face, and I thought he'd either totally lost his mind (possible) or was truly clueless (also possible). For a moment, I hated him; with all my heart, I hated him. And then I just wanted to wrap my arms around him.

Another slap: Andrew asked me when I was leaving.

"Why? We have an appointment on Monday to take the SUV in to the dealership." I'd purposely made the appointment so I'd have an excuse to spend some more time with Andy, in hopes of patching things up.

"I need my space." My husband looked toward the window, avoiding eye contact.

"Fine," I said curtly. "I'll pack up and go."

Andrew went off to the auxiliary kitchen on the other side of the house, while I gathered up some paperwork in the downstairs office.

A few minutes later, he poked his head into the room. "I'm going to get into my work clothes. There's some melon for you on the counter if you want it."

I walked into the kitchen and looked at the fruit he'd cut up—an odd gesture, considering he just told me he wanted me to leave. But

I didn't touch it, as the thought of putting anything in my mouth at that point made me want to wretch. Instead I went upstairs to get my suitcase.

Andrew, who was standing at the bottom of the attic steps holding wiring tools, asked me if I ate my melon.

"I feel nauseous. So, no, I didn't."

"You're not doing that again, are you? Throwing up?"

"Jesus! How long have you known me? That was over twenty years ago."

What I didn't say was, bulimia is your current squeeze's problem. That and ADHD. Quite a package you bought yourself, Andy.

After scooping up my cat and putting her and my luggage in the car, I was ready to go.

"Is there anything you need?" Andrew asked, standing by my SUV.

"You're kidding me." My voice was laced with sarcasm.

"I meant—"

"I know what you meant. But no, I'm fine," I said, which was about as far from the truth as you could get. I touched my husband lightly on the shoulder. "You do remember we have our appointment with the marriage counselor on Tuesday in New York. Right?"

Andrew gave me a disapproving look.

"You said you'd go, Andy."

"Okay." On a scale of one to ten, his enthusiasm was hovering around zero.

After bidding my husband a polite and very civil goodbye, I left Vermont feeling tired, angry, upset, and more confused than I'd ever felt in my entire life. Thankfully, I had my cat with me, which kept me calm on the ride home. And bless her unsullied feline soul, Mamie sat quietly like a little furry princess in the passenger seat most of the way back, her paws daintily stretched out in front of her. I drove carefully, as always, to ensure her safety—just as I used to do with Andrew on our way home from a night out.

SEPTEMBER 27

SHACKING UP AS A GUEST

Andrew arrived at the NY house and holed up in the guest bedroom. And even though everything felt so odd, off-kilter, my husband's presence soothed me. Tonight, I went to my friend Lena's apartment up the river. Andrew went out as well, but I had no idea where.

SEPTEMBER 28

WHO NEEDS THERAPY?

We sat facing the marriage counselor. I was on one end of her beige couch; Andy was on the other. Normally we would have settled in right next to each other, but not today. I looked over at my husband, who seemed a million miles away. Sighing, I turned my attention to therapist.

"Okay," she said, "tell me a bit about yourselves and what's going on between the two of you."

Andrew and I each gave the woman some perfunctory details on our history together. In short, my husband said that aside from the sexual issues, our marriage was "pretty darn perfect."

"So, what's the problem?" I said, shaking my head as I looked over at him. And I had to ask again. "Andrew, are you going to stop sleeping with Trudy?"

"No," he said, a little too quickly. "I told you that before."

The therapist said nothing in response, nor did I, as it was almost impossible for me to wrap my head around all this. But Andy did say that he had not completely "flipped the switch," meaning his tendency to completely shut the door on something or someone when things go awry. I recalled how he'd done that so easily with his last wife after he'd found out about her fling with their mutual friend. Even though Andy's wife wanted to reconcile, he refused; in his mind it was over, and there was no turning back. At that point, I had already moved into his house. We ended today's session by agreeing to a six-month trial separation and set another appointment.

That afternoon my business partner sent me an email asking how therapy went. After giving him a blow-by-blow account, including details of Andy's "quest for passion" and his desire to have a partner who wanted to jump his bones 24/7, Ron quickly wrote me back.

RON: *I think he's really missing the big picture. In time, two months or two years, the bloom will be off the rose with Chicken Lady, and he'll wake up and realize that he's deluded himself. All that shit is fine if you're an A-list actor/player, but they know that marriage isn't for them. That and they can partake of an endless supply of super-models.*

If you want to be in a marriage, you have to face what we all face: the sex changes. The freaky-deaky wild abandon gives way to utilitarian sex, without exception. What happens is you get a partner to share your life with—someone to help you realize your potential, create good stuff with;

it's about mutual support and the safety afforded when someone has your back when you fail; it's also about having someone to share the joy with when you succeed. But I think you guys had a pretty good marriage, and he's going to trade that in for a little boo-pah? If he had any nuts, he would have banged her, zipped up his pants, and walked out the door. When she asked where he was going, he would have said, Home.

I'm sorry. And he's going to be sorry too. Hang in there. Ronnie

A few hours later, Andrew shot me an e-note on his cell from the guestroom down the hall.

ANDREW: *I will always care deeply for you.*

"Well, Andy," I said, quietly, out of earshot, "you sure have a funny way of showing it."

SEPTEMBER 29

HAPPY BIRTHDAY TO ME

We took my husband's car over to the mall, not for any kind of celebration, but to pick up some vitamins that we both needed and to grab some lunch. In the past I almost always did the driving, due to an inner ear problem that causes mild vertigo when I ride as a passenger. But things had changed. My husband was now in the driver's seat.

I tried to keep the conversation light along the way, but the knot in my stomach was huge. There also seemed to be more than the usual amount of litter along the road, which intensified the anger that had started to rise up inside me.

"You're smoldering," my husband said.

"Yeah, Andrew, I'm smoldering. What do you expect? That everything is just hunky dory? Good God."

He did not respond.

We ate lunch at the sushi place and made small talk, both he and I picking at our food. So much was left unsaid—just like, I suppose, it had been for the last several months before the blowup. Or maybe things had been festering inside of Andrew for some time. I silently reflected on the mistakes I had made, particularly when I told him I'd never really fallen in lust with him the way I had my former boyfriend. I thought honesty was, as they say, the best policy between partners. And then there were those times when he would awkwardly grab at me in bed, and I'd tell him I felt like I was with my little brother. I wished I could take it all back.

Early evening, I went into the city to be with my friend Gaby. Before I left, Andrew informed me that he was going out. Again, he offered no details as to where or with whom, and I didn't ask. This, I was sure, would be one birthday without any kind of acknowledgement from my husband. There was actually one other, when I told him not to bother getting me a card—or anything else. I said it didn't matter. When he took me at my word, I got mad and told him so. We used to laugh about that quite a bit. Now there was no mirth.

SEPTEMBER 30

WRONG COLOR—GAUGED RAGE

I walked into the kitchen to find Andrew sitting at the center island doing some work on his computer, eating a breakfast of mixed nuts. He looked up briefly and slid a brochure across the counter as I put some glasses in the sink.

"This is the woodstove I'm going to get," he said. "I refuse to freeze my ass off up there."

"No one is asking you to." I picked up the pamphlet and scrutinized the picture. "The stove is <u>blue</u>?"

"It's the only color available in this model," he said. I could tell he was ready to go on the defensive—or offensive.

"Andrew, I spent so much time coordinating the colors in the living room. Blue would be disastrous." I could not help but take this as another assault, another act of indiscretion.

But my husband didn't give a damn about color coordination and said he was going to get the stove—regardless. I now realized more clearly than ever that we were in a power struggle, which until a few weeks ago was a non-issue. Before the breach, I'd always been the decision maker on all things domestic and otherwise.

"Jesus! You've thrown a complete shit bomb into my life," was all I could manage as I clomped back up the stairs. I said no more, but silently thanked Ron for providing me with that very apt expression, which I suspected would come in handy going forward.

At around four o'clock, Andrew told me he was going out. Again, I had no idea where or with whom.

An hour later, I headed for NYC to meet Robin, my college friend, who had spent time with me and Andy when we came into the city. After we settled in at the Roosevelt Hotel bar, I gave her the lowdown on my crumbling marriage.

Like everyone else, she was flabbergasted. "<u>Andrew</u>?"

"Yeah," I said. "Everyone is shocked. No one saw it coming. Least of all me."

Later, on my way home on the train, I received an email from my husband. In the subject line was one word: *Leaving.*

ANDREW: *I couldn't handle the anger.*

My face and ears began to burn, and I fired off a response on my cell.

ME: *And you think I wouldn't have some anger at what you're now doing? Get real...We had a life.*

I managed to get home in one piece and pulled into the garage. But my insides were roiling.

"Great," I said, noticing that Andrew had forgotten to turn off the overhead garage lights.

I got out of the car and slammed the door shut. The place was a mess; my husband's tools, planks of lumber, wood scraps, and empty cartons and Lord knows what else were scattered from one end of the garage to the other. In my attempts to maneuver my way over to the light switch, which was buried behind heaps of crap on his workshop counter, I managed to twist my ankle stepping over a stack of pine flooring.

"You make a fucking mess out of everything, Andrew!" I yelled, certain that my husband was by now shacked up with Chicken Lady.

My head was pounding from the fury that was now consuming me. I knew full well that it was not healthy to repress extreme emotion, so I grabbed a metal stool and heaved it at his workshop door. BAM! The door dented slightly, but it was not enough to satisfy me, to alleviate my rage. I picked the stool up again and hurled it. BAM! Another dent. Once again. BAM! Another.

I spotted the sledgehammer on the counter. Even better, I thought as I zeroed in on the large, bright red unit with long steel bars, which was part of my husband's mini sawmill. I did an assessment—sledge hammer on thick, heavy-gauge steel=minimal harm, excellent emotional release—a deductive process that took milliseconds in reality.

Raising my arm, I brought the sledge down. "Mother-fucking cocksucker!"

I began to wail, and I hit it again. And again. And again. And again. One more time and I stopped—as I didn't really want to do any irreversible damage. So maybe I wasn't as mentally imbalanced as I might have thought a month or so ago when I was so obsessed with BDSM and Carl. I did have the capacity to control my behavior, after all. (Yay, me.)

But, apparently, I wasn't done. When I closed up the garage and headed inside, the emptiness of the house overpowered me, and the anger kicked in when I went to brush my teeth. Now the tube of toothpaste was my target, and I slammed it down on the marble floor. Its plastic lid popped off and hit the ground with a plunk. I picked the tube up and slammed it down again. This time the toothpaste burst free of its casing. But it did not quell my wrath. I needed something more. I needed to throw, smash, destroy something bigger, something more substantial. I went into Andy's office and found the perfect object—the telescope that was given to my husband for his ten years of service at work. I hated the thing, which had been sitting there for years collecting dust; but more than that, I hated the idiocy of what had happened to my marriage. I grabbed the contraption by the neck and methodically began slamming it—hard—into the floor, over and over. "I hate you, I hate you, I hate you!" I yelled, howling like a crazed animal, my eyes stinging with tears, my face now streaked with black mascara.

The plastic cylinder broke into pieces, the glass lens shattered. I kept going at it until hardly one part remained intact, and the telescope's wire guts hung lifelessly from what remained of it. Finally, I was spent, exhausted; there was not another drop of water left in me to cry out. But I felt better.

The hardwood floor, however, had suffered a bit of damage, so I made a mental note to color in the nicks with some cherry-colored stain. (Another indication that I still possessed a bit of sanity.)

I took the remnants of the massacre out to the recycling bin and put the thing to rest. Andrew, I was certain, would never notice that the telescope was gone. It was a useless piece of junk that he used solely as a drying rack to air out his sweaty tee shirts.

OCTOBER 2

HOLY TREES

I was sitting in my office sorting my email on my laptop when the wind kicked up. Startled, I looked out the window. The afternoon sky was rapidly turning a deep blue-black. The tree tops began whipping back and forth, and my heart began to hammer. I grabbed Mamie, bolted downstairs, and together we huddled in the middle of the living room. Within twenty minutes, what appeared to be a microburst had moved on through, the darkness and wind now having receded.

Later, before I went off to bed, after binge-watching a couple of lame comedy shows on TV, I checked my phone messages on my land line. There was voicemail from Lori, my tenant in the cottage out back. "Holy crap, Batman," she said. "Have you seen the backyard? It's unrecognizable."

OCTOBER 3

MESSES, MOTHS, AND MAGGOTS

"Good God," I mumbled, surveying the damage behind the cottage. Lori was right when she said it was analogous to the mess that was now my marriage. Three massive maples had been uprooted by the intense downdraft and were now lying on their sides, along with several other large trees that had been in their path when they fell to earth. One victim was a beautiful, gentle fir. It looked crippled, sad, and my heart ached for the tree.

On the drive into town, I shook my head furiously to get rid of the disturbing image that had been seared into my brain. Thankfully, I had my writing workshop and lunch with a friend at a Japanese restaurant afterwards.

'This pain is just temporary," she said. "Everything happens to bring us to a better place."

I took what she said to heart. Or rather, I chose to. It was just too bad it was a little too early to start knocking back sake.

Later at home, as I went to scoop out Mamie's litter pan, a task that I now had to perform on a bi- sometimes tri-daily basis, due to my cat's advancing kidney disease, I spotted something foreign.

"What the hell is that?" I said, looking down into the pan, realizing that muttering to myself was quite the norm these days. Odd, unfamiliar clumps were scattered on top of the wheat-based mix. I looked closer. It appeared that some kind of bug had gotten into the litter, probably during the manufacturing or shipping process.

"Damn it." I happened to look up and could not believe what I saw. The wall was covered with small triangular, dark-brown shapes. They looked like moths, but not the kind of moth I was used to seeing in the pantry. "Oh, no," I said, sighing loudly, as I spotted strings of maggots, some alive, some dead, in the creases along the ceiling and walls. My stomach turned.

Hands shaking, wishing to hell I could find the humor in this,

I fired up the vacuum cleaner and sucked up as many of the live invaders as I could. I sprayed down the walls with Windex and manually scraped off the dead bugs and maggots that were stuck in the seams. The remaining kitty litter got bagged up, and I replaced the mixture in the pan with a clay-based, not-so-natural product.

I dumped the litter in the garbage can in the kitchen, thinking that was the end of it.

OCTOBER 4

THE WEEPING GARBAGE PAIL

It wasn't. Having drained the last bit of orange juice to take my AM vitamins, I popped open the lid of the garbage pail with my foot to stuff the carton inside.

"Oh God. What now?" The inside lid dripped with a clear, liquid-like substance—almost as if the trash can was weeping.

I yanked the plastic bag out, tied it up, threw it outside, and dumped the pail onto the driveway.

"This is fucking insane," I yelled as I blasted a stream of water at the can from the garden hose.

After I'd washed down and sanitized the garbage pail, using up an entire bottle of kitchen cleaner, I hauled it back inside and replaced the trash bag.

It was like the awfulness of what was happening between me and Andy was manifesting all around me in the most bizarrely metaphorical ways.

"This really is an unrelenting shit storm," I said to my sister on the phone when she called to check up on me.

OCTOBER 5

MORE TEARS

I was completely stymied. The inside lid of the garbage pail still dripped this mysterious liquid, and again I removed the trash bag and replaced it with a fresh one. It just didn't make any sense—nothing did. So where was it coming from? It seemed like something out of a sci-fi flick, and I began to envision an Alice in Wonderland sort of scenario, where the pail just kept on dripping, more and more profusely, until the alien substance was spurting out in torrents, flooding the entire house all the way up to the second floor. (Make that the third floor.)

It began to freak me out and, in spite of my search efforts on Google, I found no answer. But I knew that if Andrew were here, he'd be able to figure out what was causing this phenomenon. I was certain of that. There was a reason I called him "Mr. Science."

Thankfully, by the end of the day, the garbage can seemed to have finally stopped weeping. I wished I could have said the same for myself.

OCTOBER 12

OUT OF THE BLUE

I was so happy to see Bennie, my friend and former musical director on my play we showcased in NYC. Nestled in at a bar near Grand Central, a martini in both our hands, I brought him up-to-date on the latest with Andrew.

"I think your husband has lost his marbles," Bennie said. And like everyone else, he was stunned it was Andrew who left. "He adored you. It doesn't make sense."

"Life is just full of little surprises," I said. "But I guess I kinda lost my marbles for a while, too. But every couple has glitches. I'm just so, I don't know...I'm totally freaked."

After a few hours of solid conversation, during which I provided the gory details of what led up to our break-up, Lenny said he had to get back to make dinner for his paramour of many years.

"I hope you know how lucky you are to have a life partner," I said.

"I do. Especially after he almost died." Bennie's paramour battled cancer several years ago but was now in remission.

"You know, I think about that sometimes," I said. "I'm so afraid I'll meet someone else, fall madly in love, and then the sucker will die. I'm just not sure I could take another hit like that. Jesus, talk about abandonment issues."

Bennie nodded knowingly and patted me on the hand.

After we paid up, my friend and I walked over to Grand Central, where he planned to hop on the subway to the upper east side. We kissed each other on the cheek and said goodbye. I was a bit sad to see him go, feeling, once again, that raging emptiness and anxiety start to overtake me. My train wasn't leaving for another forty minutes, so I wandered up the stairs to one of the bars, which I quickly saw was closed for the evening. It was probably just as well since more alcohol would only exacerbate my dark mood.

I leaned against the railing and pulled out my cell phone from my purse. As soon as I turned it back on, it began buzzing with life, downloading email after email from the server. I clicked away, deleting a string of messages, since they were mostly junk, but found myself still waiting for that incoming missive from my husband that would change my life—back to the way it used to be.

"Hey," said a voice from out of the blue.

I looked up from my device. An attractive man in a grey suit and purple tie stood before me. His hair was a light brown and was slightly receding. My first guess would have put him at around age forty-five.

"You look trendy. Want to have a drink?" he asked.

(Trendy?)

"Sure," I said, feeling desperate for distraction of any kind to assuage my tremendous heartache.

We walked over to the bar at the Hyatt next door to the station, making small talk along the way, and grabbed a couple of stools. He ordered a gin and tonic; I asked for a glass of Chardonnay. My new friend gave me a nutshell view of his life: he'd been married once, was now divorced, was fifty years old, Jewish, and a corporate lawyer. He was also a Libra, like me.

After a pleasant twenty minutes of conversation, I found myself becoming increasingly put off not only by his slightly arrogant attitude, but his small, tight mouth that reminded me of a hyphen. I wanted to get out of there and told him that I needed to make my train, since it was one of the last ones to Tarrytown.

"Are you sure you don't want to stay in the city?" he said. It was clear what he had in mind.

"I really need to get home."

"Okay, your call," he said, handing me his business card.

On our way out, he moved in front of me and explained that a man should always go through a revolving door before the woman. I didn't know if that was really the case or if it was an act of passive aggressiveness since I wouldn't sleep with him.

"Libras make good friends, not lovers," I blurted out, completely killing any chances for much of anything with this guy.

My new friend (probably soon to become my new ex-friend) gave me a look of displeasure. "Okay. See ya," he said and hurried toward the escalators. So, I wondered, should I have been flattered that this man approached me or morbidly depressed that I was so obviously alone—alone and emotionally raw and desperate for distraction;

one of the walking wounded, which, according to my friend Adele, made me the perfect target for guys looking to get laid. "Men can smell the vulnerability," she'd said. "And most women in that position can easily be led into bed. They want to bolster their self-esteem, prove they're still desirable."

Being dumped by my husband, however, had quite the opposite effect on me. I really didn't want to sleep with anyone but Andy.

OCTOBER 15

TRAFFIC CONES AND ROOSTERS

It was now 1:30 AM, and I was heading across the Tappan Zee Bridge thinking about the man with the hyphen mouth and chastising myself for being overly judgmental.

Without much warning, the traffic came to a complete standstill because of the ongoing construction to repair the bridge.

"Crap," I mumbled. Twenty minutes went by and nothing; no movement whatsoever. And there I was, stuck, along with hundreds of people in cars and trucks, vehicles idling, toxic fumes spewing out into the atmosphere—and I had a very full bladder.

A surge of heat shot through my body, and I was hit by an overwhelming impulse to jam my foot on the accelerator pedal and smash into the traffic cones that had been set down to block off every single lane but the one I was in. I wanted to destroy all of them and any person who might try to stop me.

I knew that the trek home, which should have taken me twenty minutes, would now extend to almost an hour. I also knew from past experiences that along the four-or-so-mile span across the Tappan Zee, there might be one utility vehicle and two people working, and most likely on the lanes going in the opposite direction.

As the traffic finally began to creep along and I headed west, it turned out I was right. And I found myself hating, loathing these white and orange plastic monstrosities that looked like witches' hats and the bastard union workers who had aligned the cones in picture-perfect rows along the highway. "You mother fuckers!" I screamed, shaking my fist, my voice bouncing off the closed windows as I drove by.

My rage made me sweat, but I knew if I acted on it and did what I really wanted to do, I'd end up in jail, and I sure as hell did not need that—particularly now since there was no one to bail me out. A little over a month ago there was. And suddenly it struck me why these orange and white pylons triggered such wrath. On a subliminal level, they must have reminded me of Trudy, my husband's lover who kills roosters by yanking their heads through the small ends of traffic cones. (And Andrew always said he was an animal lover. Fuck him...God, how I missed him.)

PART III—LOOKING FOR MORE DISTRACTION(S)

A NOT-SO-HIP-AND-HAPPENING BAR—AN ORTHODOX JEW

Angie, my Paris-based writer friend who had encouraged us to settle in the Hudson Valley, was in NYC for a meeting with her publisher. After dinner, we decided to go to a bar someone had recommended for another glass of wine. Supposedly it was the hot spot of the moment. Naturally I was game, so we walked over to the place, which was in the west village.

The tech-noir watering hole was surprisingly empty except for a handsome gay couple, who wore slick, rectangular glasses and identical white-and-black checkered scarves looped twice around the neck. Within a couple of minutes, a bearded man in a black coat, black pants, and a yarmulke slid onto a stool at the far end of the bar. He was either an Orthodox or Hassidic Jew. Angie and I guessed the former since he was without curly side-locks, but neither of us really knew the culture all that well.

Looking over at the man with the beard, I impulsively nodded "hello."

"Hi," he said, smiling. "How's it going?" His voice was soft and youthful, and he appeared to be open to conversation, as was I, since I tried to maintain the philosophy that you can always learn something from everyone you come across. Or maybe it was simply another welcomed source of distraction.

The bearded man, who had a cherubic face, moved over to the stool next to me and offered to buy both me and my friend a glass of wine.

"I know this is probably a bit presumptuous of me, but are you old enough to drink?" I said, with a trace of humor.

"Twenty-five," he said. "But I won't ask you how old <u>you</u> are."

I laughed; the kid obviously had some class.

"So, are you Orthodox?" Angie asked after the three of us indulged in a brief discussion about the Jewish religion.

"Eh," he said, waggling his hand side to side. Neither Angie nor I were quite sure what he meant. I gave him a quizzical look.

"Rabbinical studies." He paused a moment and out of the blue told us he had a girlfriend, but that the physical component was missing between the two of them.

I had to wonder if he was "fishing."

"Do you really have to do it through a hole in a sheet?" Angie asked, her eyes filling with mischief.

He smiled but didn't answer.

We also found out his name: Yehowah. I had a hard time getting it to stick in my brain, for some reason, and messed it up several times. "Yahoo-huh?" I said.

After the three of us finished our drinks, Angie announced that she had to get back to her hotel to prepare for her meeting the next day.

"Guess I'll head to Grand Central," I said.

Yehowah's eyes lit up. "I can take you. I have my driver with me." (He definitely was fishing.)

"Sure," I said. "Why not?"

Yehowah paid for our drinks, and we thanked him politely.

Once we were out on the street, I kissed Angie goodbye on the cheek. As she wandered off, the young man with the beard and I piled into the back of the town car. Yehowah's chauffeur, a black man with a stunning smile, greeted us cordially.

"How are you?" I said to the driver as I leaned back into the leather seat.

"Just great!" he said.

As the car veered out into traffic, Yehowah moved closer to me. He gently put his hand on the back of my head, pulled me toward him, and placed his lips on mine. His mouth was soft, his lips full and sweet. For the next twenty minutes, we made out like teenagers until we got to the station.

"We can drive you home. We'd have fun, you and me," Yehowah said.

"No. It's okay. Really. I'll take the train."

"Come on. Please?"

"Can't," I said and moved in for one final, deep kiss, breathing in the musky but pleasant smell of his beard.

The driver, who I was certain had been grinning all the way over (for obvious reasons), had pulled up on the south side of the street.

"Wait! What's your cell number?" Yehowah asked as I grabbed the door handle.

I rattled it off twice, gave him a peck on the cheek, and jumped out of the car.

On my way home on the train, I heard the plink of an incoming text on my phone. It was my young friend with the yarmulke.

YEHOWAH: *Was really amazing meeting u, someone so gorgeous and wise and passionate.*

(He sure knew how to pour it on.)

ME: *I hve to apologize, I can't remember ur name. Ack!*

YEHOWAH: *U could call me Mike ;)*

ME: *Ha-ha.*

YEHOWAH: *I think if we could spend the night together, we would gain a lot from each other.*

ME: *Weeeeeee! But, might hv to thnk about this.*

YEHOWAH: *You're a great kisser! What does weeeeeee mean?*

ME: *U r a good kisser, too. Weeeeeeee! Now do you understnd the meaning of weeeee?*

YEHOWAH: *:-) LOL yes, mama.*

ME: *And there u have it, Mike.*

YEHOWAH: *Okay, Carla ;-)*

ME: *Haha. I won't b able to txt anymore as I hv to drive. Getting off train.*

Within twenty minutes I was home, and the texts kept coming.

YEHOWAH: *When should I come to Piermont? U in bed?*

ME: *Yes, moving toward pillow land. Sweet dreams, Steve. Or is it Mike? I forget. Ha-ha.*

YEHOWAH: *What do I do about my girlfriend?*

ME: *If u really feel something is lacking...do not compromise. You will pay in the end and so will she.*

Pay in the end. Interesting (and "punny") choice of words, I thought. I was honestly a bit startled at what I'd written; perhaps I was really talking about myself and how I felt when I first met Andy. I began ruminating on the subject that I often discussed with my friends: that of chemistry, or lack thereof, between romantic partners. I had managed to convince myself it didn't matter, since physical passion can often result in unwise choices. As it has been said by many, lust is disguised as love and love is disguised as lust. I had been there and done that with the lusty love. And besides, I reasoned, things change; you can't be hot over someone around the clock. No one would survive it. So, what was most important in a marriage? Trust? That had gone out the window. Friendship? Loyalty? Both of those had been tossed in the crapper as far as Andy and I were concerned. I fell asleep feeling deflated, regretful, confused, but wishing more than anything that my husband was in bed next to me—he was, after all, my mate, my companion for almost two decades.

OCTOBER 17

PERSISTENCE, PERSISTENCE

My cell phone plinked at 9:30 AM, alerting me to an incoming text from my very persistent friend.

YEHOWAH: *Good morning. How was your sleep? I can come to Piermont today. I need your insight and energy!*

(He obviously wanted to get laid. Badly.)

ME: *I can't today. Maybe we can figure something else out. I hv to run but will be back late afternoon. Then off to the mountains tonight.*

YEHOWAH: *Can I come?*

ME: *No, silly.*

YEHOWAH: *Okay. What's 2moro like or after dinner?*

ME: *Can't. Busy.*

YEHOWAH: *What's wrong with after dinner tonight?*

ME: *Boy you are tenacious. The impatience of youth! U cn wait; the world will not end.*

YEHOWAH: *It won't end, but my gut tells me that if it doesn't happen very soon, it won't happen, and I don't want that...*

ME: *Don't worry. I will meet u.*

YEHOWAH: *Ok. I'm just thirsting for ur presence. What about your friend from Paris?*

(I guess any attractive, willing woman would have sufficed. So, what was I thinking? That he would make a suitable boyfriend?)

ME: *She is leaving today :-(*

YEHOWAH: *Ok. I will be in touch.*

OCTOBER 18

A SLAP IN THE FACEBOOK

As I was waiting at Flanagan's for my friend Sarah—who I often described as a soulful hippie child stuck in an older woman's body—I got a text from Andrew's daughter.

COURTNEY: *I'm so sorry this happened.*

It sounded like Courtney knew. I hadn't wanted to tell her as I felt it would hurt her. I also had no idea what her father might have said. I decided to play dumb.

ME: *What are you talking about?*

COURTNEY: *Dad's cheating.*

After furiously texting back and forth, I called Courtney, since my fingers were beginning to cramp up, and filled her in on some of the details.

"I knew something was wrong when I spoke to you on your birthday," she said, crying into the phone. She told me she couldn't stand to get to know another woman.

"I certainly understand, but I'm upset too."

"Dad's sick. He needs therapy."

I had to agree with her and said I felt the same.

Courtney said that she was absolutely certain that her dad had cheated on her mother, Andrew's second wife. So maybe that was why his ex tried to run him over with her car and threatened to chop him up into little pieces in the middle of the night while he slept.

127

The extent of her ire had never made sense to me. Now it did.

"Did you know that Trudy friended you on Facebook?" I said, unable to imagine that Courtney would have accepted the request.

"What?! I thought she was one of Dad's colleagues from work!" Courtney one-upped me: apparently Andrew had asked his parents in D.C. if he could bring Trudy down to visit. Now I was ready to go ballistic. The body wasn't even in the ground yet! My body!

When I got home, I wrote an email to Andrew. I started off in relatively pleasant tone, but it didn't last long.

ME: ...*I understand you asked your parents if you could bring Trudy down to D.C. with you. I think that is absolutely audacious. We are still married, and so is she. She is trying to ingratiate herself into your life and your family (my family, too). And it is extraordinarily hurtful to me, Courtney, and your folks. Please use your head about this. It was also quite tasteless of Trudy to friend Courtney on Facebook. Has she no empathy/integrity? What was she thinking? What are you thinking?*

I was about to hit the send button, but decided against it, as I was afraid to sabotage any chance of reuniting, since I knew Andrew could not handle great displays of emotion. Courtney, however, who at that point had more chutzpah than me, wrote a letter to Trudy on Facebook for all eyes to see:

REASONS I AM NOW DE-FRIENDING YOU FROM MY FACEBOOK PAGE!

Reason 5. I have no room in my life for people who try to steal other people's mates, under the guise of friendship.

Reason 4. I had no idea my father was cheating on his wife with you. I simply thought you were a "friend" of his. That is deceitful.

Reason 3. You made no attempt to set any record straight with me, nor do you care about my feelings.

(It's all about Courtney. But I love her, anyway.)

...and you are being nothing but selfish trying to encroach upon my family in this manner.

Reason 2. Women do not do this to other women. Period. I will not spend my time upset and risk an aneurysm...

(It's all about Courtney. But I love her, anyway.)

...because you want to get frisky with a man that has had 4 marriages. He is wrong, and you are even more at fault for upholding this behavior. He will abandon you too! Just like he has abandoned every other woman in his

life, with the exception of his mother who will also not abide by this kind of wrongdoing.

Reason 1. I WILL NOT TRUST someone (you) who remains in a marriage for over 10 years to get her husband's pension. This is despicable. Get a clue and leave my family the hell alone.

You have not known my father long enough to understand that he doesn't even knows what love is, which I am telling you as his daughter he does NOT. The only thing that brings you together with him at the moment is SEX! This will ruin any relationship eventually, and I have absolutely no room for it in my shortened life.

(It's all about Courtney. But I love her, anyway. Dearly.)

OCTOBER 17

MISPLACED BLAME

"Way to go!" my therapist said when I gave her a blow-by-blow account of Courtney's tirade on Facebook. "But what does she mean by a 'shortened life'?"

I explained that Courtney had been challenged by one medical issue after another. "I think much of it was a need for attention and love she felt she didn't get from her mother. She herself said one-time she thought she brought it on herself. That's pretty hard to swallow, but..." I said. "And then there's the fact that her dad walked out on her when she was seven. But she does have a condition that affects the spinal fluid. She's had several shunts put it to regulate the pressure in her brain. Poor kid. Poor everyone."

Picking up my cell, I read aloud some of the emails that had flown back and forth between me and Andrew earlier in the day—including the string that had started when he blamed me for Courtney's outburst, saying I had goaded his daughter into unleashing her wrath, and that her Facebook rant really hurt Trudy's feelings.

"Trudy's feelings? What about mine?" I said.

I mentioned that Andy was supposed to come down tomorrow to cut up the damaged trees behind the garage and read her the next email.

ANDREW: *Why should I come down and help you? Tell me why?*

"Uh, because it's your property too, Andrew?" I said to Katarina, my voice laced with sarcasm. I told my therapist that I had finally managed to talk him down via email, but that he didn't say anything about making the trip.

At that point, I could have cared less about the trees, but my stress levels were at an all-time high.

OCTOBER 18

FROM SAFE TRAP TO SNAP TRAP

My body tensed up when I spotted Andrew's Honda on the lawn outside the house mid-morning. A few minutes later, the doorbell rang.

"You could have let yourself in," I said, after I opened the front door.

"I wanted to be respectful."

"A little too late for that, Andy," I mumbled as I turned around and went inside.

My husband seemed somber. But I couldn't say I was exactly a happy dancing poodle, either.

Andrew brought his bag up to the guest bedroom, where he changed into his scruffy clothes and went out to the garage to get the chain saw.

After I finished up some editing work, I walked outside to see how he was doing with the fallen trees. It was clear he'd made good, solid progress and I said so. We obviously had things to discuss, like how we planned on managing these two houses and all the repairs that had to be made, but I really wanted to do it in therapy tomorrow when we had our second session. Andrew, however, saw things differently.

"What's the point of doing therapy?" he said.

"Andy, you said you'd go."

My husband said nothing.

"Okay, if that's how you feel." I sat down on a log, my heart sinking. I couldn't force him into therapy, but I still didn't understand why this was happening and why we couldn't repair the rift. "Aside from the sex, what were the issues?"

"Well, for example, you said you would help me out here with the trees," he said. "I sent you an email asking."

"I never got it," I said, stating the truth.

So, was this why he wanted to dissolve the marriage? Because he felt like I didn't help out? What was he talking about? That was one of the sorriest excuses I'd heard so far. I'd managed the finances all the while we were married and still did, along with the house;

I worked in the gardens, weeding, which I hated doing—and there were a whole lot of gardens and a whole lot of weeds. I'd also spent days, weeks, months editing his book, going through it multiple times. There were also the many years of deconstructing and reconstructing the NY place—not to mention shoveling the back-breaking, wet, slushy snow on the ridiculously long driveway because Andy was too cheap to hire a plough service.

"Andrew, I never got the email," I repeated as I got up to go back inside. "All you had to do was come and ask."

Within a few minutes I was out behind the garage in my old jeans and sweatshirt to help him stack wood. We both remained relatively quiet until the task was completed. It took about an hour.

I pulled off my gloves and brushed some wood chips from my pants. "I need your engineering genius. I can't figure out the damn mouse trap and the mice are taking over the house."

"Okay." Andrew's tone was neutral.

"I'll go get it."

The cruelty-free Havahart trap was in the front hallway, the top open. As I went to pick it up, I noticed a tail. "What the hell?" It looked like a mouse had committed hari-kari by ramming itself through a small, thin opening on the inside of the box where the trapping mechanism lined up with a metal plate. Its head had been flattened, making it appear like a piece of cardboard. The critter, I reasoned, must have been in such an extreme state of panic, in such a state of despair that he took what he sensed was the only way out. Ironically, he could have jumped over the side since the lid was open. It now seemed at every turn that the world around me was reflecting my inner and outer life.

I brought the trap out to my husband and handed it to him. "Andrew, there's a mouse..." I said, beginning to tear up, unable to complete my thought.

My husband looked into the box; evidently it upset him too. "I'll take care of it." Andrew turned away from me and headed off deep into the woods. I went back to the house.

After he finished with the trees, Andy packed up and informed me that he was leaving. I asked him if he was able to remove the mouse.

"Yes," he said.

"Could you show me how to put the top back on the trap? And reset it?"

"I'll take it up to Vermont. I can use it there. You can get something at Home Depot. Get snap traps."

"Snap traps?" It was obvious to me he was being influenced by the compassionless rooster-killing woman. "I would never do that. I can't kill anything. You know that, Andrew."

"I would never do that either," he said, his voice tinged with sadness.

OCTOBER 21

A DREADFUL PARTY, ANOTHER DISTRACTION

After a drink at the Yale club with my widowed college friend, Pran, and his cousin, who just flew in from Europe, we all took a taxi down to a party in midtown. Pran showed us the flier on the way over. "It's for single Baby Boomers."

"It sounds perfectly dreadful," I replied.

It turned out I was right. The event, which was held in a dark, unappealing bar/restaurant in midtown NYC, was populated by a crowd of lonely, desperate people. (Welcome to my club.)

We sauntered up to the bar, where I bought the boys a round. A song by a contemporary pop singer came over the speakers.

"Great tune," Pran said, mentioning that he liked to dance. I ignored the comment; it was the last thing on earth I felt like doing.

After we'd had a couple of drinks each, Pran's cousin, who was fighting jet lag, begged off and left to grab a taxi. My college friend and I decided to stay, found a spot by a table and talked about the passing of Pran's wife and my recent separation. Although we'd each experienced a great loss, we agreed our situations were somewhat different.

"There's nothing you can do if your spouse dies," Pran said. "The door is shut. There's no chance or hoping that they might someday come back." He paused. "In some ways it's easier."

"Maybe I'll take a hit out on my husband," I said. "Just kidding. Sorta."

We moved away from the dance floor and the loud music, ending up at the far side of the bar near the front door. My friend leaned into me and planted his arm above my shoulder, pinning me against the wall. There was a look in his eyes—and it was one I recognized.

"Do you want to kiss me?" I asked, sliding down several inches to accommodate for the height difference between me and my college pal.

"Yes."

Pran's lips were smooth and sensual, but I knew on a gut level that this was another distraction to keep my mind off what was happening in my life.

After a half an hour or so of making out, Pran poured me into a taxi, and I headed for the train.

When I got home and logged on to my computer, I opened up my Outlook and saw an email from Pran in which he said he'd love to jet off to some tropical island with me.

"Oh dear," I said to Mamie who was now in my lap. Along with the height difference, this could be a deal breaker since I was prone to skin cancer and avoided the sun like a vampire. I responded immediately and apprised him of my dilemma, diplomatically of course.

PRAN: *I will hold an umbrella over your head when we are on the beach and will teach you the fine art of shade-walking.*

His words were sweet and touching, but for some reason it made me feel even bluer.

OCTOBER 22

GOOD JEW, BAD CHRISTIAN

While sitting at the bar at Joe Allen's in NYC with a friend, I got a text from Yehowah/Mike/Steve.

YEHOWAH: *My soul is bursting!!! I will explode if I don't see you! Can we spend some time 2night?*

(He sure knew how to work it.)

ME: *Actually I'm in NYC. So, sure.*

(And I agreed to meet him, because…? Oh right. It was a distraction.)

We decided on the Hyatt next door to Grand Central. After making my way through midtown, I went inside the hotel and parked myself outside the second-floor bar and called my friend Adele who was coming to visit me the following week.

Within ten minutes, Yehowah/Mike/Steve came up the stairs in full regalia: black coat, white shirt, black pants, yarmulke. He spotted me immediately. His face looked flushed, his cheeks splotched and rosy from the cold night air.

"Hey," I said. "Let's go get a drink." I desperately needed to tamp down the flutters I felt in my stomach. But why was I so nervous?

Perhaps it was the absurdity of the situation, or perhaps it was because of our ridiculously huge age difference. And for sure, if I told my young friend I was more than thirty years his senior, he'd flee, screaming in abject terror. I decided on the spot I wouldn't tell him—ever.

Once we were seated at the bar, where I'd previously had drinks with the hyphen-mouthed man who taught me about revolving-door etiquette, I ordered a glass of Pinot Grigio. Yehowah/Mike/Steve asked for water. He was a good Jew; he didn't drink and drive. I was a bad Christian; I did drink and drive. We talked a bit, and he repeated what he told me the week before—that he was involved in "rabbinical studies" and might possibly become a rabbi.

He leaned toward me and peered deep into my eyes; I could almost feel him inside.

"Your eyes are soulful," I said.

"All the girls tell me that."

"Do you want to make out?" I asked, laughing, because I sounded like a high-school student. (I was also acting like one.)

"I'll get the minivan," he said, grinning broadly.

Yehowah/Mike/Steve picked me up in front of the Hyatt. We headed south and parked on a quiet, dark street below 38th. My young friend hopped out of the driver's side, came around to the passenger door, took my hand, and gently guided me out of the car. After we climbed into the back seat, we began making out. The kisses were passionate, perfect. Yehowah pulled back, his eyes now pouring over my face, and dove in for more. Our embrace became fevered, our lips hungry, moist, our mouths open. In one skillful move, Yehowah/Mike/Steve ripped off his yarmulke and tossed it like a Frisbee into the rear of the van. Our lips locked once again, and he tenderly placed a hand on my ass. His palm felt nice, warm, but although my body craved a deeper level of contact, I didn't want to take this any further—at least not at that point.

"I have to go," I said, pulling away.

"Why don't you let me pleasure you? We can pleasure each other." His voice was soft, velvety, like his lips.

"I really have to get going."

After a brief kiss, I tumbled out of the car. I had no idea if we'd ever see each other again. But I wasn't sure I cared all that much.

OCTOBER 26

TIME FOR A REFILL

"What's the problem?" asked the woman on the other end of the phone.

"High levels of anxiety. I sometimes feel like I'm having a heart attack." The receptionist booked me an appointment to see Dr. Simmons at 3:30 PM. But this time, the need for a visit was not to get more Xanax to help me cope with the stress around an impending spanking/discipline session. It was to get more of the pink pills so I could get through the day without feeling like I was one thought away from the looney bin.

After an hour of working on my laptop at Main Street Café, I walked the block and a half over to my doctor's office.

Seeing Dr. Simmons was like meeting up with an old friend. "So how are you doing?" he asked.

"Doing the best I can under the circumstances."

"I'm sure it's hard on you," he said.

"What happened just doesn't make any sense."

I had no idea what motivated me, but I mentioned to my doctor that I never felt I could see into my husband's soul. Maybe I was trying to rationalize the separation, make it okay, justify it. Like, it had to happen because my husband had some wires loose and I'd be better off without him.

Simmons told me about his first wife, a manic-depressive, who was in and out of psychiatric hospitals. "She was off the charts. It was very difficult." He said that he too felt he could not see into her. "There was always a wall up; a disconnect."

As my doctor handed me the small state-authorized prescription form, he leaned into me and looked deep into my eyes like he was trying to establish a connection. It was fleetingly successful, and I could feel that invisible sexual energy pass between us. I immediately went into lockdown.

"Thanks. Take care," I said and bolted for the door.

(No doubt in my mind, I was now officially the poster child for the walking wounded.)

OCTOBER 27

OLD DOM, NEW TALK

My former dom IMd me. I had finally told him what had happened between me and Andy. Our e-talks were now vastly different.

CARL: *How are you doing? I hope things are looking better. Any news with your husband?*

ME: *Not really. The same. It's been really rough.*

CARL: *I feel so badly about what happened. I feel responsible.*

ME: *Don't. You didn't force me to do anything.*

CARL: *I kind of goaded you into it.*

ME: *I made my choices. I'm a big girl. A big girl who got her kicks acting like a little girl. I still can't believe any of this.*

CARL: *I really am sorry. Let me know if I can do anything.*

ME: *I will.*

After we'd signed off, I realized that the unrelenting anxiety I was now experiencing being away from my husband was similar to what I felt when Carl seemed to be pulling away. Except in this case, with Andy, the feeling was magnified a thousand times, and I knew I was suffering from a combination of post-traumatic stress and extreme separation anxiety. Feelings of abandonment were at an all-time high as well.

OCTOBER 28

DESPERATE PEOPLE, DESPERATE THOUGHTS

I finally decided to see a lawyer—in part to appease my brother who told me that I must take care of myself, and in large part to alleviate some of my own paranoia, since I didn't feel as though I knew who my husband was anymore, or of what he might be capable.

The lawyer was handsome and smart, but unfortunately short and very married. (Yes, desperate, tall, lonely people such as myself have desperate thoughts.)

"So how can I help you?" he asked. The attorney got right to the point, avoiding the usual pleasantries of "How are you doing?" knowing that such provocative questions could potentially trigger a flood of tears in newly separated women. And what guy wants to deal with that?

"I just need to know what my options are."

He asked for the details.

When I told him how many times Andy had been married, he rattled off a story about a friend of his who became the sixth wife of a successful lawyer. "I told her, look at his track record. Don't do it. But she went ahead and married the guy. It lasted a year and a half. Next!"

"You know," I said. "I never saw it coming. And if we do divorce, well, it's a first for me."

"It happens. It is what it is."

(Very Zen, this lawyer.)

So, what I found out was this: if we went through a divorce now, the courts might force us to sell both our homes. They would also make sure, since Andrew had been the main breadwinner, that I was taken care of going forward. Our assets would also be equally divided. The attorney made it clear, however, that divorce was probably not a smart financial move and would dramatically impact both of us. I totally got that. Andrew did not. Maybe he never would.

I felt somewhat relieved but a little guilty that I kept the appointment with the lawyer. I was also happy that my friend Adele was here visiting as I had developed a desperate need to fill the house up with people—loving people.

Around 8:00 PM, I went to meet Amy at the River House for drinks since Adele was in New York for a dinner meeting. We settled in at the bar, and after I successfully tore up the cork coaster in attempts to release some nervous energy, the bartender ambled over and chastised me, a scornful half-smile spreading across his face.

"But they're throwaway, right?" I asked, feeling contrite.

"So typical of you people these days. The throwaway society."

(Yeah, and Andrew just threw me away. Maybe someone needed to discuss this issue with my husband.)

The bartender took a step toward me, his eyes narrowing.

"You need to be taken in the back and spanked for destroying the coasters, missy."

"What?!" I couldn't believe my ears and covered my face with my hands, wondering what kind of a vibe I was putting out or if I was tainted with some weird psychic residue left over from my foray into BDSM. The bartender leaned over the bar and whispered, "There's a jail back there," he said, winking. "We could get out the leather zipper mask."

It was definitely time to go.

I said goodbye to Amy and headed home to find a tape in the mailbox from Edna, a woman in her eighties (hence the tape) who communicates with entities in the spirit world. I'd been consulting with her since the late 1980s and had always been intrigued by her abilities and the uncanny accuracy of the messages she pulls through. But writing to her this time was most certainly an act of desperation; I needed advice, and I needed insight. And it didn't matter if the source was living or dead.

Adele, who was getting ready for bed, heard me charging up the steps and came out of the guest room.

"I got it. The tape from Edna!" I said, recalling that it was Adele who introduced me to the medium.

"Great!"

I located the CD/tape player, which had plaster all over it, courtesy of Andrew, and plugged it in. I slid in the cassette and hit the *play* button. Nothing! It wouldn't move. "Shit." I frantically tried to eject the tape. "Goddamn it, Andrew. You fuck everything up! Including my future, which is on that tape!" Now I was mad.

"Let's try a knife," Adele said.

"On Andy?"

My friend smiled, went at the device with the knife, and managed to spring the tape loose. I put it into another older player and felt relief flood through my body as I climbed onto my bed with the boom box to listen.

EDNA: *Spirit is telling me that you have been distracted for quite some time. They were trying to communicate with you to get you back on track.*

(I did not mention a word about spanking in my letter to her.)

EDNA: *Your marriage and your creative work have suffered.*

(More than a little bit true.)

EDNA: *You also haven't been taking care of yourself in the way you need to.*

(True, again. I was going out way too much.)

EDNA: *Your husband is coming back.*

(Yeah, right. To get his tools.)

OCTOBER 29

MORE MADNESS

Wishing that my friend Adele could have stayed longer, I sat frozen at my desk not quite wanting to believe my eyes and ears. Every few minutes, huge tree limbs snapped off and plummeted to the ground. CRAAAACCCKKKK!!! The trees, which had not yet shed their leaves, could not bear up under the weight of the heavy, wet snow that had arrived way too early in the season. My hearing-impaired cat of course didn't register any concern, and for a moment I envied her.

Since the electricity was still on, I decided to do something to divert my attention away from the chaos outside and the turmoil within me and joined match.com. After I'd uploaded my picture and answered all the annoying little questions ("I'm spiritual, not religious; I like cats, dogs, and horses; drink socially to moderately—okay, right now, I drink like a fish; am in shape, don't want anyone who is not in shape;" and so on), I heard this loud mechanical noise—like a gigantic metal snow plough scraping concrete. Looking out the window, I spotted a blue light pulsating in synch with the groan, illuminating the surrounding woods on the far side of my neighbor's property. Pulsate. Groan. Pulsate. Groan. The effect was alien-like. It was as if the world had gone mad.

"Oh, my God." I sat stunned, watching as orange flames shot up from the ground. It looked as if a tree had taken down a utility wire. The groaning became louder as the fire began to attack the wooden fence between my neighbor's house and the one next to theirs.

I grabbed my coat, ran over to Brad and Jackie's, and banged on the front door, working hard to repress my tears. I felt like a child—a frightened child left to fend for herself. And I was angry. Angry that my husband was not here to tell me that everything was going to be okay.

"There's a fire," I said to Jackie as she took me inside.

My neighbor told me an emergency crew was already on its way, led me into the kitchen, and opened a bottle of wine. It was only 5:00 PM, but under the circumstances, I could certainly justify imbibing. Jackie's kitchen felt welcoming and warm. Her house was filled with life, with people—unlike mine. And it felt safe.

I commented on my friend's two boys who were out on the front porch, watching the swelling fire, jumping up and down with glee.

"I taught them to not be afraid," Jackie said.

"Lucky kids," I replied, wishing someone had taught me that. I felt afraid now—all the time.

After the storm had subsided, I went back to my house, trudging through the slushy snow. Thankfully, and miraculously, the electricity had still not gone out on our section of road, although it had mostly everywhere else in town, according to the local news.

I turned on the lights in my office, checked my email, and saw that I'd gotten several messages from guys on match.com. Most of them had too many red flags in their profiles, like the one guy who wrote: *I'm healthy (well, physically anyway).*

But this one man seemed interesting. I replied, and he asked me if I wanted to see some pictures. *Sure,* I wrote.

OCTOBER 30

INSANE.COM

At around half past midnight, I received the photos with a note.

NICK: *Hi Deborah, here are my pictures. One just now from my phone. One is at a family reunion in Maine last November, the other from one of those goofy little photo booths on Coney Island.*

It was the eye thing again. And something bothered me, so I launched an email, acting not only from impulse and too much wine, but from a deep intuitive feeling.

ME: *Hi Nick, thank you so much for sharing those pictures. This is what I feel: you are very sad and hurt. I can see it in your eyes. I think you are still reeling from whatever happened in your marriage. It's not to say that I don't have sadness, anger, or upset. I most certainly do. We are only human. I just see it quite intensely in you. It also came through in your profile. But, before any of us can successfully move on to another relationship, we need to confront what happened and deal with our feelings, take the time to heal our hearts. I hope this makes sense to you.*

(Oh boy. Me and my big, damn mouth.)

NICK: *Thanks Deborah, But... you are so totally wrong about me, how I am, how I feel, and the incredible optimism I have for my future... and most importantly what I have to offer a very special lady... to make her incredibly happy. I take a lousy picture... period. As for my profile, 9 out of 10 women say I should do a stand-up routine, that I'm the funniest profile and guy (once we meet) they've ever come across. They tell me I turn their lousy days into good ones.*

(So, if all these women thought he was so funny and so great and can turn a crappy day into a good one, why was he still on match. com and looking?)

The others are too dumb to get the tongue-in-cheek and just say I have a

140

huge ego, not even understanding that the profile is nothing but a comical farce on profiles. I think you're accustomed to "judging people" and doing so based on your own gut reaction. My suggestion: never judge anyone or anything based solely on one source of information, particularly if it's your own. Thanks for the insights, even though they were unfortunately dead wrong.

All the best to you, Deborah. You missed out on a real catch. All the adjectives about me are entirely accurate. In fact, I really was being humble in the profile.

(Not so humble now.)

Best always... with a huge smile,

Nick

I felt badly and wrote him back.

ME: *My sincerest apologies, Nick. I just had a visceral reaction for some odd reason. All the best to you, too. Deborah*

(But the show must go on.) He wrote me back right away.

NICK: *I was going to let it drop as you seemed like a nice person. But since your reply was so incredibly stupid, I'm now compelled to.*

(It was stupid? Because I apologized?)

Just as you took (huge) liberties "psycho-analyzing" me, I'm sure you do it to everyone. Hint: they don't like it, either. And if they haven't said "you're an ass" to your face, know they're (all) thinking it and saying it to your ass as you walk away. After never meeting or speaking to me but rather only reading my (intentionally jocular, goofy) profile and being one of the "ten percent" idiot women who didn't see it for what is was, let me try to now return the favor and help you.

Do you realize how stupid and/or exploitive it comes across to know you lured me into providing more insights and pictures of myself after you had, and which I now learned, an initial "visceral" reaction to my profile?

(Yes, that gut feeling. Guess I nailed this one.)

You have unbridled gall. And, regardless of whether your gut was right or wrong, why not just move on to another? But you can't and couldn't.

(I was the one not moving on?)

You're one of those "know it alls" and just had to voice your moronic, offensive, and totally off-base opinion. Insightful you are certainly not.

(Come on, Nick, maybe just a <u>little</u> anger in there?)

You're really nothing but an oblivious, dumbass narcissist. So, thanks for the "diagnosis," Doc. Unfortunately, I'm not paying for the visit as I don't pay for (gross negligent) malpractice.

Bottom-line, Deborah, get over yourself... quickly. Your friends, family, and everyone else you come in contact with have a very different opinion of you than what you think. Trust me.

Love,

Dr. Nick (Specialist in Narcissism Counseling)

My face flushed. And although he was "the total ass," I still felt like a jerk. And this blatant, raw invective from this match.com lunatic, who probably had an AK-47 under his bed, made me miss my stupid, errant husband more than ever, so I shot off an email.

ME: *Andy, I know you have seemingly made up your mind, but I would like to share a few things with you: 17-18 years of loving someone is not easy for me to throw away. I know I took a walk on the dark side with the spanking, but in all honesty, I did not think it would threaten our marriage; at the time I thought it was somehow helping us. I also understand how it could have made you feel that you were not enough and probably freaked you out. It freaks me out now, to tell you the truth; in fact, I feel like something took over me and I became this rabid, obsessed person. Coincidentally, since this huge life-changing "avalanche" and divestment of my soul (okay, that's a bit dramatic), I have had no interest in that activity (spanking) whatsoever.*

But I have to take some responsibility for what happened, yet what stymies me is how much I feel we really did love each other and care for one another. And we always had fun. I remember telling you many times that I always loved being with you. And that is the truth. I also told you how I had grown to love you deeper and deeper over the years and how I was so proud of who you had become—with your work and your amazing artistry and your growing confidence.

In my heart of hearts, I want our marriage; there was so much that was good. I know it wasn't perfect, but no marriage or relationship is...Andrew, you are/were my heart and soul. And for the record, let me say: I want you in my life. I want my marriage.

I guess I didn't do such a great sales job: I heard nothing back from my husband.

A VERY MERRY HALLOWEEN COSTUME

Not being one to give up, or perhaps once again acting out of desperation and extreme loneliness, I decided to get together with another match.com guy who called himself Bob, as his Russian name was too difficult for native English speakers to pronounce. According to his online profile, Bob was a globetrotting executive banker and was looking for someone who felt comfortable in high-profile social situations; someone who was *presentable*. I was pretty sure I could pass muster and asked him in an email if that meant *no drooling or belching during state dinners.*

The match.com man and I agreed to meet in Grand Central at the clock tower. I got into the station right on time and spotted the banker, who said he'd be wearing a red scarf. He looked older than his picture and had a Bronx accent.

"Where should we go?" Bob asked.

"Doesn't really matter," I said, but suggested the Hyatt next door for the sake of simplicity.

"Sounds good to me."

We headed to the bar area, grabbed a table, and each ordered a glass of wine. I quickly found out that he was not a banker at all but worked in the information technology department at a bank. His "international travel" mainly included trips to Texas.

I asked him about his marriage.

"Been divorced ten years," he said.

"Oh. It's been a while, then. Do you mind my asking what happened?"

He paused and blinked a few times. "Well, my wife had some issues with me."

"Oh?"

"She just couldn't deal with some things."

"Do you feel comfortable sharing?" I said, leaning in toward him.

Bob tugged on his earlobe. "Well, she didn't particularly like the outfits—you know, the little outfits I like to wear. On occasion."

"Okay. I think I get it," I said, visualizing him dressed up like Little Bo Peep.

He smiled tightly, and I could see the sadness in his eyes.

"I've lost you, haven't I?" he said.

"Well," I replied, which was about all I could drum up.

I struggled to stay put for another ten minutes and excused myself politely, telling him I had to get a train. We both knew it was end of the line. (Pun intended.)

On the way home, I received an email from Pran. He wanted to know if we'd had any damage from the storm and if I was okay. Pran was more concerned about me than my husband, my partner of almost two decades. Something about that was very disturbing. Andrew had simply stopped caring in a span of a few hours after I found out he had slept with Chicken Lady. But he was so good at that: compartmentalizing his feelings; shutting them off. I wished I could do the same.

NOVEMBER 1

IT'S ALL IN THE STARS

Frantic to find comfort and guidance wherever I could, I headed for a popular astrology site on the Internet. As I logged on, it dawned on me: I was now visiting web pages on astrology and spirituality and looking for tips on things like how to emotionally survive a separation or divorce and sudden spousal abandonment without pitching oneself off a bridge—a stark contrast to my behavior of months ago, when I would frequent sites like spanko.com.

Clicking over to my November horoscope, hoping that it would deliver some good news, I glanced at my cat who was sitting in my desk drawer, staring at me. "Well, astrology is sort of a science," I told her. "And it has been around for thousands of years. Kind of like religion."

Mamie looked at me like I was nuts and started licking at her paw. Nuts or not, I boldly continued my pursuit. Taking in a deep breath, I read:

If your birthday falls on September 26, or within five days of this date, you will benefit the most. I am happy to say this, for you have been dealing with far more than your share of tension lately.

(No shit.)

Finally, you are about to get a break—luck is coming your way.

(Bring it on.)

Day by day, the pieces of your grand plan are falling into place, dear Libra, and any fears you have of experiencing a shortfall of cash will soon prove unfounded.

(My husband had better keep his hands off our savings account.)

Keep making plans for an improved lifestyle—those dreams are very much within your reach.

(Grasping—desperately.)

NOVEMBER 2

NO SPANK YOU

After drinks with my college friend Robin at our usual haunt, the Roosevelt Hotel, I went to meet Carl, who was in NYC for a conference. My feelings were very mixed.

I called his room on my cell when I got to his mid-town hotel, and he told me to come up.

"No, I'll meet you outside." Much better choice, I thought; safer, since I had no intention of playing or getting spanked.

I waited for ten minutes and no Carl. "Fuck it," I grumbled and took off for Grand Central.

I soon got a text message.

CARL: *Where are you?*

ME: *I left. I did wait and thought—well goodness knows what I thought. I guess I overreacted. Not much patience for anything nowadays. Where are you now?*

CARL: *Back at the room. My wife kept me on the phone for 15 minutes. I knew she was suspicious. I ran down to the patio several times. I know you had good intentions, but I knew it was a long shot in seeing you.*

I texted him back and in so many words said that when you are deeply connected with someone, referring to his wife, the other person intuitively knows when something is up. I also told him that maybe that was the reason my marriage busted up. Maybe Andrew sensed, as Adele had suggested, that I was exploring this fetish with a man and thought I was having an affair.

"Oh!" I mumbled to myself as it hit me like a truck full of rocks: The name of the company Carl worked for was called Katalyst—how utterly, blatantly ironic. (The catalyst that broke up my marriage.)

Another tape from Edna was waiting for me when I got home. She still maintained that Andrew would be coming back, but said my lesson now was to learn to be alone. (I'd rather learn how to clean out cesspools.)

BACK IN LOVE WITH HUMANITY—FOR A MOMENT

Pran looked handsome tonight. I also liked the fact that he was a lawyer with liberal leanings. I just wished he was taller. Or I was shorter.

At the Mexican place on the ground floor of Grand Central, Pran and I had two Margaritas each. We talked and laughed, and he told me funny stories about road trips. I recounted my recent match.com adventure with the Russian but did not offer up any details about my twenty-five-year-old Orthodox Jewish friend. Maybe it was because I was embarrassed, or maybe it was because it made me sad that in all likelihood I'd never see Yehowah/Mike/Steve again.

For dinner, Pran and I settled in at the bar for food and drink at my favorite Indian restaurant near Union Square. Within minutes we struck up a conversation with a professor from Dartmouth. He was engaging, as was Pran, and we talked politics and discussed issues stemming from over-population. After the man left and Pran and I had more wine, my friend confessed that he'd always had a thing for me.

"You didn't know that?" he asked, responding to my surprised look.

It never crossed my mind, even though during the summers when we were both in the Boston area, he would ride his bike twenty-five miles one way to come see me at my parents' house.

The kisses began. They were fleeting, but tender and sweet. Yet I found myself still missing Andrew and his quiet intelligence.

After dinner, Pran and I grabbed a cab that dropped me off at Grand Central where I managed to catch one of the last trains back to Tarrytown. I was exhausted from the ongoing anxiety and probably too much wine, and for the first time in my life, I fell asleep and missed the station.

I woke up close to the last stop, jumped up out of my seat, and searched for someone who seemed lucid and not three sheets to the wind after a night of NYC barhopping. A man told me that if I got out at Croton-on-Harmon I could find a taxi there.

Once out on the street, I spotted several town cars and picked the one that didn't have any dents,

thinking that it might increase my chances of getting back in one piece. "How much to Tarrytown?" I asked the driver.

"Forty," he replied.

"Forty <u>dollars</u>?" I said, knowing full well it couldn't be forty cents. I really didn't want to spend that kind of money, but I had to get home, so I climbed in the car.

The driver was nice and respectful and on the way to Tarrytown, we got into a political discussion. After it was clear we were on the same page about most issues, I told him I could not believe I fell asleep.

"A lot of people do," he said, which helped me feel a little less like an idiot.

When we got to the train station, he drove me right up to my car, making sure I'd be okay.

"Oh my God," I said, digging in my purse. "I don't have forty dollars. I only have thirty. Thirty-one. I am so sorry!"

"It's okay," he said. "Really."

"Thank you. Thank you so much!"

For a brief moment I was back in love with life, but when I got in my car, I began to sob, and I couldn't stop. I missed my husband so deeply I felt like I was going to disintegrate, fall apart in bits and pieces, melting into a waxy blob of human flesh. But thank goodness there was no construction on the bridge tonight, no traffic cones, no delays, and no union workers threatening the health of my urinary tract.

When I arrived home, I went into my bathroom to pee and then wept for another ten minutes while I cleaned out the kitty litter and put on my pajamas. I wanted my husband here. I wanted him here, so I could tell him to stand up straight and take the right vitamins and to make sure he knew how handsome he looked when he wore his beret backwards.

NOVEMBER 6

EVERYONE HAS BEEN THERE

I didn't want to go, but I went because I didn't want to be alone and because my friends and neighbors, Ted and Eva, were being honored for their work with The Wittingham Arts Center at a country club up the Hudson River.

"Can I park my car somewhere near?" I asked the valet. "I might need to escape early."

"Sorry," he said. "No can do."

Not what I wanted to hear, since I knew that when I went inside all those feelings I used to have about being the proverbial third, fifth, seventh wheel (always the bridesmaid etc.) would coming flooding to the surface. It was guaranteed the place would be filled with couples.

As I entered the lobby, I saw that I was 100% correct. I immediately spotted a former theater colleague and friend, headed over to say hi, and filled her in on the latest as her life partner went off to get a drink.

"Wow," she said, "I really think guys just snap when they get to a certain age."

The same thing happened to her years ago. One minute her husband was at home, acting as normal as can be; the next day he said he didn't want to be married anymore, gave her some lame excuse, and moved out. She too didn't see it coming.

"You know, I think it's far more devastating when that happens. It's traumatic, the sudden loss, the abandonment. It's like life as you knew it blew up in the blink of an eye," my colleague told me. "It's totally different than when a couple divorces after years of not getting along."

One of the event organizers picked up a microphone and announced to the crowd that we needed to move into the dining room and find our seats. I went looking for my allotted place and realized they forgot to set one aside for me; I felt more alone than ever. So that was it. Snap decision: I was out of there.

But the girl from the coat room was no longer behind the counter, and I couldn't locate my jacket on the racks. I fluttered about looking for someone to help, but to no avail. "Oh, just buck up," I said to myself and went back into the dining area and grabbed a glass of wine.

The redheaded hostess approached me. "Do you have a seat?"

"No. I was thinking of leaving."

"Why?"

"I know it's silly, but I'm recently separated and am having a really hard time," I said, leaning into her, speaking quietly. I didn't mention that I continually fought to ward off panic attacks. Nor did I tell her that anytime a casual acquaintance simply asked about my well-being, I was pushed to the verge of an emotional, tearful breakdown.

"Oh, I know how you feel," she said, her eyes lighting up, but not in a merry way. Her husband, she told me, left her years ago with two kids and no money.

"Jesus," I said. "Is this an epidemic or something?"

The redhead smiled. "Let me find a spot for you." She touched me lightly on my sleeve. "You know, mostly everyone I know has been through something like this. And guess what? We all survived. And most of the time, life actually got better."

"Really?" I said, not quite believing it.

"Just wait. You'll see."

NOVEMBER 7

MORE THERAPY

"How are you doing with the plates? And the pants tugging?" Katarina asked.

"I can't stop. Don't think I will either. After all, when I did stop, my marriage busted up."

"I'm not sure if you're serious or not," my therapist said, her eyes narrowing.

"Somewhat serious," I replied, knowing that I would continue to tug at my underwear while driving on the highway and carefully select just the right plate from the stack—just in case.

Switching gears, I mentioned to Katarina that I had found this new shampoo. "It's natural and doesn't contain any sulfates. But the odd thing is, it has a different chemical effect compared to the commercial shampoos, so my scalp has a different scent. I now smell like my husband."

"No way." Shaking her head in mild disbelief, my therapist leaned back in her chair.

"Just another little irony slapping me upside the head."

NOVEMBER 8

THE JERK, THE MUSICIAN, THE DEAL BREAKER

Ned, a lovely man in his forties, who is physically handicapped from a tragic accident during high school, was there at his usual table at Flanagan's for Wing Night. And, as usual, my friend Sarah and I joined him. Our conversation was light, and Ned asked me how Andy was doing. But he didn't call Andrew by his name. He now not-so-lovingly referred to him as "the jerk." But he always said it with good humor, and it always made me laugh.

On the way out after dinner, I stopped to say hi to Henry who worked part-time at the local music store. Swinging around on his barstool, he smiled sweetly and began to update me on the latest news with his band. I stood and listened attentively at first but found myself wondering if Henry was a good kisser. He certainly had nice teeth, which I liked. As I watched his lips move, I wondered if maybe, just maybe, he'd be open to making out a little. Maybe we could do that on a regular basis. And maybe if it all went well, we could start dating. Henry would also be a good antidote to my anxiety, since he was mellow to the point of seeming stoned. So maybe we'd be a good fit. And maybe if all proceeded smoothly, we could get married. Problem was, Henry was about thirty years younger than me.

I stuffed my hands in my jeans, said goodbye and left, feeling rather pathetic.

NOVEMBER 10

TALKING BUSINESS

"We should talk business," my old friend Dustin, a struggling actor, said. "About me moving in on the third floor."

He seemed agitated tonight, but it was probably because he was on the verge of losing his apartment. I thought it might be nice to have someone around the house, but my gut was telling me to not jump the gun.

I did the roommate thing in LA and had a preconceived notion of what happens when you room with people. They inevitably go psycho on you, such as this one guy who became convinced I was stealing his live-in girlfriend's underpants—an absurd notion considering her rear end was at least three times larger than mine. (Okay, like the broad side of a [insert any type of building].) So he put a lock on his door. When my scarves and a few other items started to disappear, I put a lock on mine. We did not part all that amicably, although he did invite me to his wedding during which he got up and sang "Breaking Up is Hard to Do" with the band. He was a bit of an odd duck, but I really did like him.

"Let me think on it for a few days," I said to Dustin.

He nodded and brought his lips up to my ear. "Everyone is staring at us. I think they think I'm your boy toy," he whispered.

"Now that might be an interesting arrangement. How much more would you pay a month?"

Dustin gave me a look.

"Just joking, love," I said, making a mental note to ask my numerologist if it was a good or bad idea to have my friend move in. "By the way, Dustin, when is your birthday? And what is the name you were given at birth?"

(God, how I missed being married.)

NOVEMBER 11

OH, FOR AN AGENT TO LOVE ME

A seventy-something artist friend of mine and I headed off to a French restaurant in SoHo. He seemed distracted, and I knew it was because his financial situation was tenuous. And although at this juncture I was not financially challenged, I was scared to death my husband would stop working, go berserk, and wipe out our savings. Then we'd have to default on all our bills and mortgages, and I'd end up on the street. It was almost too easy for me to visualize myself living in a cardboard box. But at least I'd be sure it was gaily painted and peppered with fake plants and a few tasteful prints.

Next stop: a Greenwich Street restaurant for post-dinner drinks. The joint was packed, but the fates intervened, and two stools opened up at the bar as we walked in. We pounced immediately.

"Ask, believing, and ye shall receive," I said to my friend, as I reminded myself to quit thinking about taking up residence in cardboard boxes and focus only on that which was good and positive. Not always an easy task. Especially now.

The bartender, a tall man with a shock of wiry black hair, immediately came over and playfully asked me if I could guess his age.

"Not a clue," I said. I also had no clue why he would bring his age up to begin with.

"Sixty-one," he said, showing me his license.

I couldn't see a damn thing without my glasses but nodded and smiled.

"He likes you," the girl bartender told me.

"Well, then, we should get married," I replied, smiling at the man behind the bar.

The bartender cocked his head, grinned broadly, and raced around to my side of the counter. "We'll put that to the test." He pulled me off the stool, stood me up, and kissed me on the mouth. It was a strange sort of "kiss-muss" test, and I didn't know what the results were. But he smiled, went back to his station, and poured me a glass of wine, which I accepted gratefully. Nothing else was said, which was fine by me, since the kiss was a bit wooden. (But apparently we were not going to get married.)

"Hey," I heard someone say and turned to my right. The man sitting next to me reminded me of a very good friend of mine in LA who died of AIDS in the early 1990s. Coincidentally, I found out that the man with the longish brown hair was in town from Los Angeles for a meeting with the NY arm of the talent agency for which he worked.

The man ordered another drink, said he liked me, and told me I had pretty eyes.

"Wow. Thank you," I replied, feeling a bit nonplussed, since my eyes were really an unspectacular green/brown/grey mix. I figured it must have been the double coating of mascara, or maybe it was the booze talking on his part. Or maybe it was that "walking wounded" thing again.

After another half hour and another round of drinks, I noticed that my new friend's effeminate side was starting to come through and figured he was probably just another bisexual on the loose. But there was something quite appealing about him and I told him so, in so many words: "I would love to drag you outside and kiss you," I said, realizing that this had now become my nighttime modus operandi to stay sane.

"My hotel is right across the street," he said.

But doing anything with this man was a moot point since I only had only so much time to make the last train. And I didn't want to leave my car parked on the street overnight. And there was the fact that I didn't do one night stands very well, and I knew that I would leave feeling emptier than ever.

"I have to go," I said.

"Why don't you stay?"

Wishing I could muster the gumption to throw all caution to the wind, I kissed the agent goodbye on the cheek and went over to my dinner companion. "I didn't mean to ignore you," I said, wanting to explain my dire need for "safe" romantic distraction.

"I was fine," he said, indicating the woman to his left. "I had a good conversation."

I touched my friend lightly on the shoulder and saw the sadness in his face. "It's going to be okay. For both of us," I said.

On the cab ride to Grand Central I talked freely to the driver who had large, liquid brown eyes and a luminescent smile. I could easily see the beauty inside of him.

"What the world needs is for people to love and tolerate and accept one another," he said.

"Amen to that."

He felt like a kindred soul, and we communicated like long-lost friends. Under other circumstances we probably could have been friends. But there was one thing I knew for sure: I didn't want to make out with him. So, maybe I really wasn't all that whacked out.

But the energy tonight most definitely was, and about five stops from Tarrytown, a very upbeat conductor with blond hair dropped all his tickets in the aisle next to me.

"That wouldn't go over too well in a poker game," I said. "Especially if you were the dealer."

He smiled and asked me if I played cards.

"Sometimes," I replied.

After he collected a few more tickets from passengers, he came back, sat beside me, and started chatting me up. Although I was slightly inebriated, I managed to sound coherent and asked him how long he'd worked for Metro North.

"About eight years." His eyes lit up and he said, very proudly, that he was forty-four and had never been married. "What about you?"

I told him that I'd recently separated from my husband. He gave me a look and literally jumped up from the seat and bolted into the next car without another word.

For the rest of the train ride to Tarrytown, I puzzled about his bizarre reaction and came to the conclusion that people were unpredictable by nature (like my husband). But you'd have thought I'd told him I had a highly contagious disease that turns your brain into mush and causes bleeding from the eyeballs.

My mood was momentarily elevated when I got to the Tappan Zee Bridge and found that the traffic flowed freely. I arrived home in good time, tumbled out of the car, let myself inside, and got ready for bed. But I remembered I needed to feed Mamie and went down to the kitchen to get some cat food—nothing out of the ordinary, since I often refuel her late at night.

When I got back upstairs, I saw that my bedroom door was closed. And I could not get it open. "You have got to be kidding me," I grumbled.

Somehow, I'd managed to lock myself out, and everything I held dear and necessary, including my cat and my purse, was inside. I wrenched the doorknob this way and that; I shook it and pulled at it, but I could not get back in. I retrieved a paper clip and inserted the tip into the small hole in the middle of the doorknob—a trick I had learned from my husband. But it didn't work, so I got a screw. Same result.

I mentally listed the other options: (1) I could try and kick the door open—but figured that would not be a very good idea, as it would likely end up costing me an expensive trip to Home Depot, not to mention a broken foot; (2) I could get a ladder and crawl in through the unlocked second-story bedroom window—another bad idea since that too would probably result in a broken bone or two, since admittedly I was a few sheets to the wind; (3) I could call 911 or the fire department, but I had no phone. My cell was in my purse, and we'd gotten rid of the land line in the kitchen years ago.

Only one other option remained: I would go over to Jackie and Brad's house, even if it meant having to wake them up. I grabbed a pair of my husband's sneakers from the hall closet and ran across my lawn into their yard, squeezing between the evergreens that my neighbors had planted along the property line. I didn't bother putting on a coat, even though all I had on was my pajamas. At this point I was frantic and could have cared less if my breasts were flopping around like water balloons.

Thankfully, the downstairs was lit up.

I peered into the dining room window and spotted Jackie and her two friends, one woman and one man, playing cards. There were piles of poker chips and a lot of cash on the table. I rapped lightly on the windowpane. "Jackie, it's me!" For some reason, the three of them all ran into the kitchen, which completely confounded me. I clomped over to the front steps and knocked on the large, mahogany door.

The lock clicked and Jackie opened the door, her hand over her heart. "I thought it was someone trying to break in," she said. "Or the cops."

"Why? Is betting illegal at home?" I asked.

Jackie didn't respond but pulled me into the dining room and sat me down. As she poured me a glass of wine, which I certainly didn't need at this point, I explained my dilemma.

The guy who was losing his shirt to his female opponent said he used to break into houses when he was a kid and was more than happy to help me out. "I can get you in. No problem. Let's go."

I flounced along behind him in my PJs, and when we got upstairs, I handed him the paper clip; he opened the door in less than two seconds.

"Impressive," I said.

He did exactly what I did, but apparently you had to have that magic criminal touch.

After I fed my cat, I headed back to my neighbor's for an infusion of "people" energy to ward off a tremendous surge of melancholy.

NOVEMBER 12

IT'S NOT IN THE CARDS

Jackie called me in the morning and asked me what time I went home.

"What do you mean? What time did you all quit the poker game?" I asked.

"You slept on my couch. I put a blanket on you. You must have left in the middle of the night."

"You're kidding?" I had no recollection whatsoever of going home.

So, did I sleep walk? I didn't even remember being on her couch. Was Edna the spiritualist right about how I needed to learn to function alone? I _thought_ I was learning. After all, I _did_ manage to deal with the locked door—admittedly, with a little help from a former delinquent. But I didn't fall apart, and I didn't call Andrew. Yet, was I _really_ learning how to be resourceful, to be on my own? Or was I learning how to become a full-fledged alcoholic?

At 4:00 PM, I picked up the phone and dialed up the 503 area code for a tarot card reading. (Once again: desperate measures for desperate folks.) My tenant's aunt who lived in Oregon and was supposedly very good at her craft, picked up immediately.

"Hello, Deborah," she said, her voice gravely and raw, due to what I suspected was years of smoking cigarettes.

"Hey, how are you?" I asked, feeling the butterflies of anticipation flare up in my stomach.

"Doing okay," she said, a sigh punctuating her response. "So, I'm going to shuffle the cards, and when you feel compelled, tell me to stop." I heard the shuffling over the phone line and after a few moments, I told her to stop.

She sucked in a sharp breath. "Hoo boy."

That wasn't exactly what I wanted to hear. "Should I start putting my affairs in order?"

Lori's aunt laughed but did not tell me I shouldn't.

"Okay," she said. "First thing I see in tarot is that you are very creative. And you have a pretty face."

(I suspected she felt she had to say something positive to counter her initial reaction.)

"It's time to purge yourself of anything that's not working."

(Like my husband?)

"It's a time of change. You are due for another life change in three to four years," she said.

(Maybe if I managed to live through this one.)

"Don't get so bogged down by responsibilities that you cannot see what's ahead. Delegate and give some of these up to God. Don't take them all up yourself."

(Yo God. Down here. It's Deborah. Can you hear me now?)

"There's an element of grief that seems to be lifting, and good times are on the horizon. You may change your thinking about the type of person you are interested in."

(You mean someone who has the courage to work through issues within a relationship? That would be nice.)

"You worry about a pet."

(I was worried. My beautiful Mamie seemed to be losing more and more weight.)

"You're not having sex. That's good, because if you were, you would get yourself into a lot of trouble."

(Perhaps I'd better stick to making out for now.)

"They're telling me that you are a very strong person, with a good self-image. You are ready for something very, very positive and new. I see a very nice outcome. You just have to get past this time in your life."

"What about my husband?" Lori's aunt knew that he took off and was living in Vermont.

I heard her flip some cards over. "They are saying that right now he's stuck where he is, and it is of his own making, and he is asserting himself. But he's into something new."

(Correct. The rooster killer.)

"It is uncertain whether he will come back."

I sighed loudly.

"But what is interesting, here, is that if he does, you might not be so sure you'll want him back."

"Hmmm," I said. "Could you ask the cards about this woman he's with? Trudy?"

She shuffled the cards once again.

"Oh," she said. "I'm seeing something really negative around her. I see issues. She's erratic. She's not very stable. It is not a match made in heaven. They do not live happily ever after. I think it's temporary."

(Hallelujah. I could now go to bed and perhaps sleep peacefully.)

Apparently, however, that was <u>not</u> in the cards, and somewhere near midnight I awoke from a dream in which I was yelling at Andrew. "Spanking does not lead to sex!" I screamed. "I gave you the fucking handbook! You should have read it!"

NOVEMBER 13

RED—THE COLOR OF BLOOD AND BEAUTY

My cell phone was quiet; there were no incoming texts and not much in the way of emails, so I had a lot of time to think as I waited for my train, and I came to the conclusion that I really didn't have that spanking gene, as Carl had said. Otherwise I wouldn't have been able to stop. I also didn't talk much anymore to my former dom, nor did I particularly want to at this point—especially since the last time he IMd me he told me about a woman he was seeing and described in vivid detail how he'd caned her until the welts rose up on her bottom like *angry red worms*, her skin broken and bleeding. So how in God's name, I wondered, could I have let myself get drawn into that? The thought of what I did now repulsed me, and it all seemed so dark. I also felt tremendously guilty that I'd gone so far as to meet Carl in that hotel room.

I expelled the thoughts from my mind and looked up at the sky and was startled by what I saw: the sunset was magical, an almost other-worldly display of rich pinks and blues. It was so magnificent that I had to mention it to the woman sitting next to me. She briefly looked up and went back to texting on her cell phone. The colors intensified within seconds, and I wanted to shake her and say, Look, look! You must look before it goes away forever. Because you know it will!

The blues, which now appeared in swirls, were quickly morphing into brilliant purples, the pinks moving toward a deep magenta. The blend of colors reminded me of the fuchsia flower, but the effect was neon-like, with the perimeters of the clouds lit up by the setting sun that glowed golden behind them.

And I could not help myself. I lowered my head and let the tears fall freely, touched by the exquisite beauty of the natural world and overcome with sorrow that there was no one with whom to share the sunset.

NOVEMBER 14

SORT OF DATING

Pran said we were "sort of dating." I didn't know what to call it; nor did I want to attach a label to it, but I knew I needed him on some level—perhaps to fill in the emptiness. It wasn't that I didn't like him. I did. Certainly, our conversations were always stimulating, and the fact that we had a past that went back decades consoled me in an odd way.

Tonight I took him to my favorite NYC pizza place, which my Paris-based friend introduced me to. I missed Angie in many ways, especially since she and I made such good wingmen.

"We make good wingmen, too," I remarked to Pran, who sat to my left at the corner of the bar. I appreciated the fact that I could be honest with him and told him that I had no idea what the future held or how I felt about what we were doing.

After polishing off a flat-bread pizza and a bottle of wine, I once again asked Pran if he wanted to kiss me. He said he did and leaned in to me. Our noses touched briefly; our mouths met. My friend's tongue darted in and out, and we gently moved our lips back and forth in a light sweeping motion. I liked the sweetness, the softness of the kiss. And even though Pran and I were once again displaying affection in front of strangers, I didn't care. I felt completely comfortable being with him—as I always did with Andrew. But I had never kissed my husband in public like this. Not once.

NOVEMBER 15

WRITING GROUP FOR SPIRITUAL SEEKERS

Today found me a bit more morose than usual, so I was thankful for my writing group.

Before we got started, Maddie, who was also a speech pathologist, brought in a client of hers for a brief introduction. The woman was beautiful, but had difficulty talking and walking due to a stroke she'd suffered years ago when she was in her thirties. She was feisty and had an amazing sense of humor, despite her disability.

And it certainly put things into perspective. Although my heart was heavy, I had nothing to complain about: so what if Andrew left me? This woman had to raise a daughter, who was only two at the time, completely on her own, since her husband left her shortly after she'd had her stroke.

Meeting Maddie's client also triggered my desperate need to understand what this life was all about. Does each soul choose its journey to learn some profound lesson? Or to help others learn? I wanted some answers, but no one or no "thing" was talking. My thoughts began to pull me deeper into gloominess, so thankfully when our colleague read the opening to her one-woman show, we collectively started working on a fix to tighten up the first chunk of dialogue.

We approached the issue methodically, but the session deteriorated into hysterical laughter, as we struggled to find the grammatically correct way to say, "But don't worry, I wouldn't be able to tell if you aren't wearing underwear."

"Wait, or is it, I wouldn't be able to tell if you are wearing underwear?" I said.

I was glad to focus on less gut-wrenching things like finding the right words and was momentarily able to overshadow the angst and fear that were consuming me pretty much around the clock. By the end of the workshop I was more upbeat, and we all left feeling empowered—as creative people, as women—and I was once again reminded of the healing power of the arts.

Tonight, I was supposed to go out with my poker-playing neighbor, Jackie, but instead I forced myself to stay in, watch TV, and drink water. (The healthy choice.)

After I got settled in my bed, I tried to distract myself further by reading some chick-lit. It seemed to do the trick, and I was finally relaxed enough to go to sleep. My cat was now resting peacefully beside me on her large animal print pillow, her eyes closed, her breathing rhythmic, even though her physical health was declining. I pushed at and plumped up my pillows until they were just so and looked to my right. Where my husband once slept were piles of books and a few notepads that I used to capture ideas that often sprang up in the middle of the night. I had now staked claim to the entire king-sized bed, but I was far from relishing my newly expanded territory.

I shut out the light, flipped one way and the next, to find the most comfortable position, and felt myself start to drift off. But I was quickly jerked back into full consciousness by this scuffling noise at the other end of the room by my desk.

"What the hell?" My heart started to hammer.

It sounded like something was crawling up the wicker chest that held my office paraphernalia. Or was this thing rustling about in the dead leaves on the plant that sat atop the unit? It was too noisy to be a mouse. So, what was it? And why wasn't Andy here to tell me to not worry, that it was probably a (insert some kind of furry, non-threatening animal) and he'd check it out in the morning?

I stayed quiet another moment, afraid to move. Another rustle. What did it want? Food? (Was I on the menu?)

"Mamie, go fight kill," I said, poking at my cat. Too old to rally, she raised her head and went back to sleep.

I listened again for the source of the scratching sound and reached for my bedside lamp, knocking it over. "Crap." I felt around for the flashlight that I kept next to me on the bed. I tried to turn it on but could not find the on-off button. I realized why: it was not the pink metallic flashlight. It was my vibrator.

"To hell with it," I said. "And to hell with the healthy choice." I got up, popped a Xanax, and climbed back into bed. That night I dreamt of behemoth mice attacking my house.

NOVEMBER 16

A CLICK TO SAVE THE WORLD

It was a cloudy morning, which didn't help my outlook. Nor did the e-alert from the Natural Resources Defense Council letting me know that the polar bears were now drowning at an unprecedented rate due to the warming global temperatures and melting glacial ice. The council, of course, wanted me to help protect the bears and sign yet another petition.

And that upset me even more since it was now hard for me to muster up the energy for much of anything other than staying sane.

It was like Maslow's hierarchy of needs: When I was with my husband, I felt grounded, solid, loved. My emotional needs were met. I also didn't have to worry about money. And because these core but critical needs were satisfied, I had the energy to e-lobby for green causes, animals, and sociopolitical issues. Now, if it took more than a click of a button online—if for example, the site wasn't programmed to automatically pull up my name, address, and other vitals as a repeat visitor—I said screw it. I simply didn't have the patience to complete the form.

So, because of my errant husband, the polar bears might go extinct, women could lose some of their rights, bullying will go on in the schools, cows and other farm animals will continue to be mistreated and abused, and the coal firing plants will keep right on polluting.

"Oh, all right," I said, caving in to an overinflated sense of responsibility. I took a breath, went to the site, and filled in the petition to support the polar bears, but I didn't personalize the "attached letter" to my congressperson.

"Let some other idiot who has a stable, happy marriage and a bountiful life do that," I said to my cat.

NOVEMBER 17

KINDRED SOULS

Learning Protools, a software program that I wanted to master so I could start composing again using my Mac desktop, was clearly going to be an ongoing battle as well as my efforts to stay emotionally intact. During today's workshop in the city, I countered my ineptitude by making jokes about being "techno-tarded." But I liked coming here to the studio. I liked being with the guys: my musical director friend, Bennie; Al, a cardiologist/wannabe composer; and Chip, the studio engineer and our instructor.

Afterwards, Bennie and I went out for coffee in Chinatown. The place was swarming with people. The weather was nice, so the humans had come out en masse like bugs from the woodwork. Vendors were also out on the street hawking all sorts of goods, from bok choy to knock-off Rolexes.

"So, did Andrew comes to his senses?" Bennie asked as we sat down at a small table.

"No," I said, "But I have to take some responsibility for what happened."

He wouldn't hear of it. "But you didn't fuck anyone. Your husband did."

"No, I didn't. Not really," I said, frowning.

"And you were willing to work things out."

I shrugged, mentally throwing up my hands.

Once I'd ingested a second cup of Chai, Bennie and I headed uptown on the subway. After kissing my friend goodbye on the cheek, I got off at St. Marks Place to meet Pran.

At the neighborhood bookstore I spotted my old college friend and jogged up to him. Pran broke into a big smile. I, too, was smiling. We settled in at a low-key bar with a chatty bartendress and stools that were too high for the counter. I couldn't cross my legs and made a joke about talking to the management about "raising the bar."

"What's going on with Andrew?" Everyone, it seemed, wanted to know.

"I honestly couldn't tell you," I said. And that was the truth, since my husband didn't share much of anything with me anymore, unless it was "business-related."

"I bet he'll be back," Pran said.

I wasn't so sure. But what I did know was that my friend wanted to sleep with me. The problem was, I was still shutdown sexually. After seventeen, almost eighteen years of knowing only one man's body, I didn't think I could make the switch so easily.

The bartendress, a spunky woman with a penchant for red lipstick, leaned into me and said she felt some sort of strange connection with me. It was totally out of the blue, but I felt it too.

"We're soul sisters," she said.

It happened like that with people sometimes. And although by the end of the evening, Pran had kissed off most of my lipstick, I didn't feel that same kindred connection with him.

"Do you want to come home with me?" he asked.

"I can't leave my car at the station," I said, which got me off the hook.

After we paid up, Pran and I took a cab to Grand Central. The taxi dropped me off and Pran continued on to the Upper West Side.

On my way home, I got an email from my husband.

ANDREW: *You go girl.*

That was his response after I told him about the book I was writing and how it never would have come out of me had we not broken up. I fired off an email.

ME: *BTW, I will always honor what we had together. I am simply making a positive out of a seeming negative. There is not a day that goes by that I don't think about you and reflect on the good things we shared, the life we built. And sometimes it's the little things that one remembers most fondly...*
x D

NOVEMBER 18

HAVE FUN, MY ASS

I received an email back from my husband early morning.

ANDREW: *Understand fully and feel the same. Write the book and have fun!*

Have fun? That hit me in about the same manner as *You go, girl.* I didn't reply but what I really wanted to say was, I most certainly will have fun, and I hope you're doing the same with your bulimic little chippie with the ADHD.

And I had to laugh when I got an image of this possible wife number five with her head in the toilet, secretly barfing up her sandwich made from her very own chickens. Andrew, nearby, slept fitfully, his C-pap machine working overtime, obliterating the sound of Trudy's last gagging breath as she choked on her vomit.

Two hours later I got a text from the twenty-five-year-old future rabbi, Yehowah/Mike/Steve.

ME: *Mike/Steve! What a delightful surprise. What is happening in ur corner of the Universe?*

YEHOWAH: *Just the usual...is your hubby still living with u?*

ME: *No. He is in our place in VT.*

(I knew what was coming next.)

YEHOWAH: *So that means I could come over.*

ME: *I'd rather meet in the city. But I hv nothing free til after next Sun.*

YEHOWAH: *I would love to just come over to your place late night and sleep with u even without intercourse, just to cuddle; there's time for that...*

ME: *U r very persistent. I have to run to a play reading. Can resume later.*

YEHOWAH: *Ok.*

After the reading, I had dinner with my actor friend Dustin to continue our discussion of him becoming my roommate. But he said something that bothered me. He called a woman friend of his "a cunt." (Guess I'd be staying in that big, old, empty house by myself.)

NOVEMBER 19

CRUMBLING CALF'S LIVER

Tonight, I hit the pillow around midnight and shortly bolted awake from a disturbing dream. In it, I was kissing Pran. It felt nice at first, but his tongue began to fragment and crumble, like an overcooked, desiccated piece of calf's liver. And I wondered if the dream was not a sign of things to come—a sign that our relationship would ultimately disintegrate. But if it wasn't meant to be...que sera and all that crap.

NOVEMBER 20

EVERYTHING SEEMS BROKEN

Groggy from a heavy dose of melatonin, I dragged myself out of bed. After getting dressed, and before I left to meet my friend Maddie, I spotted the now-leafless grapefruit tree from my upstairs office window. I had forgotten to take it in when the weather got cold, and it was now lying on its side on the cement patio. I went outside, stood the tree upright, and attempted to bring it into the house, but it was too heavy. Next to the patio furniture, the small portable grill was lying upside down, and I saw that one of its side flaps had been damaged. I instinctively looked up. The berry tree also had been damaged by that dreadful winter storm that came through way too early. Its limbs hung down to the ground, broken. Everything seemed broken—everything inside of me and outside of me. I began to cry, the sorrow eclipsing whatever hope I had garnered from a dream in which Andrew and I were back together, holding hands like we used to. But what made me most sad was the grill because it reminded me of my husband—because Andrew loved to barbeque.

I flashed on the time that he went to fire up the large standing grill on one of the first warm days of the season and found a family of bees living inside. Instead of killing them, he went to Home Depot and bought the portable one. I just wished I could block out all these memories that continued to haunt me. It was just too bad they didn't perform lobotomies any more. Or maybe they did. (Note that for further research.)

NOVEMBER 21

BIRDS, BALD HEADS, AND HAIR-Y TOADS

Early evening, Carl sent me an email, reaching out to me as a friend, and I felt obligated to respond.

CARL: *What's going on? Are things getting better for you? Where do things stand at the moment with your husband? I'm sure you're still reeling from*

all of this. I'm still seeing my teacher pal, but I'm meeting another lady.
Very hot. She's not necessarily a spanko (more into heavier S&M) but is
very interested. I don't know if it's just me getting older, but these girls/
women have some serious baggage. Head cases. Not that I'm a poster boy
for sanity, but damn... That's the latest. I really hope you're doing better.
Please let me know.

ME: *Things are basically okay. I am adjusting...or trying to. Not surprising*
that a lot of people into "S" are dragging around a lot of baggage. That
can't surprise you. Although I think Brenda and I were/are extremely well
balanced individuals :-) Keep me posted. Have a wonderful Thanksgiving.
I'm heading up the river (no, not to prison) to be with friends.

(I realized I couldn't even write or say the word "spanking"
anymore.)

My former dom emailed back:

CARL: *You sound good. I know things will work out for you. Have a great*
Thanksgiving. And yes, you and Brenda were two of the sanest ladies to
have their bottoms set on fire. I'm actually leaving work early today to see
the teacher. It feels wrong sometimes, but I can't stop. I'm totally in the
zone right now and that's never good for the lady over my knee. I think you
can attest to that, miss. Remember LA?

ME: *Yes, I think I can attest to that.*

CARL: *Good girl.*

ME: *Uh-oh, here we go again.*

CARL: *So, there's no way you would think about being hauled over a man's*
knee and having your bottom bared and getting your tender cheeks spanked
raw? That complete loss of control? The understanding that you're going
to be disciplined hard and there's nothing you can do about it but surren-
der? I'm sure that hasn't crossed your mind. Or has it?

I told him that the only thing that had crossed my mind was that
nothing was certain in my life—absolutely nothing.

The night turned dark and rainy, and dreariness quickly settled
inside the house, so I called a friend of mine and we met for drinks.
After a few glasses of wine, I left feeling a little better and slightly
potted.

On the way home, what looked like a frog or a toad jumped into
the road. I swerved to avoid it, almost taking myself out instead.
Thankfully, I missed it, and the small creature survived.

When I got upstairs, I shot Andrew an email and asked if we had toads or frogs around here this time of year. He responded right away and said, yes, but only if it was warm. But it wasn't. It was freezing cold. So perhaps it was just a leaf blowing in the wind. I knew I could have found the answer on Google, but I felt an aching need to reach out to my husband. I also had to wonder what he thought when he got these emails from me. Maybe he was as confused as I was. Or maybe he just didn't care.

I later had a dream that I put my wedding band back on my left hand.

NOVEMBER 22

A DECISION, BUT DO NOT RESUSCITATE

At nine-thirty in the morning, my husband, Andrew, called from his parents' house in D.C. and left a message. He needed to ask me a question, he said. But why did he call? Was he reaching out? Or was Chicken Lady with him down there? I had a sense she was not. But I didn't want to call him back, which I realized had become a pattern, since I was afraid of what he might say—or not say. And how foolish I felt since I was still operating on the hope that he would see how senseless this all was. So, I sent him an email instead asking what he wanted. He responded pretty quickly.

ANDREW: *Mom has made a decision. Need the FedEx number so she can send you something.*

I began to fantasize that his mother wanted to send me a plane ticket down to D.C. for Thanksgiving so I could be with them and Andrew—and we could perhaps resuscitate our marriage. My fantasies were quickly shattered: his mother wanted to send me her iPad, which she didn't use. The device had been a present from Andrew to his parents. But I felt as if gifting me with it was her way of demonstrating solidarity.

I missed his parents a lot. Sadly, mine were long gone.

NOVEMBER 23

S&M HITS THE STAGE

Venus in Fur, which touched on the subject of dominance and submission, was generating great reviews—and a lot of attention. After I told Pran about my experiences with the two dommes (choosing not to tell him about Carl), he was determined to take me to the play "as sort of a joke." He also said he didn't quite get why spanking would turn me on. Or why it would turn anyone on, for that matter. I couldn't really explain it. As Carl had said, anyone outside the scene (or anyone who hadn't played before) just wouldn't—or couldn't—understand.

Throughout the show, the female co-star wore standard BDSM attire: leather corset, fishnet stockings, and miniskirt (all black), while the actor was dressed in street clothes. During one particularly intense scene, the male performer seductively slid the woman's thigh-high patent leather boots onto her legs and slowly zipped them up while she laid on a divan, her head flung back, her eyes closed in semi-rapture. There was no dialogue. You could have heard a pin drop in the audience.

Pran didn't particularly like the play. I found it very entertaining, but like him, felt it was lacking in heart and didn't feel a thing for either of the two characters. "Maybe S&M simply doesn't have any heart," I said on the way out.

"So why is this play doing so well?" Pran asked.

"You know," I remarked, "this fetish just might be more mainstream than I thought."

My mind was again flooded with questions: So, was what I did so bad then? But what about when Carl recently said he "feels it's wrong sometimes?" I guess the main difference was, what we saw tonight was a play; it was not "real life." But then again, BDSM was not real life either. It was play, and it was consensual.

I shifted my attention back to my friend, and we headed on over to a local watering hole. Pran and I snagged a couple of seats at the bar where I ordered a coffee martini and checked my messages. There was a voicemail from a woman who worked at Flanagan's. "Deborah, I made a pie for you. You were supposed to pick it up yesterday." Her voice was stern and reprimanding, which ironically I now found aggravating. A few months ago, it would have turned me on.

I laughed inside at my reaction, flashing back on the two dommes, and made Pran listen to the recording as I didn't want him to think I was lying and making another excuse to not go back to his place. (Silently, however, I thanked my lucky stars that she'd called.)

On my way home, I picked up the pie.

A DAY OF THANKS AND NO ANDREW

I refused to think of all the Thanksgiving dinners Andrew and I had at our house. I refused to think of his gravy and how much I liked it, unless of course he put in too much sage. I refused to think about how much fun we always had shopping in preparation for the annual feast. I refused to think about how helpful he always was around the kitchen. I refused to think about the soup he loved to make out of the turkey carcass. I refused to think about how good our stuffing was. I refused to think about him.

Instead, I headed up the river to Gaby and Claire's house, where I planned to spend the night.

The dinner table conversation was charged and animated. The food was fabulous. But the pie I brought from Flannagan's did not go over well. Gaby asked me if it was okay to give it to the raccoons.

NOVEMBER 29

PROFFERED PLEASURE

I shot my globe-trotting friend Angie a text on Skype to check in with her.

ANGIE: *So, what's the latest with Yehowah? Have you slept with him?*

ME: *Nope.*

ANGIE: *Are you tempted?*

ME: *Yes, but I'm so much older than he is.*

ANGIE: *Ask yourself what a man would do. Why should we deny ourselves proffered pleasure? No guy would turn it down.*

Angie and I disconnected from Skype and I ran through my email. I had sent Andy a note asking him where I could find replacement filters for our water system in the kitchen, but I hadn't heard anything back. Even though our marriage was now in shambles and I felt tremendously abandoned by my husband, I still worried about him and began having images of him lying frozen, dead in a snow bank somewhere in the wilds of VT. After I sent him another email expressing my concern, he responded, and for the first time in months, he asked me how I was doing.

ME: *Doing well. Under the circumstances.*

(That might have been just a slight exaggeration since I still I cried like a baby on a daily basis.)

Later, at 7 PM, I met Sarah at Flanagan's, where we broached our usual subject of how our thoughts created our reality.

"So, on some subconscious level, I must have wanted to push Andrew away," I said. "But if that's the case, why is it so damn painful without him?"

"Because you got used to him."

"Maybe," I said. "But I really did grow to love him and our life together. I just wish I didn't feel so shut down."

"It's understandable."

I leaned into her from across the table. "But I think I'm going to go forward with my twenty-five-year-old friend. Perhaps it will shake something loose."

Over the course of dinner, I drank a bit too much wine, but congratulated myself for not finishing my last glass. I got home safely, took my vitamins, and ate a few nuts. It didn't feel so bad tonight being in the house. So maybe I was starting to be okay with being alone, and I remembered Edna's message about learning to be by myself. So, what would happen when I "got it?" When I finally was able to function on my own without feeling like I was going out of my skin with anxiety? Would someone miraculously come into my life? Would I reunite with Andrew?

Screw it. I didn't want to think about it anymore. I took a Xanax and settled in with my cat beside me on the bed and a book by Jane Fonda about love and sex in the golden years, or prime time, as she calls it. Thank goodness, I was not seventy years old. Because right now I knew I couldn't deal with the fact that my tits would surely be hanging down to my belly button and my ass down to my knees. Forget my arms. They had already morphed into wingspans. Hopefully by the time I reached that age they would have come up with a pill: "Here take this. Within six weeks your skin will be taut, your hair will be thick and shiny like that of a twenty-year old, and your boobs will be perky, your booty rock solid. And how wonderful that will be, since your brain will still be intact, and you will still possess the wisdom gained from years of emotional torture and pain."

All of a sudden I became depressed about the whole idea of aging and pushed Jane's book off the bed to the floor. It landed with a clunk. (But, as a friend of mine said, at least Andy didn't leave me when I was one stroke away from the nursing home.)

NOVEMBER 30

NO MORE HEARTACHE, PLEASE!

The café was cozy and inviting, so I didn't mind waiting for my play-writing friend, Julie—until an old, heart-wrenching song came over the speaker and I lost it. Spotting me, my friend slid into the booth and hugged me, which made me weep even more.

"Goddamn Andrew," I said.

"Here," she said, taking out her bottle of Xanax.

"Why doesn't he get it? Even the President gets it when he says he was lucky enough to marry his best friend."

After regaining my composure, which required about ten napkins to sop up the mess on my face, Julie and I again talked about love and how lust is blinding and that practical choices in a mate make much more sense when we get older.

"I miss the companionship," I said, my insides aching. "I miss being with him. I don't know what to do. I don't know how to deal with all this grief."

"Why don't you come to church with me?" Julie had converted from Judaism to Catholicism.

"I could do that," I said, knowing that I'd probably never go.

"It's only when I connect to God through prayer that I feel okay." My anxiety surged, and I wanted to pop another Xanax. I wished I could believe fully in God and find comfort in prayer. I wanted to pray, I did—especially now, but I was a little dubious about it all, due to what happened a year ago. I had read a book by one of my favorite memoirists, where she recounted her life as an alcoholic and her experience with AA. Like many addicts, she went kicking and screaming to the twelve-step meetings and felt the idea of pray-ing to a higher power was ridiculous. But she finally relented and began putting her hands together. At the time, she was a struggling writer, and not too long after she adopted a daily ritual, she received a $30,000 grant. Someone she knew, a professor, had submitted sam-ples of her writing to a particular organization on her behalf, unbe-knownst to her. When I read that, I thought, okay, maybe there was something to this after all. I decided to experiment and put this prayer business to the test, adopting the clinical approach that I learned in undergraduate and grad school. So, each night thereafter, with my husband sleeping beside me, I'd roll on my side and clasp my hands together, just like I did as a child when I'd petition God to "please make mommy start talking to daddy again."

But I felt a little uncomfortable calling God by his real name, so instead I addressed the almighty as "George." I also decided to chronicle my experiment and title it, aptly, *The God Experiment*. My research didn't last too long. Within a week, my flat-rate salary for my editing work was reduced by $300 per job and my theatrical producing partner informed me that she "had to move on to projects that pay well," since her financial situation was precarious. I was crushed, devastated—on both counts. And I quit praying. This was in February, which coincided with my venture into "the dark side."

I didn't share this information with my friend. Instead we talked more about my husband.

"You know," Julie said, thoughtfully, "if Andrew is not able to really see what you had in these seventeen, almost eighteen years together and is not willing to make amends, then there is something in him that is damaged, and you need to let go."

I looked up at the TV that was playing silently in the corner of the café and saw the phrase *So Wrong*. "I think the universe is trying to tell me something," I said to my friend. (But what was it that was wrong? That he left, or that I wanted him back?)

DECEMBER 3

THE MAN WITH THE LARGE WOOL HAT

Pran and I headed off to our favorite haunt on the corner of Ninth and Third Avenue and sat down at the bar.

"I find you sexy," he said.

Instead of giving me a boost, his comment triggered an unwelcomed surge of gloominess, so I forced myself to find joy in the moment and in him. It really was not that difficult.

The night began to feel right, and we were both sorry to see it end, but I told my friend with the nice, thick head of hair on the way uptown that I was just not ready to spend the night at his place. Pran was very understanding, and I was grateful for that.

After kissing him on the cheek, I slid out of the cab, feeling good, uplifted—until I walked into Grand Central. Unable to stop them, they came: the tears, the unrelenting tears. Perhaps it was the Christmas decorations or the onslaught of memories of me and my husband racing through the terminal, our fingers entwined.

I found my train, which was leaving in fifteen minutes, grabbed a seat, and put my hand over my face, my head against the window.

The sobbing became almost uncontrollable, but I had worked hard at being a relatively quiet crier over the past several months, since the floodgates often opened up when I was in public places.

Finally, the train began to move. I wiped at my face and gave my ticket to the conductor, clenching my jaw in attempts to stop crying, forcing myself to think about something, anything, other than my husband. It didn't work, and the tears came again, my chest heaving up and down as I took in great gulps of air. Thankfully, no one seemed to notice—or cared to.

Two stops later, a tall black man with a wool hat that looked like it was covering up a small flying saucer sat next to me. He wore clothing that said "homeless," yet here he was on the Metro North local. I could feel him staring at me, and I found myself wondering if he was connecting with my pain. He too, I imagined, had had a lot of sorrow in his life. Or maybe that was a projection on my part. Maybe, as the whack job from match.com said, it was a symptom of narcissism. But, despite my intellectual ruminations, I continued to weep.

The man, who had kind but red-rimmed eyes, finally asked if I was okay. His concern made me sob even harder.

"Yes," I said, with great difficulty, turning toward him. "I'll be fine."

Our eyes locked, and I impulsively extended my hand. He took it and gently squeezed my fingers. His hand was cool to the touch, like mine was usually, and I could feel his calluses.

"Thank you," I said.

"God will take care of you."

Within moments, a sense of calm settled over me and the tears dried up. I felt as though I should say something else but realized there was no need.

I looked out the window and began to breathe rhythmically and deeply, my hands now folded on my lap.

When the train came to a halt at Tarrytown, I saw that the man had fallen asleep. I gently touched his leg, and he moved to let me out.

"Be well," I said. These were the same words my husband used in an email to me a few months ago. But I knew, in this case, the words were appropriate, since I had only been in this man's presence for twenty minutes, not seventeen years.

As I maneuvered past him, our eyes met once again, and I sensed a deep connection that went well beyond the physical plane. And

I thought to myself that maybe we were never really alone. Maybe we were all "one." And maybe there really was a "God." And maybe, just maybe, the black man with the soft brown eyes wore the hat to cover up his halo.

DECEMBER 4

SPLIT LIPS AND PING PONG

I slept until noon, wanting to avoid the day, my thoughts, but the memories kept pulling me into consciousness. And I wandered back to the time I had to bring my husband to the hospital after he split his lip open on the kitchen counter. We'd been down at one of the local joints listening to our friend's band, and by the time we'd gotten home, we were both a little tipsy. And like a bunch of kids playing a game of "catch me if you can," we started chasing each other around the downstairs.

Andrew would go one way; I would go another and quickly switch directions, both of us squealing with laughter. When I came at him from the dining room after he'd bolted into the kitchen, he slipped. His face hit the corner of the counter, and blood began pouring out of a gaping slit on his top lip.

"You need stitches," I said without pause.

Andy put a hand up to his mouth "I'll be okay."

"No. We're going to the hospital. Now. I'll grab a towel."

On the drive over, I was shaking like a leaf inside, but I worked to maintain a steady demeanor as I didn't want to frighten Andy. Once there, I stayed with him in the examination room and held his hand after the doctor came to stitch him up. Sadly, the surgeon was not the greatest, and Andrew ended up with a rather visible scar. I often wondered if he thought of me when he looked in the mirror. My guess was he did not.

Finally, after tumbling around with more memories, I got up out of bed and noticed that I felt a bit stronger, more centered, even though I had a stuffy nose. I knew it was probably the cat dander that was stopping me up, since I hadn't washed the sheets in more than a month. But every time I thought of it, my cat happened to be asleep on her bed pillow, and I hated to disturb her. Or perhaps it was just an excuse. Even the most menial chores seemed daunting.

Around noon I headed for downtown.

Main Street Café was busy today, which was good, since I had a pressing need to be around people. (Lots of them.)

173

As I was about to take my first sip of my tongue-scorching Chai, I got a text from Yehowah/Mike/Steve, who was waiting to board his plane in Miami.

YEHOWAH: *I'll be back in the city tonight. Would love to see you*

When I told him I was not going to be around, he said I was playing hardball.

ME: *Come on, I do have a life outside of Yehowah/Mike/Steve.*

Then, being silly, I told him to ping me, or pong me, sometime this week.

YEHOWAH: *I'd like to ping your pong :)*

(Oh, for fuck's sake.)

DECEMBER 8

THE CRAYONS THAT KEEP ON GIVING

After dinner and in between spurts during which we reconfigured my Mac that now sat on the kitchen island table, my tenant, Lori, and I shared a bit about our childhood experiences and how they affected us. (I called it being programmed.)

"When I was in first grade," I said to my friend, "my teacher took my crayons away from me and gave them to my best friend to keep. They were a birthday gift from my parents, and I'd brought them to school and spent a good half hour sharpening each one to perfection. I made a mess on my desk, and the teacher got pissed."

"Did you tell your parents?"

"No, I thought I had done something wrong. It took me a long time to overcome the belief that everyone but me deserves the goodies."

And isn't it ironic that decades later, Carl, my dom, would "punish me" with a task that required colored crayons. (They just seemed to keep piling up, these little ironies.)

DECEMBER 9

A BUBBLING UP

Yehowah/Mike/Steve must have had me on his mind.

YEHOWAH: *Were you at Pret à Manger last night in the city?*

ME: *No. It was probably my doppelganger.*

YEHOWAH: *LOL.*

ME: *You should have said hello and hooked up with the woman.*

YEHOWAH: *No.*

ME: *Why not?*

YEHOWAH: *I want you.*

Even though I still had no interest in sleeping with anyone, something tingled in my nether regions.

I later met Pran for dinner during which he told me about a group therapy home that he lived in during the 1980s. The leader, a relatively well-known psychotherapist, encouraged intimate interaction between the participants, both emotionally and sexually. It helped Pran come out of his shell, make friends, both male and female, and communicate more effectively. It also taught him a little about the female body, knowledge of which he was apparently lacking.

"Andrew could have benefited from the communication part. But I suppose I could say the same about myself," I said, wondering if what I interpreted as contentment in my marriage was not that at all, but a shutdown in communication. Or maybe it's just that couples tended to get complacent over time, taking things for granted—and at times, each other. I turned to Pran and smiled slightly.

He tilted his head, then ran his hand up and down my back. I sensed a little flutter in my stomach; my body began to respond, and I realized how desperately I craved human touch.

DECEMBER 10

HAPPY HO HUM

Grand Central was mobbed, not with the usual people, but hundreds upon hundreds of Santa Clauses. But these Santas did not have beady black eyes and a penchant for BDSM (at least as far as I could tell), nor did they come bearing gifts, since it was the annual Santa pub crawl that begins in Brooklyn and ends up at some hole-in-the-wall bar in Manhattan. The crawl started at ten in the morning, so now that it was around 3:30 PM, many of the Santas and their elf helpers, both male and female, were well blitzed and more than a little unsteady on their feet. Under other circumstances, I probably would have been amused, but I only felt irritated because it was getting impossible to move through the crowd, and I was running late for my workshop. Not so coincidentally, I remembered when I found out there was no Santa Claus. In my child's mind, it was just about as devastating as the day I found out my husband was not coming home—and just as surreal.

After my Protools workshop, I went back to Piermont and headed next door to a holiday party at Jackie and Brad's. The house was alive with people, and I ended up talking with a lovely woman who had lost her husband when he was only forty years old. We discussed the initial shock of loss and how one adapts afterwards.

"You pick yourself up and go on. It's life," she said.

Even Frank Sinatra knew that when he sang the song about dusting yourself off and getting back in the race. And I suppose he did mean the "human" race.

Just when I was about ready to leave, Jackie's husband said that a friend of his had had his eye on me since I walked in the door. "Oh, that's, uh, sweet," I remarked, not exactly filled with enthusiasm.

Brad pulled me over to the man in question and pushed me down on the couch next to him. The guy was very cute and seemed nice enough. It also turned out he was pretty much in the same boat I was, being newly separated. The main difference was, he had three kids in the picture. Fortunately, I only had my cat's emotional and physical health to consider.

An hour later as I lay in bed staring at the ceiling, scratching Mamie's head, I thought about Brad's friend and wondered if I shouldn't have expressed more interest. (Loneliness sucks.) But I reminded myself of a quote I had recently come across: *Fall in love when you're ready. Not when you're lonely.*

DECEMBER 12

LIES—ALWAYS ON MY MIND

While seated at one of the bars in Piermont waiting for my friend Alexis, who was trying (without success) to convince me to take the money out of my and Andy's mutual savings account, Yehowah/ Mike/Steve texted me.

The e-conversation did not go well.

YEHOWAH: *When do you want me to come over?*

ME: *After the 22nd...unless by then u successfully find a playmate. Logistics are an issue at the moment.*

(Lies, lies, and more lies. Logistics being an issue had nothing to do with my husband. But my rationale was this: if I decided to take advantage of what the universe was putting in my path, meaning

Yehowah/Mike/Steve and a potentially sizzling affair, I should wait until Pran was out of town, since I felt a certain amount of loyalty to him. And this was in spite of the fact that I had not yet slept with him and wasn't sure if I ever would—or could.)

YEHOWAH: *Oh fuck U.*

ME: *That was very mean-spirited.*

YEHOWAH: *I'm just saying it sounds like you are constantly pushing things off.*

(He was right on that count.)

YEHOWAH: *But u do whatever u gotta do. U have my number. I'm sorry if I was mean.*

ME: *Okay. Apology accepted. We'd probably have fun.*

He did not text me back after that, so I let it go and ordered another glass of wine. Within an hour or so, mostly everyone at the bar was sufficiently tanked and talking at maximum volume.

An older man, a psychiatrist, spotted me and came over to chat me up. I told him he reminded me of Robert Duvall, but I omitted "a much less handsome version." I didn't find him appealing, but you talk anything psychology with me and I'll jump on board. I mentioned that I was separated.

"Gee. How come?" He (a complete stranger) seemed shocked as well.

I didn't necessarily want to get into intimate details, but he continued to push at me, and I relented—especially now that my tongue had become a bit looser after another half a glass of wine.

"Well," I said, "I tried to spice up my sex life and got into spanking."

The psychiatrist looked a little too pleased, excited. "Wow, I know exactly where you're coming from." He leaned in closer and told me about a problem he had with his wife. In so many words, she wouldn't go where he wanted to go. "I'm really into anal," he said. "I'm, you know...small." He paused, a look of concern spreading across his face. "Do you think anal activity is wrong?"

I had to repress a laugh: a shrink was asking me if I thought it was wrong? I said it wasn't, but I did tell him that I felt it was important to have a partner who liked the same things, or who was at least willing to experiment.

"My wife thinks any kind of anal play is immoral," he said.

(But it didn't bust up their marriage.)

The psychiatrist veered off the subject and said that I reminded him of his sister. "She died a few years ago," he said.

"I'm not so sure how I should take that," I replied with a half-grimace.

He went on to tell me that his mother also died recently and expelled a deep, fitful sigh. I placed a hand on his arm and said I was sorry, that loss is very difficult to deal with, but it touches all of us at one time or another.

Unfortunately, I carried that last bit of conversation home with me in my head and as soon as I got in the front door, I lost it.

('Tis the season. HO HO HO!)

DECEMBER 14

UNCOMMON CONVERSATIONS AND A WHOLE LOT OF QUESTIONS

Now I was really afraid of God. I began to pray, once again, looking for guidance, some relief from the loneliness and extreme anxiety. Instead, the same thing happened that happened the last time I began to petition the Lord with prayer: the company that I freelanced for decreased my salary again. Was God pissed at me for taking a scientific approach to unraveling the mysteries of "He Who is All and Everything" and for having the audacity to question His existence? Was He pissed off at me for calling him "George?" For not having faith?

It was definitely a Xanax night.

Once I was sufficiently relaxed and able to bear the disturbing quiet of the house, I slid beneath the covers to read.

"Oh hell," I said to Mamie, my cat. "I'm just being silly. I have to stop being so paranoid about God." So, instead of picking up *Traditional Home* magazine, I got up and pulled from the bookshelf a hard copy of *Conversations with God—An Uncommon Dialogue* by Neale Donald Walsch.

But I seriously had to wonder if the author was out of his mind when he wrote it, yet the ease of his dialogue with God was comforting, as were God's answers to the man's many questions (all those same questions that had plagued me over the years). And aside from a few seeming contradictions, I believed every word. Or wanted to. And apparently so did millions and millions of people all over the globe, as the author's first book in the series remained on the bestseller list for 137 weeks. (Go Neale! Go George! Oops, sorry. I mean,

God.)

I read for a while and took some thoughts to bed with me. I decided then and there that I would not indulge in despair, but trust that everything would be okay and that my life would once again be filled with love and joy—and that God, or the God of my understanding, would take care of me, like the man in the big woolen hat said.

(I sure hoped that was the case, because I was not doing such a great job on my own.)

DECEMBER 15

THE MAN WITH THE SQUIRREL ON HIS HEAD

Today it became official: It was me who was insane. I made plans to meet a man several years my senior from match.com. Why? I just answered that: I was out of my mind. (Or maybe I was looking for a father figure?) But, I rationalized, he was a Gemini, and I generally liked Geminis. They tended to be lively and engaging. (The man also promised to leave his cane at home, so at least he had a sense of humor. I just hoped he didn't show up hobbling.)

I sent the match.com man an email asking how I'd be able to recognize him. He didn't respond, so I entertained myself with thoughts like *he's in the hospital having an emergency heart transplant/hip replacement/colonoscopy [fill in the blanks] and can't get to his cell phone.* I also realized my cynicism was based in my own fear of getting older.

Assuming all systems were in gear, I took off for the city anyway. Once I was at Grand Central, I called the man to tell him I was wearing a grey jacket and black skirt and was standing by the clock tower.

"Hi there."

I turned toward the voice and fought the urge to pretend I was someone else. It wasn't because he was old and looked nothing like his photo; it was because he sported one of the worst toupees I'd ever seen. He also had dead blue eyes and a mouthful of unnatural-looking dentures that I suspected were installed decades ago before they were manufactured to look like real teeth. But there was more. When he spoke, he made a clacking sound, the source of which I could not identify. I did my damndest to not judge, but realized it was way too late for that. However, I did make an effort to smile, although I knew it looked stapled on.

We walked over to Starbucks and grabbed a couple of seats. I told the man with the bad hairpiece, which looked a bit too much like a dead squirrel, that I had an event to go to at nine o'clock. He probably knew I wasn't telling the truth. I might be a good actress, but when it came to lying I wouldn't win any awards for best performance. I thought about my husband and wondered if we wouldn't still be together if he'd just fibbed about sleeping with Chicken Lady and carried on until it ran its course (I could not for the life of me imagine it could be true love).

So, what was I going to say to this person who I had no real desire to get to know? Turned out I needn't have worried. The man liked to talk.

"I'm an actor," he told me. "I saw that you're a producer."

"Sometimes. I'm focusing on other things right now."

When the man asked me what went into making a film, I deduced he wanted to know if I was "legit"—if, as my profile on match.com said, I really did produce film and theater. I gave him the lowdown in a nutshell and told him I was pretty small potatoes in that world. But soon I came to realize, after a bit more conversation, that he was not just an actor; he was a desperate actor looking for a job. I also intuitively knew he didn't live in Gramercy Park, one of the swankier sections of NYC.

At that point, I was not so sure I could agree with my novelist friend's philosophy to take advantage of whatever the universe puts in one's path (like I felt I was doing with Yehowah), even if it was self-orchestrated. I think you sometimes have to go around (avoid) what's put in your path, run it over, or flee. Tonight, I chose to flee and headed off on the S train to go to a party, which started at ten o'clock. It offered a nice distraction for a few hours.

On my way back to Grand Central, I came upon a homeless person who had the most astoundingly beautiful eyes I'd ever seen. A pale, pale green, they lit up with a purity that was almost tangible.

"Hey," he said as I passed by.

"Hi," I said, smiling, regretful that I didn't have any cash. But it didn't seem to matter. His face beamed with joy, and I could tell he harbored not one tiny bit of bitterness or self-pity. So maybe, if it did come to it, life in a cardboard box wouldn't be so bad after all. At least there was a good possibility I'd have some cool neighbors who just might have a better handle on life than many of us.

When I got home from the city, I logged on to my computer, opened up my Outlook, and spotted an email that was sent through match.com.

MATCH.COM MAN: *It was nice meeting and talking with you tonight, but I sensed you weren't interested.*

I wrote him back immediately.

ME: *I'm just not ready to start dating yet. But I truly wish you all the luck in the world with your acting career.*

My heart ached for the man with the bad toupee. It ached for all the lonely people in the world.

DECEMBER 16

STOP THE MOVIE!

After a few glasses of wine at the Yale Club, Pran and I wandered off to find some food. More than ever, I was aware of our height difference. He held my hand as we walked down the street, but our step and gait were out of synch; it felt extremely awkward.

We ended up at a French restaurant in midtown, and later at its bar where I had two espresso martinis. I recalled the train ride home, but I could not remember how I got to Grand Central. Maybe it was because Pran and I were now doing habitual things—things that eventually would begin to define our relationship. We were also, in effect, creating memories. And that could be wonderful, but I would have given anything in the world to wipe away my memories of all those years with Andrew. The mornings were the worst, since every day I'd wake up and my mind would fill with images of the places we'd been and experiences we'd shared together in Vermont, in Connecticut, in California, in D.C. and Georgia, in New York, and in Europe. And there was that wonderful trip to Costa Rica, where we had (surprise!) some stunningly hot sex, which for some reason Andrew had forgotten about. It was like an ongoing movie that started the moment my eyes snapped open, and no matter what I did, I could not shut off the projector.

DECEMBER 17

A DAY OF MANY CULTURES

I realized I'd left my notebook in Pran's backpack, so I arranged to go up to his apartment before I headed downtown.

After taking the subway up to 103rd street, I walked north through a neighborhood that lacked the hustle and bustle of midtown. Within five blocks I was at Pran's building where he had lived for more than thirty years.

I woke my friend up from a deep slumber when I rang the outside buzzer, amazed that he could nap so soundly during the day in the same bed where his wife of twenty years had passed away. I found myself thinking that it must simply be how the male animal was programmed, how their brains were wired; they seemed to be able to fall asleep easily and, most of the time, within seconds. Just like Andy did at the bar in VT.

After being buzzed inside, I worked my way up five flights of stairs, my lungs pumping overtime due to a lapse in my daily exercise routine on the elliptical. That was one good thing about getting spanked: I had a much greater drive to stay in shape. As I told my husband, if someone—even if it was a woman—was going to be looking at my ass, it had better be tight. Now I could have cared less; let the sucker sag.

I knocked on the door to apartment 5F and felt a heaviness deep in my gut. Maybe it was the dinginess of the walls or the palpable silence that permeated the hallway.

Pran opened the door, his face still heavy with sleep. "Hey. Come on in." I walked into the living area and was immediately transported to an unfamiliar world. The apartment was bedecked with a multitude of paintings, artifacts, and candelabras from India. But there was an erratic quality to it all. Although the colors were bright and bold, nothing seemed to go together. Everything felt "off."

"Oh, I have one of those at home," I said, pointing to a statue of an elephant with its trunk in the air. "But mine's small; a little marble thing."

And I had a thought: perhaps Pran and I were together for one reason—to help each other through this transitional time, as friends, and not as lovers. Otherwise, as soon as I had walked into his apartment, I was pretty sure I'd have thrown myself at him, and we would have headed straight for the bedroom. Instead, we ended up at the deli next door.

"Is it safe to eat here?" I asked when we went inside. The deli was not the cleanest of places, and three bouts of food poisoning within a year and a half had made me a bit paranoid. Pran told me it was okay, that he ate there all the time, and he was still kicking. I decided to trust his judgment, so we feasted on tabbouleh and hummus and talked about his upcoming trip.

After lunch, we walked to the subway station, but this time we didn't hold hands, so perhaps he sensed my ambivalence.

At the entrance, I leaned down and kissed him, intentionally missing his lips, and wished him safe travels to Malaysia where he would be directing a play he wrote. "Goodbye, sweetie," I said.

"We'll talk before I go."

I almost told him to keep an eye open when he got to Malaysia; that there just might be a sweet Indian princess looking for the love of her life.

Next stop: my Protools workshop, during which I forced myself to focus on what I was supposed to be learning and thought about the top-of-the-line Mac computer and keyboard that Andy bought me so I could compose music. I felt guilty that I'd barely touched it. (I probably should have traded it in for a new TV—or a new husband.)

Two hours later, and after our heads were filled to the brim with technical information, us three "students" and our instructor, Chip, gathered around the reception area outside the studio.

"So, what's everyone's doing for Christmas?" Chip asked.

I sucked in a breath.

Al said his family would be together and talked about the difficulties of buying the right gifts for his daughters. Bennie said he and his partner were planning to have the people from next door over for dinner. Chip turned to me.

"Uh, not sure what I'm doing." I smiled tightly, knowing I had to get the hell out of there before I came unglued. "I really have to go," I said, indicating the clock on the wall. "Thanks everyone. Have a great holiday."

Bennie took a step toward me as I headed for the door; I could tell he saw my pain.

"I'll call you, Bennie," I said quickly.

And I was off, out of the building, racing toward the subway, choking on the emotion.

"Fuck. Fuck Andrew for doing this," I grumbled, sounding like some stoned-out lunatic. "It's fucking Christmas!"

On the way home, I texted Amy. She said she was depressed and was not sure she wanted to come out. I convinced her otherwise, offering to essentially pay for her company. She relented. I knew she liked being around me, perhaps because we both shared similar neuroses, including the fear of death. Right now, however, what I feared most was living in this continual state of despair.

We met at a local Japanese restaurant and, a few sakes later, the melancholy lifted.

"Have you heard anything from Andrew?" Amy asked.

"Just business stuff. The usual."

"Really?" she said, her eyes wide with surprise. "He doesn't even ask you how you are doing?"

"He did once."

"Wow. How are you coping with all this?"

I shrugged and told her that I was not exactly brimming with joy.

Over eel and salmon rolls, Amy talked about moving out to LA, suggested I do the same, and share a place with her. I was not thirty-years old anymore, and I simply did not want to live with roommates.

"Can I please have my life back?" I whispered to myself when Amy took off to the restroom.

A voice in my head said "no."

DECEMBER 18

AN EVER-PRESENT GHOST

I woke up feeling like I had a cold. I didn't know if it was from the booze of last night, although I didn't feel hung over; or the sleeping pill; or the cat dander, which was now probably at near toxic levels. (Note to self: wash the bedclothes.)

Today was particularly bad; my husband's ghost was ever present in the house and, once again, I had to get out.

As I was leaving, I heard the phone in my office ring and stopped to listen to an incoming message from Bennie. "Hello, honey. Just checking in with you. I love you." He cared seemingly far more than my husband of almost fourteen years.

So, what happened to me and Andy, I once again asked myself. What happened? I snapped. He snapped. We all snapped.

DECEMBER 22

BE BOLD, BE DARING

"I think Andrew has a mild form of Asperger's," I said to my friend Maddie over lunch, trying desperately to better understand his behavior.

My therapist had made the observation after I told her about Andy's social and physical awkwardness, a trait that was countered by his vast knowledge of science and the natural world.

"When I first started going out with him," I said to Maddie, "we were at a party, and when they brought out the food, Andrew asked when they'd be serving the pig's guts. On the way home, I lit into him. Why would you say something like that? I'd said. That's something a child would say! And we hardly know those people."

Thinking back on it now, though, I felt sorry that I was ever bothered by his ineptness. "He simply can't help who he is," I said to my lunch mate.

"You know, people with Asperger's also see things as very black or white. That's why they can compartmentalize so easily. Also, once they make a decision, it's locked in."

"That doesn't bode well for me, for our marriage."

My cell phone suddenly pinged. I gave my friend a look, and she immediately knew who was texting me.

"Here's what you do," Maddie said. "Ask one of your guy friends to call him up and announce that he's in the disposal business. Know what I mean?"

I'm not sure I liked that idea. Something kept pulling me to my twenty-five-year-old friend, so on my way into Grand Central I texted Yehowah/Mike/Steve.

ME: *Since my husband and I are working to figure many things out over the holidays ('tis the season, after all), the best I can do is meet for a drink. Not what u want tho.*

It was a fabrication, yes, but a part of me was hoping it would put the final nail in this twisted, sordid little coffin, ridding me of this ongoing tentativeness. No such luck. He phoned me at seven o'clock, but I was at a bar having a drink with my college friend Robin, so I ignored the call, letting it go to voicemail.

I told Robin about Pran. "We're sort of seeing each other," I said.

My friend, who acted in a lot of shows with Pran in college, busted up.

"Oh dear. That is not a good sign." I said, laughing myself.

"I just can't see the two of you together."

"Yeah, I know. We're kind of like Mutt and Jeff."

We talked a bit more and after we settled up the bill, Robin headed downtown, and I began the trek across 45th Street to Grand Central and got another text from my persistent friend.

YEHOWAH: *R u in the city?*

ME: *Are you psychic? Yes. Am in city.*

YEHOWAH: *Wanna grab a drink or go for a ride in my car? I'm meeting someone soon but wld love to c u before or after.*

ME: *Cn mt u for a drink now.*

He called my cell and told me he was at the Hyatt. I snaked my way through the crowd at Grand Central and out to the street, in through the hotel's revolving doors, and up the escalator where Yehowah/ Mike/Steve waited. We sat down at a table outside the bar. I didn't need another drink but wanted one. He didn't want one since he was driving. As always, he was being a good Jew, and I was being a bad Christian.

After I'd ordered a Chardonnay, we talked very seriously about relationships, and he brought up his girlfriend once again. "Something is missing, but I feel I have to stay with her," Yehowah/Mike/ Steve said, which told me it was most likely an arranged marriage. And, out of the blue, he told me that he had "control issues."

"Oh," I said, knowing that this could mean a million things. But I didn't press him for more, since I was not sure I wanted to know.

Yehowah/Mike/Steve pulled me in with his eyes, and I flashed back on what the train conductor said to me coming into New York when I handed him my ticket: "Why thank you, young lady." People never say that to young people. They always say it to older people, and I suddenly felt ancient compared to my friend. But Yehowah's thoughts were apparently elsewhere, and I felt a zing pass between us as he leaned in closer to me. I almost bolted from the chair but remained seated. I did, however, sense what was up ahead; maybe not tonight but at some point, we were going to consummate this relationship—or whatever the hell you'd call it.

"I have to meet my friend now," Yehowah/Mike/Steve said.

He seemed nervous, but I was not sure why. Maybe I intimidated him. Or maybe he was finally coming to his senses and wanted to run for the hills. But as we got up, our eyes locked, and I felt that electrical current pass between us once again.

When we got outside, Yehowah took off to the east, and I headed west toward Grand Central.

Halfway home on the train, I felt compelled to text him, to explain a comment I'd made earlier.

ME: *When I said u were amusing, I didn't mean it in a bad way, tho u r funny. I meant the sitch is amusing. I fnd u very attractive tho we are very age disparate.*

YEHOWAH: *I hope we have a sleep-over soon.*

I looked out the window and saw that it had started to storm.

ME: *Okeeeeee!!!! It is thundering and lightening up here: the gods must be happy that the Christians and Jews might be getting together at last. Ha-ha.*

YEHOWAH: *Yes maam!!!! Let me know when works for u.*

ME: *I will. Enjoy your evening, u cwazy wabbit.*

I decided I would not contact him again and would instead wait for him to make the next move. Maybe on New Year's Eve it would happen—my fourteenth wedding anniversary. I played a scenario out in my head: I'm at Ted and Eva's up the road. We're raising our glasses of wine or champagne, toasting to the coming year—a year that promises joy, good health, prosperity, and peace. It's two hours before midnight when the ball will drop in Times Square, signaling the leap into the month of January, and I get a text from Yehowah/Mike/Steve asking where I am. I give him the address. He has his driver bring him up in one of his fancy cars. I don't want him to drive himself, since that means he won't drink. He needs to imbibe—to obscure his vision. That or I lock him in a dark basement, and we do it there. Yehowah/Mike/Steve gets to Ted and Eva's just after midnight. I race to his car—a roomy Lincoln town car—which is parked down the drive. His chauffeur gets out, opens the door to let me into the back seat. I tell the driver to go enjoy himself at the party inside. He smiles, shuts the car door, and saunters up the small hill toward the house.

Yehowah/Mike/Steve and I, finally alone, begin to kiss. It gets heated. But it is filled with that kind of passion that makes you feel like your head is going to spin off into space. And even though we kiss more feverishly, I am aware of the sweetness of his lips. Though hungry to tear at my flesh, he gently glides his hand up and down my body and lightly traces the roundness of my breast. And then my fantasy shatters: he asks me to give him a blow job.

I still could not imagine doing that with anyone other than my husband. Maybe I needed to make that clear before anything happened; maybe I needed tell my young friend that I have to know someone for a while before I venture down that road, or perhaps I should say, venture up that pole.

I was staring to freak out. But I was getting way ahead of myself—

way far ahead of myself. But okay, I thought, this guy keeps putting himself in my path, and I've made no effort to shut him out. So maybe I just needed to follow through. And hopefully he was of sound mind, and I wouldn't end up in his mother's potato latkes.

The rain stopped when I got to Tarrytown, but it was oddly warm for this time of year. The traffic across the bridge remained light, since it was still relatively early in the evening, so I felt happy about that. I got home, parked the car, and headed toward the house where I spotted a small evergreen tree on the front steps, replete with tiny red and green Christmas bulbs and a card. This was not what I needed. "You are not going to cry. You are not going to cry," I said, repeating my new mantra over and over.

I read the note, which was from my sister, Wanda: *I wish I could be there to give you a big hug.* And that did me in, and I found myself weeping and projecting all my sadness onto the tree, which seemed so small, vulnerable, and alone. I loved my sister for doing this, but at the same time I wanted to figuratively smack her. I was also astounded that I had anything left in me to cry out after several months of sobbing (but the human body just keeps right on giving).

As I placed the tree in the sink to mist its branches, I reminded myself how lucky I was to have my sister in my life; my brother, too, to whom I'd become much closer since my separation. (Nothing like a little crisis to bring a family together.)

DECEMBER 23

SURVIVAL AT WHOLE FOODS

Andrew and I used to shop at Whole Foods for holiday meals, a luxury I always looked forward to. It was one of my favorite grocery stores, and one place that I didn't mind overstaying my parking welcome of one hour—or overspending on food.

Today, however, I almost blew the limit on both counts. But I felt proud of myself: I didn't blubber. Instead, I wandered the aisles and marveled at the beautiful soaps and fancy containers of nuts. I smiled when I saw the fresh fish laid out like they themselves had willingly sacrificed their lives for our human consumption. And I didn't cry when I walked by the beer aisle where Andrew used to spend a good ten minutes making just the right selection. And I didn't get all weepy when I ordered a Chai latte with soy milk at the coffee and tea counter, which my husband and I always used to do, or when the checkout person was extra nice to me. I was even able to drive home safely without being blinded from tears. I wanted to say, Yea! And so, I did.

Later, after I exercised and did a little editing work, I drove up the river to Gaby and Claire's house.

The night with my friends and their guests, Paul and Kathy, was lovely, but I had to keep telling myself I was not going backwards in time to the days of being the extra wheel, like tonight. However, I got a little dose of hope. Momentarily.

Kathy, I came to find out, met Paul on match.com, and he actually seemed normal. But it was more than that: in addition to being sane and stable, he was smart, he was cute, and he had a good job.

"I spent ten years looking," Kathy told me.

"Ten years? Ten?" I said and repeated what the tarot card reader had said. "Hoo boy."

DECEMBER 24

IT'S ALMOST OVER! YIPPEE!

I could not wait for Christmas to be over. This was the first time in my life I had felt like this, and I left Gaby and Claire's in the morning, not wanting to say goodbye.

At 5:30 PM while I was sitting at my desk at home, I got a text from Yehowah/Mike/Steve.

YEHOWAH: *Happy Holidays to you and your family.*

Wow, I thought. There was not one peep from my husband, and this kid I barely knew.

After going on a cathartic cleaning rampage, I stopped by the cottage to give Lori a gift before heading off to a small gathering a few towns away.

Lori's mother, a lovely woman in her early seventies, quickly came up to me and gave me a hug. "I'm so sorry about you and Andrew," she said. "But you'll be better off."

I wanted to believe her, but I was not quite sure I felt that way. She pulled me aside and told me about the breakup with her husband, Lori's father. She, too, inadvertently found out her mate was shacking up with someone else.

"I made the mistake of asking him if it was the first time he'd had an affair," she said. It was not. She leaned in to me and said that he'd started sleeping around right after she'd had her first child. "He seemed proud of it. I'm sorry I ever asked."

I decided right there and then I didn't really want to know if Trudy was the first time Andrew strayed. Like Andrew said about therapy, what's the point? (At this point.)

I hugged Lori and her mother goodbye and wished the rest of the family Merry Christmas.

On the drive through the small towns along the river, I peered in the windows of the restaurants. They were all filled with families enjoying a holiday meal. I was touched by the sight of these people smiling and laughing yet saddened that I was without any family on this holiday. Andrew really was my family. *Oh well*, I sighed. *Oh, fucking well.*

I got to my destination and parked across the street from the house—a charming three-level structure. The river view was spectacular, and the owner had decorated it beautifully.

My stay was short, however, since the cigarette smoke proved more than a little irritating, and I was starting to feel emotionally drained. I said goodbye to the party goers and wished them a Merry Christmas.

As I pulled up into my driveway, I saw that the party at Lori's was still going on. My energy suddenly returned, and I invited myself inside. Tonight, these people were my surrogate family. I felt welcomed and happy.

DECEMBER 25

WE WISH YOU A MERRY

At 5:00 PM on the dot, Lena and her boyfriend, Lawrence, arrived at the house. They must have split up at least a dozen times since they met nine years ago. But somehow, they'd survived the chaos. This time, Lena told me a few weeks ago, she was going to stick it out. They were adults—committed adults, and committed adults made an effort to work things out.

We went into the kitchen, and I bemoaned the fact that my husband always monitored the turkey as it cooked in the oven, and I was not so sure I knew what I was doing. I also mentioned that I had no idea when the twenty-four-pound bird would be done.

"Fifteen minutes per pound," Lawrence said, making me wonder why it was that guys seemed to know more about cooking turkeys than women. Lawrence did the math and said it should be done within forty-five minutes or so. I mentioned that I had set the oven to "convection roast," thinking that that was a smart move since I was "roasting" a turkey. Lawrence gave me a concerned look.

"What's wrong?"

"That makes it cook faster," he said.

"Oh shit." I immediately envisioned disaster—an overcooked, shrunken turkey the size of a pigeon. But we got the bird out just in the nick of time, so the three of us poured wine and toasted to good times ahead and an edible turkey.

Lena put her glass down and wrapped her arms around me. "I am so sad for you," she said. She began to cry, which of course got me going, but thankfully, we were distracted by the doorbell. Our fourth guest and mutual friend, Sarah, had arrived.

The night was good. We ate, we drank, and we were merry. And I was glad to have my friends around my table. Our conversations were cheerful, light-hearted—until the subject rolled around to Andrew. Lena finally got me to admit that my husband and I were mismatched physically, as she knew how I had often struggled with our sex life. Yet it didn't mean I did not love him and miss him.

"But, really," I said as an afterthought, "what couple is perfect?"

"Certainly not us," Lena said looking over at her squeeze. "But I think it's important to have that initial physical connection."

"So, what do you think you're going to do going forward?" Sarah asked.

"I don't know. Everything is so up in the air," I said. "But in the meantime, maybe I'll go have some hot sex and get myself the hell out of this funk."

DECEMBER 26

ALWAYS ON MY MIND

I decided to contact my young friend, breaking my vow to let him make the next move. But before I could say "Yehowah/Mike/Steve," I got a text.

YEHOWAH: *So what's up? When are we gonna meet?*

ME: *End of week. You know this is nuts, right?*

YEHOWAH: *It's nuts but who cares.*

ME: *U only live once (tho not totally sure that's true). I thk I knew u in a past life. I hope I was good to u:)*

YEHOWAH: *LOL. I will rent a hotel room.*

ME: *U cn come up here if you want. Don't want to rent a room.*

YEHOWAH: *Tonight?*

ME: *You need to listen more carefully, cwazy wabbit. End of week. Friday late night, perhaps, since I will hv guests.*

YEHOWAH: *I understood, but what's wrong with late tonight?*

ME: *My husband. That's what's wrong with tonight.*

(And the lies just kept on coming.)

YEHOWAH: *LOL. Ok. Will be in touch. Enjoy the week.*

I hoped I would enjoy "the ride" when the time came. Yehowah, I thought, somewhat amused, would make a good name for a motor bike.

DECEMBER 27

WISHFUL THINKING

Before I even mentioned what was happening with my twenty-five-year-old suitor, my friend Adele said that now was not the time for me to get together with anyone who just wanted sex.

"It's important to be honored and respected," she said.

I also agreed with her that it was very difficult for most women to have sex and not get emotionally attached. After we hung up, I promised myself to work on sustaining a certain level of optimism; it was, after all, better for your health.

But I still could not get over the fact that my husband had simply stopped communicating with me. It started a few days before Christmas. Maybe he was feeling badly. Maybe he was feeling blue. Maybe like me he was remembering all the wonderful and good things we had together. Maybe he was thinking of how we used to shop for Christmas trees, and I'd get all sad for the ones that were not going to get taken home. Maybe he was miserable. Maybe I was deluding myself that he was miserable. Maybe he was having the time of his life. "Huh?" I heard a noise, a clunk, and discerned it was not the head of the bath brush that often flopped off and hit the shower floor. But I couldn't quite figure it out, until I went into the closet to put a gift away that did not get gifted (along with all my other Christmas-reserve presents that have sat in bags for years) and recognized the source. One of Andrew's sneakers had dropped out of the shoe caddy, and the saying "the other shoe has dropped" came to mind. Something told me that perhaps Trudy was finally revealing her true colors.

THE JOKER IN THE BOX

Yehowah/Mike/Steve was supposed to contact me this morning. When he didn't, I felt a surge of relief, and then disappointment, my ambivalence once again rearing its head. Maybe he had found someone else. The idea of going through with this, sleeping with him, was traumatizing me, as I was old enough to be his mother, maybe even his grandmother. But to further exacerbate my insecurities about our age difference, I had a hair disaster in my attempts to look younger. When I mixed the color-blend formula with the bleaching component, as per instructions, I noticed the solution looked unusually blue. But figuring it was just the typical chemical reaction for this shade, I slopped it on, and it ended up stripping my hair of all its color. I now essentially had hair devoid of any hint of blond whatsoever—make that any hint of color, period. Add that to the wrinkles that had shown up on my knees, and I really wanted to leap off the bridge. And, once again, I implored, *Please, God, please, don't let him call!*, which was a far cry from what I used to say when I'd meet a guy I was attracted to in my younger years. (*Please, please! Make him call! I'll do anything. I'll help old ladies across the street and feed the homeless! I'll help orphaned children and abandoned animals if he calls! I promise!*)

The phone rang, momentarily jarring me from my thoughts. It was my sister. After we chatted a bit, she told me that now, more than ever, I needed to be my own best friend. But fuck that noise, I said. I just wanted some fucking company. And I wanted my damn husband to come home. And to further exacerbate my emptiness, tomorrow was not only New Year's Eve, it was the night Andrew and I got married. He must be thinking about it as well, I thought. But if he was, he wasn't saying. My husband still only sent me business-related emails, mostly about managing our expenses, since we now pay out more on a monthly basis due to his weekly, and costly, runs to Home Depot in attempts to avoid freezing his silly Asperger's ass off up in VT.

As I got up from my computer, I heard my cell phone ping with an incoming text. It was (surprise!) Yehowah/Mike/Steve, who I now alternately called Rabbit.

YEHOWAH: *When is your husband leaving?*

ME: *Not until tomorrow morning, Rabbit.*

(My husband was hundreds of miles away.)

ME: *It's a bit challenging at the moment. Emotional.*

YEHOWAH: *Why?*

ME: *Our anniversary is New Year's Eve (THAT holiday will never be the same—ha ha) Need some happy talk and a bottle of wine.*

YEHOWAH: *Okay. So I will be in touch.*

ME: *Sounds good. Have a great NYE. This next year promises to be spectacular.*

HE: *;)*

I kept blowing him off but couldn't help myself. It did briefly cross my mind that perhaps I could have sex with him with my clothes on. Instead of doing it through a hole in the sheet, we could do it with me fully clothed. Maybe I could cut a hole in my pants. I doubted, however, he'd think that was such a great idea.

Early evening, I drove across the river to meet a friend at a small, local wine bar.

"So, what's going on with your young guy?" she asked.

I gave her the latest on Yehowah/Mike/Steve.

My friend smiled and told me that right after she'd moved into her condo, her neighbor, a twenty-six-year-old stud, came to her door bearing a plate of chicken and fruit. They ended up having a hot and steamy eleven-month affair. She was fifty-two at the time.

"Some of the best sex I've ever had," she said, convincingly.

"Those are magic words," I said to my friend.

After I'd pretty much decided (98.9%) that I was going to sleep with Rabbit, it occurred to me: I hadn't thought about Pran since he left for Malaysia. Not once.

DECEMBER 31

NO COAT—NO "HAPPY ANNIVERSARY"

A woman wandered into Barnes and Nobles talking on a cell phone. "You starve, you freeze, your teeth hurt, and you're homeless," she said. "But I refuse to go to a Medicaid dentist. You're supposed to enjoy the holidays, not want to kill yourself. I can't stand going to the soup kitchens with all those crack heads. The people stink. They bring in bugs. I didn't get a coat this year, either. I had to sew mine back together."

She walked toward my table and stood within a few feet of me, still talking. I started to itch as I imagined kamikaze bedbugs in full attack mode, ready to launch onto my sweater, and moved to another spot. But I really did feel sorry for the woman and had to remind myself how fortunate I was to have a roof over my head and some money. I was also momentarily thankful that my challenges were what they were. At least I didn't stink, and my teeth were in good shape. Yet I had to wonder how she was able to pay for her phone bills.

At around seven o'clock, I went up the road to Ted and Eva's 19th century country home for New Year's Eve, determined that I would have a good time—regardless. I had hoped I would hear something from my husband, but of course I got no message or phone call.

The group was an interesting mix of professionals, including a particularly colorful man who just turned eighty and was still designing interiors for high end homes. When we sat down to eat, we discussed relationships, and we talked about our experiences growing up and how our parents affected us well into our adult years. After, it was on to lighter fare, which included a few off-color jokes, and laughter pierced the air.

Having overstuffed myself on dessert, I said my goodbyes and drove off down the road feeling even more progress had been made. In other words, I didn't weep (1) when they dumped the poor, very-alive black lobsters into the boiling water—which I could not bear to watch; (2) when they served the now-red lobsters with the dead black eyes—which I could not bear to eat; (3) after I had too much wine; (4) when it turned midnight and I thought about the fact that Andrew and I were now officially married exactly fourteen years; and (5) when I came home to a dark, cold, empty house.

Perhaps, as I said in a text to my twenty-five-year-old friend, this next year would be spectacular. (But I was not going to hold my breath.)

JANUARY 1

JUST "DO IT" IN THE NEW YEAR

Mid-afternoon at Main Street Café, an old friend and openly gay man came over and sat with me. In that he was well-versed in the fine art of sleeping around, I asked him if I should go ahead and have sex with this twenty-five-year old. Just to get another opinion.

"Why not?" he said. "As long as you go into it with your eyes open."

My eyes were wide open—from sheer terror. "I think I'd be more comfortable with a guy who had skin that needed a little ironing."

Yehowah/Mike/Steve ended up texting me around 5:00 PM. I had told him that today was no good. He wanted to know about tomorrow, and I decided screw it, I'd screw him for sure; get it out of my system, out of his system. For him, it was just about getting laid. For me, I didn't know what it was about. I certainly didn't need to do this to feel attractive—or whole.

ME: *Okay, Rabbit. Tomorrow, but how late and where?*

He said he'd come up to my house. I gave him the address and immediately had a panic attack, so I texted my Paris friend, Angie, on Skype.

ME: *I'm totally traumatized about Yehowah/Mike/Steve.*

ANGIE: *Guess what? Yehowah has already seen you! He knows what you look like!*

ME: *Not without clothes.*

ANGIE: *What is wrong with us women??? Men don't have that problem.*

ME: *Next life I'm coming back as a football player. A famous, hot-looking one.*

ANGIE: *Just do it!*

I later met my friend Amy at the sushi bar for a light dinner. After we talked about men, as usual, she tried to convince me to go to this steam room in one of the neighboring towns. I told her I was not exposing my body to a bunch of people I didn't know and wondered if I was somehow regressing. I used to feel so free around Andrew.

"I like your outfit," Andy would say when I'd run around naked. I always thought it was a goofy comment, but right before the split I started to appreciate it. (Go figure.) I guess I'd always had an issue with timing. Wrong place, wrong time, and now, apparently, wrong husband. I now wanted to work on "right, right, right" and be able to say, this is where I belong, and this is who I belong with. And I so desperately wanted to pray to God to lend a hand in the journey, but I was afraid my salary would be lowered for the third time—or my work would completely dry up.

Amy brought up the spa again. "You'd really like it. No one will care what you look like."

Finally, after I mentioned this horrendous rash I got from a steam room in a gym I used to go to, my friend stopped pressing the issue.

Before we left, I asked (more liked begged) Amy, who was not yet forty, to come over tomorrow night and sleep with Yehowah/Mike/Steve, since I was sure he'd be perfectly happy to accept a substitute who was closer to his own age. And she was attractive.

"I'll give you twenty bucks," I told her, joking. Part of me, however, wished she'd take me up on my offer. (She wouldn't, even though she was close to being broke.)

JANUARY 2

DOWN THE OTHER RABBIT HOLE

After picking up a bottle of Pepto Bismol, I went downtown to meet Sarah at Flannagan's for Wing Night. My stomach was churning with anticipation, even though I had not yet heard from Yehowah/Mike/Steve.

At 9:48 PM, after dinner and a couple of glasses of wine, I received a text.

YEHOWAH: *I'm on the way!!!!*

"Oh my God," I said to Sarah, reaching into my bag for the bottle of the soothing pink-colored liquid.

My friend laughed and commented that I was my young Jewish friend's prize (forbidden) ham.

"Oy," I said and shot Rabbit a text.

ME: *Thnx for the effing warning. I am out and about. How far away r u?*

YEHOWAH: *60 minutes. I could delay if you'd like.*

I thought about telling him to go home (or drive off the Brooklyn Bridge). Instead, I told him to let me know when he got close.

At 11:22 PM, I still had not heard from him and texted him.

ME: *It's getting late. Almost past my bedtime.*

YEHOWAH: *Had some traffic. I'll be there in two minutes.*

Sarah saw the terror in my face.

"I don't know if I'm going to survive this," I said.

"Did he really drive all the way from Brooklyn just to get laid?"

"Yeah. He must be pretty desperate."

My cell plinked again with an incoming text.

YEHOWAH: *I'm on your road.*

ME: *I'll be there in about 15 mins. U cn take a nap in the meantime. Ha.*

Sarah and I were now at the bar, and I had begun fortifying myself with coffee that was laced with a shot of vodka.

"I might as well get this over with," I said to my friend and asked for a to-go cup for my drink.

Sarah and I hugged each other goodnight, and I promised to call later to let her know that everything was okay and that Yehowah/ Mike/Steve had not been intent on playing out some weird Oedipal scene. I drove fast, since I didn't want to be rude and keep Rabbit waiting (why?) and spotted what I intuitively knew was his car in the small dirt parking lot about an eighth of a mile from my house. I flashed my lights a couple of times, and he followed me down the road and up into my driveway.

After pulling my SUV into the garage, I punched in the code to shut the door and cordially greeted my friend. "Hi," I said, struck by how disturbingly young Rabbit looked tonight. He was also shorter than I remembered. I was about to say "Ready?" but realized how utterly ludicrous that would have sounded, aside from the fact that it was probably an appropriate question. We walked down the drive-way in semi-awkward silence and up the steps to the front door.

"How was the drive?" I said as I escorted Yehowah/Mike/Steve inside, hoping beyond hope that the Pepto Bismol would kick in soon.

"Long," he said.

"Hope the drive will be worth it," I muttered under my breath as we settled in at the island table in the kitchen. "So how is everything?"

Rabbit told me he was doing okay and once again mentioned his girlfriend and the ongoing issues and his reluctance to get involved. "Did you have some drinks?" he asked me.

Being the consummate control freak, I knew I wasn't acting drunk, so I figured he could probably smell it on my breath.

"Yup. I was at a jam session at a bar," I said. "Do you want some wine?"

Rabbit declined, which told me that he was planning on going home afterwards as he didn't drink and drive. I did get him a glass of water, however, and offered him a sip of my coffee concoction. He took it, having no clue it contained vodka. I also fought off the temptation to abandon all restraint and get rip-roaring drunk, fig-uring that if this resulted in some truly amazing sex, I wanted to remember it—relive every single, tantalizing moment. But some-thing told me it wasn't going to go that way, and I was struck by an odd feeling that Rabbit might possibly be a virgin.

When I stood up to get some water, Yehowah/Mike/Steve pulled me to him, and we began to kiss. It was not as tender as the last two times; the connection now felt different—less intense, less impassioned. Perhaps it was me. Or perhaps it was because I knew that he had come here for one reason and one reason only. And that didn't feel so great. (But neither did my stomach.)

We went upstairs, and I ushered him into the guest bedroom.

"I'm going to brush my teeth and you should too," I said to my friend.

"Oh." He looked momentarily puzzled.

"Fourteen years of marriage and some habits are deeply ingrained. You know, like brushing your toothies before bedtime," I said, sounding like a flaming idiot and flashing back on my husband's proclivities for tacking on IEs to words. I also had no clue why I would even ask this of him. It's not like he had bad breath.

Further questioning my good sense, or lack thereof, I went into the master bath and retrieved a complimentary packet I'd gotten from my dentist that contained a toothbrush and a mini tube of toothpaste and gave it to Yehowah/Mike/Steve. He obediently took off to the guest bathroom.

"Oh, for God's sakes, no," I grumbled as I felt a loud rumbling deep within my intestinal tract.

After grabbing a bunch of baby wipes that I kept by my toilet, I hightailed it to the downstairs bathroom where I had a raging attack of diarrhea. It took me a few minutes to clean up.

"Oh hell, oh shit, oh damn," I muttered, wishing I'd grabbed more baby wipes.

"Where are you?" my impatient friend called out from upstairs.

I flushed the toilet, hiked up my pants, and stepped out into the hallway. "Be right there," I yelled. I began to panic and considered leaving altogether, maybe going back to Flanagan's, but remembered that Rabbit's car was blocking my side of the garage. "Fuck." I decided to forge ahead and get this over with and dashed up the stairs.

My friend stood at the bedroom door, fully clothed, and led me inside. As I reached over to turn off the lights so I could hide behind the darkness, Rabbit pulled me into him before I could hit the switch. We immediately began kissing and rolled onto the bed. I flashed on the words of my dermatologist who injected me with RADIESSE©

every six months or so to fill in my facial lines: "Don't bend over and look at yourself in a mirror. You'll look like a deflated old tire." Seeing that Yehowah/Mike/Steve was neither farsighted nor wearing a blindfold, I flopped over on my back, encouraging my twenty-five-year-old paramour to get on top. He assumed position and straddled me like he was riding a horse.

And, just like the time in Rabbit's minivan, the yarmulke was the first thing to get tossed aside. But now, instead of flinging it into the air like a Frisbee, Yehowah/Mike/Steve dropped it on the bed. Next, he focused on my boots.

"Gotta get rid of those. Bad luck to do it with your shoes on. Seven years of lousy sex," I said, noting that this was probably not the best time to be making lame jokes.

Rabbit ignored my comment, probably figuring that any sex is better than no sex at all. He quickly relieved me of my ruched top, stretchy black jeans, and undies and threw them over his shoulder; my bra was the last thing to go and gave him a bit of a challenge, which I found amusing. Still straddling me, he took off his coat and tasseled undergarment. But, for whatever reason, Yehowah/Mike/Steve left his medium-blue underpants on.

I scanned his hairless body. His skin was smooth and youthful, his belly round, portending a middle-age paunch, but his arms were strong, which I liked.

We kissed again, and I fluidly wrapped my legs around him. He slid lower, put his mouth on my breast and within a few seconds began the trek downward, kissing my belly.

Momentarily freaking that in my haste I didn't do the greatest job with the baby wipes and possibly stunk to high heaven, I grabbed Rabbit by the hair and dragged him back up, which seemed to confuse him. We kissed again, and I reached down and felt him over his underpants; his penis was hard to the touch. It was also small; its head felt strangely triangular, reminding me of the mushrooms that grew in our yard after heavy rains. He pulled his member out through the leg hole, perhaps thinking that this was a practice round for what lay up ahead for him: sex through a hole in the sheet.

"Condom," I muttered.

Yehowah/Mike/Steve stopped, blinked a couple of times, and said he'd only use one if he had to worry about getting a woman pregnant. Now I really felt old, since he obviously thought that impregnating me was far from the realm of possibility.

(It was. Totally!)

"Not a good idea to not use protection since you don't know where people have been." Including my husband, I thought to myself.

Rabbit creased his brow and shrugged. He clearly didn't seem to care, and I decided I didn't either. He touched me between my legs, but I knew I was dry as a bone, most likely due to my complete and total inability to relax.

Time began to accelerate. Yehowah/Mike/Steve locked his lips on my mouth and grabbed me around my middle, emitting a few little grunts here and there. He began panting, rubbing his body against mine, and all I could think of was that line from *The Three Little Pigs* nursery rhyme: "I'll huff and I'll puff 'til I blow your house down."

Within thirty seconds, and without entering me, he came, his warm, sticky wetness dribbling onto my thigh. Is this what he was trying to tell me when he said he had control issues? Whatever it was, it didn't matter. I didn't feel much of anything—emotionally, physically, or otherwise. So, fait accompli. We had done the deed, or at least a variation thereof.

Yehowah/Mike/Steve rolled to his side and sat up on the bed. "Interesting," he said, which was exactly how he'd described my house when he first arrived.

As my friend began to dress, I could feel him shutting down, and I didn't know if he was feeling embarrassed or disappointed. After adjusting his yarmulke, he looked at his cell and said he had to go. At one o'clock in the morning, he was going to drive all the way back to Brooklyn.

I leapt off the bed, went and grabbed a robe from my room, and led him back downstairs.

"Drive carefully," I said, opening the front door. "There are lunatics out there." There are lunatics in here as well, I thought.

Rabbit's face was expressionless; he nodded and scurried down the front steps.

I closed the door behind him, went upstairs, and noticed that he had left the toilet seat up in the guest bathroom. I briefly wondered if that was consciously motivated—an act of disrespect—but realized that he hadn't yet been trained by a woman and didn't really know any better. I supposed there were a lot of things he didn't fully grasp or understand, but that probably applied to me as well. I mean, what was I thinking would happen? That he would spend the night and we'd have a pajama party and talk well into the wee hours of the morning, discussing love, religion, politics, sex?

After knocking back the rest of the coffee drink, I took a sleeping pill and called Sarah to let her know I was still alive. I also told her I was certain I'd never see my young friend again.

JANUARY 3

BACK FROM THE RABBIT HOLE—BUT NOT INTO THE LIGHT

I woke up at six-thirty in the morning and felt the sadness start to spread throughout me like a putrid infestation. It wasn't that I particularly cared about what happened last night—I felt I had to see it through—it was just that I was reminded of what I really wanted in my life, and it was not just sex. I wanted companionship. I wanted friendship. I wanted to share my daily life with someone I loved and cared for.

The loneliness was now making me bitchy, and I began to understand why some people were inordinately irascible. They were either in extreme physical or emotional pain. I got it. And it was rotten.

My irritation came out when I took my cat to the vet. After a brief checkup and a blood test for hyperthyroidism to determine if that was the reason behind her weight loss, I got hit with a bill for over $250. I told the receptionist in a less-than-polite tone that it was ridiculous how much they charged and forced myself to bite my tongue to keep from announcing to the entire waiting room full of people and animals that I would never come back here again.

"Fucking bullshit," I said to my cat as I got into my car, cradling her in my arms. "It's all fucking bullshit."

As I plopped Mamie on the front seat, I was hit by a surge of guilt and felt badly that I was not pleasant to the receptionist. I considered going back to apologize, but assumed she was probably used to dealing with disgruntled pet owners, as the clinic had a reputation of being a bit of a rip off. I also figured that it was probably not necessary since karma would likely kick back.

And it did, after I dropped Mamie off at the house and went to Best Buy at the mall to see if we had a warranty on our DVD player that was giving me problems. The sales guy was cold and not very accommodating and said he'd help me after he took care of this other customer, a short, scrawny man with a hyperactive child. The Best Buy employee transacted the sale, chatted up the customer—for a ridiculously protracted period of time—and, without saying a word to me, went off to help the man to his car with his purchases.

I waited for another fifteen minutes, periodically checking my cell phone, hoping to see a text from Rabbit, but there was nothing. Ten minutes later I was still standing there, staring at one of the flat screen TVs that was airing some dumb reality show, doing my best to remain patient. But it seemed the salesperson had decided to either take a lunch break or had quit his job on the spur of the moment.

This, I thought, was my karma kickback. What goes around comes around and so on and so forth. However, I did make an effort to reach out to a little boy who was crying because he couldn't find his father, figuring that it would somehow karmically offset my earlier behavior. I also made a vow that no matter how dreadful I felt, I would be nice to everyone I came across going forward.

I took off to Barnes and Noble to catch up on some reading and drank too many Chai lattes, which, along with the overdose of Pepto Bismol, wreaked havoc on my digestive system. Within the hour, I got a text message from Courtney, Andy's daughter, and it warmed my heart:

COURTNEY: *Love you, thinking about you, and hope things are going okay! Thanks for being a wonderful mentor for me over the years! You are amazing and deserve only the BEST!*

(I guess she felt her father did not qualify as "the best.")

I stayed at the mall for several hours since I could not bear the thought of going home. For some reason, I had begun to loathe the house, a house I was once so proud of—a house that used to be so full of joy. I used to feel secure there, and I felt whole. Not anymore.

After I'd shut down my computer and packed up, I left B & N and headed down the escalator. As I was about to make a beeline for the parking lot, I impulsively made a U-turn and went into Bed, Bath & Beyond to buy some candles—thinking they might help bring some warmth into the house, figuratively speaking of course.

I was halfway to the candle section when I ran into Willy, a man who might briefly be described as a pot-smoking, streetwise, spiritual seeker; eccentric ex-actor; insightful, sensitive liberal; highly educated Jewish boy from the Bronx. He was intense and passionate in his search for understanding life.

"So, what's the good news?" I asked, referring to a message he'd posted on Facebook the other day.

"I might finally have a job," he said. "And I really have to say that this good fortune has to do with the spiritual work I've been doing over the past five years." Willy tried to talk me into smoking pot, which he said was very different today and was tailor-made to give you the high you desired. (Want to feel smarter? Want to feel more physically adept? Want to relax and get laid? Want to just get laid? Light up a joint!)

He also talked about the nature of personal reality and our challenges as emotional beings. "It all starts up here," he said, pointing to his head.

Willy said he felt it was all about controlling your reactions to the events around you: Someone cuts you off on the highway, you can hold onto that anger for the next hour, triggering a massive release of cortisol, the stress hormone, through your bloodstream, which over the long-run can prove damaging to the body. Or you can choose to let it go. (You could also smoke some weed.)

"You know," Willy remarked, "the simple act of smiling can release a flood of endorphins into the brain." (As can pain, I thought, reflecting on my BDSM days).

An hour went by quickly as the words flew between us, and I ended up feeling uplifted. He also reminded me that people, like my husband, were all doing "the best they could."

I nodded. "I forgave my husband almost immediately."

"That's good," Willy said. "Resentment and bitterness is like wishing the other person dead and swallowing the poison yourself."

"Well said." I also realized that I needed to find a way to forgive myself for what I did.

We made a promise to keep in touch and, as I walked to the car, I silently made a vow that when I got home, no matter how bleak it felt to be in the house, I would smile. I silently thanked Willy for that—and realized that this man was simply another angel put in my path—albeit a pot-smoking, white-haired, balding angel with probably no more than twenty bucks in his pocket.

PART IV—THE CLIMB OUT OF THE ABYSS

THAT BASTARD PLANET SATURN

Email check: not a word from my husband (since what was now last year), not even in response to my reports on the bills I'd paid and the increase in New York state property taxes. Trolling around the net, I saw on weather.com that the temperature up in Vermont had dropped into the negative numbers in the past few days. So, I shot Andrew an email:

ME: *Please just let me know you are okay. I worry about those extreme low temps up in VT. People can freeze to death. You get very sleepy and then go into hypothermic shock. And we ain't in our twenties anymore, either.*

He finally responded.

ANDREW: *Not cozy but doing fine. Periodically I get a pipe that freezes up, but I always get it going again. The wood stove is definitely a life-saver. I'm doing most of my cooking and water heating on it as well. No question this is roughing it, but I'm up to it.*

And that was it. That was all he wrote. No *How are you doing?* or *I hope your holidays were okay*. Maybe he really was lacking that sensitivity chip a friend of mine complained was missing in the men she met. Who knows? I just wished I could find some source of comfort and had some answers. So once again, I did what many of us women do during times like these, I checked my horoscope. Ironically, or maybe not ironically at all, it rang true, but did not exactly elicit levity:

By now you have been directly touched by the vigorous challenges of Saturn. Do you find that you are busy reinventing yourself by learning new skills and easing into a new life role?

(I couldn't exactly call it "easing.")

If so, you have this taskmaster planet to thank, as it teaches us that we are capable of much more than we assume. While we sometimes do not find Saturn's methods to be easy, we also learn that the things we work hardest to achieve are ultimately the ones of which we are proudest.

Saturn won't leave Libra until October but after he does depart, you will emerge as a new person: tougher, sharper, and more able to take on all that life throws your way.

(Fine. I was all for emerging as a new person. But October? Such a long way away.)

I surfed for more information on this bastard planet and found additional information that pertained to my husband who was in his "Saturn return" phase, which happens only two or three times during a person's lifetime, depending on their longevity:

A large percentage of marriages crumble when one of the partners is going through this phase. However, not all marriages fall apart, and some grow stronger when they make it through this maturation phase together.

Time, I supposed, would tell. And if I had to move on, then so be it. And if we were meant to be together, we would find our way back to each other.

In the meantime, I would remember to smile—long and hard—until it hurt.

JANUARY 5

SWEAT, XANAX, AND WATER

In the middle of the night I woke up sweating. Unable to go back to sleep, I broke my pledge and popped a Xanax. But I needed some water, so I headed downstairs. Rabbit's glass still sat on the counter as I hadn't had the inclination to remove it. Perhaps because it was a reminder that these types of encounters were ephemeral, that all of life was ephemeral, and we cannot hold onto anything or anyone forever. Or maybe I wanted proof that it really did happen, since a part of me could not believe that it did, that I actually went through with it. And I wondered how long I would leave the glass there. I also realized I was being silly and put it in the dishwasher.

At 10:00 AM, after dragging myself out of bed, I opened up my email. There was another "wink" (which I thought was the stupidest thing in the world) from some match.com subscriber and a note from another suitor who was pleasant looking and sounded wise and kind. I decided to write him back.

ME: *Hi Sam, thanks for the "thorough" missive. I always feel if someone reaches out, the polite thing to do is to respond. In truth, I am currently dating someone—this happened rather recently. An old college friend. Not sure where things are going. Also, match.com put me off a bit, since I came across a few people who were rather unbalanced. Alas... I wish you well and much luck in finding exactly what you are looking for.*

Apparently, he'd had similar experiences.

SAM: *Unbalanced, deceptive, manipulative, and delusional are among the choices that describe many of the people on the site. If your new relationship does NOT work out, give me a shout.*

More queries came in from match.com throughout the next couple of hours. One guy's moniker was LovePole, which pretty much said it all. Another guy, who seemed fairly interesting, was allergic to cats. And finally there was Bruce, who had posted a picture of himself hovering over his wheelchair-bound mother at a New Year's Eve party. They looked like long-lost lovers. (Oy.)

After viewing one more potential online "match," or rather, "mismatch," I decided I'd had enough and deleted myself, my profile from the site.

Toward the end of the day, I got an IM from my former dom, Carl. He wanted to know how I was doing and told me that he missed our emails and texts.

ME: *Hanging in. Focusing on creative stuff. How are things with you?*

CARL: *Work is crazy but I'm having fun. Seeing two playmates this week.*

ME: *Sounds like you are keeping busy and are well sated.*

CARL: *Do you think about it? Spanking? Does the thought of it get you revved at all?*

ME: *Not in the least.*

JANUARY 6

ANOTHER SUNSET AND A NICE LITTLE BOW

On the train ride in to NYC, I bore witness to yet another spectacular sunset—the kind that should be photographed, framed, and displayed in a museum. But this time I did not cry. Perhaps I really was getting stronger.

Tonight, it was dinner with my former general manager for a show I did in the city. We caught each other up on our lives, and my friend remarked on her struggles with relationships, with finding someone who could commit.

"Apparently, that's my issue, too," I said, half-jokingly.

I had to question, once again, if we did not subconsciously create certain experiences in our lives because we needed to grow in ways that otherwise would not have been possible. "So, did I 'cause' this breakup because I needed to take a different path? And because Andrew needed to figure out who he was?" I asked. "Are we the ultimate dream weavers? Or, as one numerologist says, is it all in the numbers? Or is it all in the stars?"

"Maybe it's a combination of everything. Karma, numbers, belief systems," my friend said.

The questions were endless, like the universe itself. And that's why it was a relief to focus on more mundane matters. Like sex. This time, however, my dinner mate did most of the talking.

When I got home, I fired up my computer and found an email from Pran, who was still in Malaysia. It was a response to a note I'd sent earlier since I felt bad I had not reached out to him in a while. He said he was doing well, and I wanted to ask if he had found his "Indian princess," but didn't. And like Carl said to me yesterday, I told him that I missed our conversations.

Impulsively, I took out my cell phone and sent a text to my twenty-five-year-old friend:

ME: *Hey Rabbit, please know that even tho it was odd, very surreal, I wish u only joy in life and a fun ride along the way:) I know u will figure out/ get what u need.*

I knew he would never respond, but I wanted to tie it up with a nice little bow. I liked the kid. I really did.

SAMMY THE ORCHID

Subscribing meaning to events around me was more common than not nowadays, but this time what happened was a far cry from maggots climbing up the walls. Today, it was Sammy the orchid, which was named after Sammy the cat.

Sam belonged to Andrew, but I bonded so deeply with the animal Andy used to tease me and say I loved the cat more than him.

When the door began to close at the end of Sam's life, due to his battle with cancer, my husband and I made the decision to keep him at home, administering morphine we'd gotten from the vet to ensure he was pain-free.

Within a week, we intuitively sensed that Sammy was getting ready to say goodbye. We also knew that animals, when they passed, preferred to do it on their own.

The day was sunny and cool and after we swathed Sammy in blankets, Andrew and I headed out to Home Depot to do some errands, both of us in a somber mood. My husband went off to find some screws, and I wandered over to the garden section displaying ceramic pots. Within a few minutes, Andrew came up behind me, carrying a tiny orchid in his hand, which was completely out of character for him. He was not a plant person. But there he was, holding this sweet, little potted plant with dark-green, variegated leaves in the palm of his hand, and we both said at the same time, "Let's name it Sammy."

Now I don't know if it happened at that exact moment, but it would not have surprised me. We left the store after we paid for our purchases and drove home, which took the usual five minutes. When we got upstairs, we saw that Sammy had gone under Andrew's desk to make his transition.

We gently wrapped his now lifeless body in a blanket and took him to the animal clinic for cremation, the two of us weeping like lost children.

About a month ago, I put the orchid in Andrew's old office beneath one of the windows with a southern exposure. Last week, I spotted some interesting new growth, and today it was confirmed: Sammy, who had grown from a two-leaf into a multi-stemmed plant, was about to blossom for the first time in six years. And this, I knew, had to be a good sign.

JANUARY 9

MORE FLASHES, MORE MEMORIES

After I reluctantly climbed out of bed at 10:00 AM, I emailed Andrew about our checking account and some expenses he'd paid out that his company was supposed to reimburse. After we got that settled, he shot me an email.

ANDREW: *What do I punch in to download Netflix up here? Winter nights are long and boring. What's the account and password?*

Now, if I'd had a brain in my head, I would have interpreted that as meaning he was not with Chicken Lady anymore.

I counted on my hands the number of months left in our trial separation: two. And I made a promise to do some living, try and have some fun, before the clock ran out—because in truth, I didn't know what else to do. And that's why I booked a flight to LA in February to see friends from my former life on the west coast. I felt strangely empowered and maybe just a little bit hopeful.

Another thing I'd started noticing—especially since my emotional landscape had begun to shift from the negative (depths of hell) back toward the oh-yeah-life-is-really-okay groove: Anytime I turned on the radio, I was not besieged by wrist-slitting love songs. Now it seemed to be all upbeat toe tappers. And it was the same station I'd been playing all along. So again, I had to wonder, does the external world reflect our internal life? Maybe more than we know.

JANUARY 10

HOPE AND HORROR

When I got to Barnes and Noble, I went off to the bathroom and impulsively pulled up my sweater sleeve and looked at my arms. Bad idea since fluorescent lighting makes everything ten times worse. I shook my one arm, observing, in abject terror, the flab that waggled to and fro.

As I walked back to my table, I made a promise to myself to stop looking in the mirror so much. But it soon became clear that age was a topic of import today.

"Clint Eastwood is eighty-one years old," said an elderly woman at the table next to me, who was probably around the same age as the actor. "He looks good."

"Whaaat?" said her husband, who had very hairy ears and an

extremely large nose.

"I said—"

"Don't yell at me!" he said.

"What's the matter with you?" the woman said, slapping him on the hand.

"Nothing's the matter with me."

"Say that again?"

One of their cell phones rang.

"Honeybunch?" the man said. "Did you say something?"

"Why don't you answer your damn phone?'"

"Whaaaat??"

"Your phone!"

"Oh, is it ringing?"

"Yes, it's ringing. Answer it, for Crissakes!"

"You know I don't answer these things."

"Then what do you have the goddamn thing for?!"

How sad, I thought as I watched the couple continue to squabble, that Andrew and I were not together anymore; we were always so civil and kind to one another. We rarely fought, and when we did, we resolved it quickly. And suddenly, the anger bubbled up again and I wanted to kill Andy for leaving me in the way he did.

JANUARY 11

A KIND OFFER, A LOVING CAT

Andrew called about a bill, and we briefly talked about politics and the recent New Hampshire primary. I mentioned that there was a super bug going around here that laid people up with bronchitis and laryngitis. He said he'd been staying healthy and was down to one hundred eighty-four pounds and that he was in better shape than ever. My heart sank; he was obviously staying buff for a reason, and it was not because he liked to look at himself in the mirror. Nor was it for my benefit.

"Why didn't you take care of yourself when we were married?" I asked, remembering how Andrew would balance his plate on his protruding stomach when we'd eat dinner while watching a movie on TV.

"I don't know," Andy said, and that was pretty much the end of our conversation.

After I managed to fill up the day, doing everything I could to sidestep an overwhelming sense of disappointment after my conversation with Andrew, I met up with a friend I'd known for years. Greg was funny and smart, although he always seemed to have relationship issues. (Welcome to the club.) Good news, though, he had finally settled down with an old flame. Prior to that, he was with a woman who, like him, enjoyed a little S&M activity, which we had discussed a while ago. Problem was, she liked whipping him just a bit too much with the birch branches she used to procure from his backyard. The main concern, however, was the age difference—she wanted kids, and he was approaching sixty. So, he finally broke up with her.

"She went ballistic," he told me. "She called me a fucking asshole and threatened to kill me. I would never go back with her after that." (He did.)

I mentioned to Greg, who knew about my own spanking experiences, that I was very calm when Andrew told me he'd slept with Trudy. "So calm in fact that Andy said, I love you more than ever."

"Then what the hell is his problem? That doesn't make any sense. He loves you, yet…"

"Exactly. Now do you understand why I am half out of my mind? Let me qualify: completely out of my mind."

"Wow," he said, which as far as I was concerned, aptly summed up the insanity of my situation.

My friend and I decided to go to a bar/restaurant where a bunch of musicians had come to jam on open mike night. Henry, from the music store, stepped up to the microphone and began playing a slow, soulful song, while we bellied up to the bar.

"He plays from the heart," Greg said.

I agreed and whispered to my pal that if I was twenty years younger, in addition to Henry, I could fall in love with the bartender.

Greg looked over at the very cute man with the long dark hair who was in the process of drawing a beer. "Excuse me." The bartender stopped mid pour. "She wants to go home with you," my friend said pointing over at me.

"Greg, shut up!" I said and whacked him on the arm.

The bartender grinned broadly. "Okay, then, let's go," he said, but I knew he was not serious. And that was probably a good thing, since I didn't need to be traumatized like I was with Yehowah/Mike/Steve.

(I just wished my body matched my mental age as of late.)

After one rather strong black Russian, I was ready to go home, even though it was on the early side. Greg said he had to get up for work anyway, so it wasn't a big deal. He walked me to my car, which was about a mile away, and I drove him back to his.

As I got out, my friend said, very seriously and empathetically, "I'll spank you if you want."

"If only it were that simple a fix," I said, laughing, realizing that at this juncture, I honestly didn't know what I needed to patch up my emotional wounds. I felt totally lost in a sea of tears.

But thankfully, I had my cat, who I loved and adored as she did me. Mamie would also let me do whatever I needed to do to help her, even if I had to flip her upside down, put her in the sink, and wash the poop off her paws, like I did tonight when I got home.

This time, however, I inadvertently drenched her entire bottom half. But she sat patiently in my lap, her legs splayed out like long skinny branches as I blow-dried her matted fur. This, I thought, was the mark of a solid, enduring relationship—one of complete trust and unconditional love. (No wonder so many single people had pets.)

JANUARY 12

A MISSED MISSIVE

After logging on to my auxiliary work email, which I rarely checked, I noticed something from my husband that was sent back in December. I had written him about some bills and mentioned how expensive yard care was and how some of the trees still need to be tended to due to *that freakoid storm that came through around Halloween.* There were a lot of large limbs that snapped high up and some smaller trees that were damaged. He had responded with: *We can figure out a time to work on them.*

I wrote an email telling him to come down, but I didn't send it. Maybe I was not ready to see him. It would, I knew, be unbearable if I found out he was still with Trudy, in spite of what he had said about the long, boring nights. I could have asked his daughter, but decided against it, as I was still operating on a modicum of hope. And that felt better than what could turn out to be the ugly, devastating truth. (What you don't know can't hurt you.)

After forcing myself to do some laundry, I figured I'd head off to the mall. As I maneuvered down the driveway, a squirrel ran out in front of the car, and I instinctively slammed on the brakes. Another attack of nostalgia reduced me to a blubbering mass (would this ever stop?) as I thought back on Lucky, a baby squirrel that my husband and I raised in the small shower in the guest bathroom.

Andy and I had rescued Lucky several years ago when we were driving over to a local theater to audition actors for a play I had written and was directing. On the way, we spotted a car stopped in the middle of the road and saw this little gray creature darting back and forth in front of the tires in sheer panic. Andrew got out immediately and scooped up a very small baby squirrel with a very bloody nose. The woman, who was sitting frozen behind her steering wheel, thanked my husband profusely and went on her way. Andrew climbed back in the car and placed the animal in the breast pocket of his shirt. The little guy stayed put the entire evening, both during the auditions and afterwards when we went out to dinner.

Once we were back home, we created a simulated squirrel habitat comprised of a few tree branches and a sock that we attached to one of the limbs to serve as a "bed," as per instructions from the local wildlife expert. We put it in the shower stall in the guest bath on the second floor.

Over the next several weeks, when we'd come into the bathroom to change Lucky's water or replenish his food, we would let him out of the shower, and he'd either sit comfortably in our hands or crawl around on our laps and shoulders.

When it finally came time to release Lucky into the wild, Andrew set up a cage in which we put some other squirrels given to us by the wildlife guy to help them adapt to the natural world and to each other. The cage had an open door and when they were ready, when they had acclimated to this new way of life, they'd supposedly leave. Within a week or so, the cage was empty.

We thought that was the end of it, until Lucky showed up at our patio shortly after the cage had been abandoned. We were thrilled beyond belief that he remembered us and, for several years running, the squirrel would show up almost every day and sit on our laps while we fed him peanuts. Eventually, though, Lucky stopped coming by, and I found myself missing him terribly. As did Andrew.

JANUARY 13

WHO WOULD FIND ME?

After an evening at my neighbor's and an intense game of poker, I walked home at around two in the morning. I dropped my purse off upstairs (making sure I didn't lock the bedroom door) and went off to the kitchen to load up on skin-firming, anti-aging vitamins and herbs. But this time I did it a little more creatively. Instead of walking down the steps, I slipped and took the flight of stairs on my butt. Assured that no bones were broken, I picked myself up, had a little chuckle, and proceeded with business as usual. But that recurring, nagging thought crossed my mind: what if I'd really taken a serious tumble, hit my head and gone unconscious? Who would know? Who would find me? And who would take care of Mamie? And what if, what if as I was lying on the floor, oblivious to the world around me, the man of my dreams, lost and looking for love, came to my door to ask for directions? I'd never know, and opportunity would have gone out the window. But I realized that that would never happen anyway as men don't ask for directions. And then there's the likelihood he would have been be using GPS.

JANUARY 14

A WINK AND A PRAYER

Convincing myself that sometimes you have to help the Universe along, kick its ass in gear, I screwed up my courage, joined another dating site, and the messages began showing up in my inbox. But I ended up ignoring them. It might have been my tainted filtering system, but I got the feeling that most of these guys were borderline and carrying around enough baggage to fill a cargo ship. Like the one man who said, repeatedly, how even-tempered he was. Translation: prone to psychotic outbursts. I just wished I could stop obsessing over Andrew.

"If I'm not obsessing about someone, I'm miserable," Amy said later at the Japanese restaurant. Her current "obsession" was this guy who was clinically depressed and would not respond to her texts or phone calls.

"As soon as he shows interest, you're going to want to dump him," I said.

"I know."

I had a thought. "Is this why I want my husband back so desperately? Because he doesn't want me?"

When I got home, I saw that my tenant had left my mail at my doorstep and spotted a small package; another tape from Edna had arrived. I thought about waiting until tomorrow to listen to it since I was dead tired, yet I was anxious for some insight. I was also a little afraid of what she might tell me. Tossing fear aside, I dashed into the house, package in hand, and bounded upstairs.

But I had to question what I really wanted. "She'll tell me what I want," I said to my cat, who was lying on her pillow. "Spirit knows, right, Mamie?" I was pretty sure my higher self knew, too (if I could only access it.) My much more easily accessible lower self, however, needed to pee and wanted a glass of wine.

After settling on the bed, I slid the tape into the recorder and hit *play*. In short, Edna the spiritualist still saw Andrew coming back— but not anytime soon.

"I still see a period of separation," she said.

"Like how long, Edna?" I said aloud. "Ten years?" I clicked off the tape recorder. "Damn it," I muttered to my cat. "Why can't the fucker get his head on straight?" (Why can't I?)

JANUARY 16

NO ONE'S PERFECT

Carl IMd me again to check in, see how I was doing. He mentioned that he was "playing" a lot more than usual, and I asked if he thought his wife might suspect what he was doing, even though when she busted him years ago, he'd told her he would stop.

CARL: *She probably does, but in all likelihood chooses to ignore it now, since it's been two decades since she and I have been intimate. I think on some level she understands that I need the outlet. An outlet. Regardless of what it is.*

ME: *Certainly makes sense.*

CARL: *She also knows I'll always be home for dinner.*

Something to be said about that. Carl then admitted to me that his wife constantly brought up his supposed betrayal of years ago.

CARL: *"Once a cheater, always a cheater," she says. It's not always fun. There's a lot of tension at times.*

The more I talked to married people, the more I realized that what Andrew and I had was pretty good. Apparently, though, my husband felt otherwise. But, if he was so unhappy, why didn't he say something so we could have worked things through?

I looked at the time on my computer.

ME: *I have to sign off. I have to get to an appointment.*

CARL: *If there's ever anything I can do for you, please let me know. Or if there's anything you need.*

At one o'clock I arrived at my therapist's office. After settling in my usual spot, I gave her an update as I hadn't seen her since mid-December. We talked a bit about Andrew, and I told her that I sometimes felt sorry for him and felt badly that I ever thought he was less than perfect.

"We often project onto our partner our own sense of imperfection, and little things become annoying," she said. "But all couples experience that to one degree or another. And guess what? No one is perfect."

"What I'm still struggling to understand is, why I was so sexually charged up for my husband when I was into the spanking?"

Katarina asked how long after a spanking the sexual urge would kick in. I said it didn't really matter. All it would take was reading a suggestive email from Carl or Santa.

"At this stage of the game, though, if Andy and I did get back together, I'm sure that a sexy novel just might put me in the mood," I said. I paused a moment. "Maybe I needed this breakup to happen to truly fall in love with my husband. I just hope it's not too late." I thought again about what had occurred to me earlier. Maybe I wanted him because I now could not have him. Perhaps that was my particular neurosis or psychodynamic—always wanting that which was out of reach. I felt very messed up.

We talked a bit more about relationships and marriage. When our time was up, Katarina ended the session by telling me I was doing remarkably well dealing with the uncertainty; together we decided that every other week was good enough. Besides, I wanted/needed to save the money. Probably a good instinct, since I learned via an email post-therapy that the writer who I normally worked with doing my bread-and-butter editing job would not be available until March—and that meant no money coming in for me. So much for no longer being "clogged up with anxiety." And I didn't want to rely on Andrew financially any more than I had to. I was not totally sure why, but I suspected it was rooted in the guilt I harbored for my involvement in BDSM and my relationship with Carl. I realized I blamed myself for what happened. (Women in general are good at that.)

JANUARY 17

BROKEN PIPES, BROKEN KARMA

It was a bit past six o'clock when I got home. As I walked through the dining room toward the kitchen, I heard a very loud swooshing noise coming from the back of the house. And I immediately knew it was not good.

"Oh great," I said, as I looked out at the patio. Water was shooting out from a pipe in a thick, heavy torrent, and goodness only knew how much water had been wasted since I'd been gone all day and had no idea when the thing broke. I immediately visualized the reservoir nearby completely drained of water and wished, once again, I could find some humor in all this. But right now, I felt like I couldn't deal with one more damn thing and wanted to kill my husband for abandoning me in this house, which was way too big and problematic for one person who didn't know jack shit about plumbing or wiring or anything else of that nature. Yet, ire aside, I wanted to call Andrew, to lament my situation, to tell him how I felt. Instead, I called the plumber who had not paid a visit in three years. I left a message and he called back in ten minutes and was at the house within a half an hour.

"Frozen pipe," Ray said.

"Yeah, I forgot it was exposed after we took down the solarium."

"Not to worry. It's an easy fix," he said, encouragingly.

I was comforted by his words, by his responsiveness, by his kindness.

After he repaired the pipe and installed a shut-off valve, I asked how his kids were doing and he told me about his daughter who was now working security in stores.

"You have no idea how many people steal," he said.

"Wow. Not a good idea. Bad for your karma. And karma will most definitely kick back."

Ray laughed. "Yeah, I believe that too. A lot of people don't. But all you have to do is observe."

Taking from real life, he recounted this story about a guy who walked out with a costly piece of equipment from Home Depot, and a couple of weeks later had his very expensive car stolen.

So, was I working out some karmic kink with Andrew? Was he perhaps the king to my queen in some past life and I had him poisoned for some unjustified malfeasance? Were we perhaps arch enemies during the Dark Ages? Did I shoot my husband through his heart with a ballista during some bloody battle over land? Or maybe I ripped it out with my teeth (Deborah the Barbarian). Edna the spiritualist said this was our fourth lifetime together. I had to wonder if it was our last.

JANUARY 18

DOES THE ORACLE REALLY KNOW?

A wave of disappointment flooded through me when I opened up an email from Andy.

ANDREW: *Hi Deb, I think it is time that we start discussing how to end our relationship. I don't want to drag this out. I've spent a lot of time searching my heart for how I feel about you, and where I am now compared to last summer. I care about you just as I have for the past several years. I would do most anything for you, but I will not spend the rest of my days pretending that there is any strong physical bond between us. I spent years trying to find a way into the real core of your heart; a place where I could make you go crazy for me. You never did, or if you did at times, I never felt it.*

Now, months after leaving you, I feel differently. I still care for you as much as we've said for years; as a companion and for 17 years my closest friend. But keeping that would cause me to lose the only chance I will have in my lifetime to find real passion. I deserve to have that, at least once, and I intend to find and keep it for as long as I can. And with all the love I have for you, I hope you will go and find the same. I know you had it several times in your life; you richly deserve to have it now, and I want that for you just as much as I want it for myself.

Enough of all that. The short version is that we cannot have that passion between us; we never did. Now we need to go through the process of dismantling the rest of that union; doing the paperwork and dividing the things. I do not think it needs to take a long time.

Let me know when we can get on the phone and start to talk about it. The first call may be difficult, but I know we can do it, and it is time.

All the best (really),
Andrew

(I was definitely glad I had plans in NYC. I was definitely going to need a drink or three.)

ME: *I wish you would have said all this before. I told you not too long ago how deeply I had grown to love you over the years and how fortunate I felt we were. This ending would make a lot more sense if there were not so many "good" things about what we had and who we were together. (Passion ebbs and flows, and even if I had it on an intense physical level with a few others, it waned and there was nothing substantial left, like solid friendship). But you have to do what you have to do, and I would never keep you from that. Maybe I shook things up for a reason. I also saw you in a different light that time I came up to VT in September, and I thought there might be hope down the road when this all blew over. But again, I can only change myself; I cannot change how anyone else feels or thinks... There is so much more to say, but I have to run.*

JANUARY 19

CHEAPER TO KEEP HER?

My heart was black, but I forced myself to go to SoHo for my Protools makeup class with Chip, during which we talked about the changes in the music software over the past several years.

"That's fine," Chip said. "I can handle that. I just don't want any changes in my life at this stage of the game." He looked at me knowingly. "Bennie mentioned you were going through some pretty heavy-duty stuff."

I nodded. "It's been pretty hard."

Chip told me that he and his wife almost got divorced years ago, but they decided to stick it out, due to financial considerations, and it ended up working out okay. That gave me a shot of optimism—just a hair more than I had for ever fully grasping the music software program.

JANUARY 20

LOVE LETTERS SHOT THROUGH THE HEART

My business partner, Ron, Skyped me to get some feedback on a movie trailer he'd filmed. I briefly gave him my opinion but told him that my mind was elsewhere since I got that email from Andrew about his quest for passion.

"Oh, for God's sake. Not that passion shit again! It lasts a year and a half! More if you're lucky. He just doesn't get it!"

Ron said he wished to hell I would just move on. "But hey, I can't tell you who to care about and who to love," he said. "When I got back with my wife, everyone told me she was crazy. She is, but I don't care. I love her."

I told Ron that I knew I probably couldn't do anything to change my husband's mind. But I could tell Andrew how I felt, which was exactly what I did in an email. I titled it *For your reading pleasure (or not)*. It might have been a little awkward, but it was from the heart.

WHAT I KNOW TO BE TRUE AND WHAT I MISS
I do love you.

I love the life we had built together.

I have grown incredibly in these past many months apart, but I have not put a wall around my heart; you still reside there.

You have grown a lot as well in the past few years; we have helped each other to become better people. That is key to a successful union. I also grew to love you deeper as your love for yourself grew.

I immensely respect your talents as an artisan, writer, and professional.

We have similar goals; we support each other in those goals.

I respect and honor you as a person.

We share many of the same values, including great compassion for animals and the natural world.

We are wonderful companions and partners.

We are intellectual equals (okay, you kick my ass in science...)

We both love old houses; I would even be willing to rehab another house.

I now understand that spanking got me back in touch with my sexuality (and again, admittedly, it was not the best approach), but it ignited something inside me, and that made me want you, which tells me that desire for you is there.

And on that note, regardless of who the people are, passion wanes, but it can be rekindled, and it can be "created," so a couple can have a satisfying sex life if each person is willing to work on it. And THAT is why there have been volumes of books written and why there are a gazillion sex and marriage therapists out there. And THAT, again, is what I was trying to do.

Andrew, I am very, very comfortable with you physically; you know my body, I know yours. I have no desire to share mine with anyone else at this point.

I made a mistake in saying you sometimes reminded me of a little brother—but there were just some little tics that pushed my buttons and vice versa. But I realize now that that was clumsy of me. I never meant it to hurt or disparage you. You are not my little brother. You are a strong, creative, extremely intelligent man, and I love you for that.

More on the physical component: We are both in our later stages of life, and to walk into our house (VT) as we did this summer and begin making out and then race upstairs to make love is pretty darn good. Keep in mind, too, that there are many people in marriages who don't even have physical intimacy let alone broach the subject or try to rectify the situation.

I miss the house in Vermont and the town. It is in my soul. It always has been, and it became even more special when I introduced you to it.

I miss the little things that make a couple a couple: the hugs in the kitchen; the trips to Home Depot; the walks down the hill in VT; dodging snow-

flakes in NYC; the laughter we shared; the tears we cried when Sammy the cat passed; the way you would salaciously lick your lips to get a rise out of me; the way we would chase each other around the house (sorry about that split lip); I miss putting my finger in your ear to let you know I love you. I even miss our Scrabble games. I miss seeing you outside working at your sawmill. I miss seeing you dressed up and looking so handsome. I miss the way you wore your hat (okay, the way I made you wear your hat). I miss holding your hand when we walked together or rode the train.

I can go on without you; but what we had was pretty special, although I'm aware no one person can satisfy all our needs, which is why we have friends. I am also willing to find that level of passion you feel you are missing, if you can open your heart to try. I want you, Andrew, as my life partner. No one else. Then, at least if it doesn't work, I can walk away and say we really did try.

My husband responded pretty quickly.

ANDREW: *You are truly in touch with your soul, and that is an awesome thing. And I won't lie; your letter made me cry. Months ago, it would have moved me right back to you.*

And no, your note doesn't displease me. I'd be disappointed with any less from you. I've grown that much as well. Not much in the world can scare me, now. I live alone in a stunningly beautiful place that could kill me if I weren't on my toes every day.

I have so much alone time to think that my brain gets tired. I am also more myself than I have ever been in my life. Not an easy transition; a lot of pain, as you know from your own experience these months, but I know who I am and what I have to have.

Now for the hard part. As much as I do now and will always care for you and yes, love you, I cannot say that our lives will continue intertwined as they have these past years. In all honesty, I do not today know with whom I will live; I do know beyond a doubt that I can and will have the passion I seek, and I will do everything in my power to hold it for as many decades as my body and mind will allow. I will never "settle." I'll live alone before I do that.

And I'll never turn away from you as my dearest friend. That's forever.
Loving you still as best I can,
Andrew

The pain that bubbled up inside me was almost unbearable, but I vowed to remain cool-headed. Within the hour, Amy texted me to see how I was doing. I told her that I felt a little sad, which was a gross understatement, and mentioned the emotional emails going back and forth between me and Andrew. She said she thought I "missed the idea of him." I felt I missed more than that. But on some level, I hoped she was right.

JANUARY 21

RELIGION—THE RIGHT CHOICE OR THE ONLY CHOICE

It was seven o'clock in the morning and I still could not sleep. Throughout the night I had taken a melatonin, OxyContin, a homeopathic remedy called Calmes Forte, and finally a muscle relaxer, since I was out of Xanax and Zolpidem, a prescription sleeping aid. My body was on fire with anxiety; my entire backside felt as if it had been charbroiled, and Andrew wanted to talk on the phone later today.

"Looking forward to it!" he'd said.

Looking forward to discussing divorce? He also told me in an email last night that his vision was to sell the NY house as soon as we could and to *Have a fine evening.* Have a fine evening with all this bullshit hanging over me? With all the recent loss in my life? Which would include the house I was living in? How could I have a fine night? I tossed and turned, pulled the pillow over my face, the sheet over my head. But there was no way I could shut off my brain, so I got up out of the bed. Feeling stoned with exhaustion and a cocktail of natural pills and prescription drugs, I fired off an email.

ME: *Here are my thoughts: If you really and truly are my friend, then I need you to give me some leeway before plunging into divorce. I am dealing with a tremendous amount of unwanted loss, of things I cherished and held dear—my husband, my marriage, and now, if it is agreed upon, the very roof over my head; a house that we both lovingly and painstakingly created over the course of 14 years. You may be battling to stay physically alive on a daily basis, but I am trying to survive emotionally. You are also living in one of the most beautiful places on the planet and, in truth, although we talked about sharing the place, I'm not sure if I really would want to go back there; another loss, since it was a sacred spot to me.*

I need to be on solid footing to move forward with my life and with all this. I suggest that we begin finishing the NY house in March, or whenever it gets warm. Once that is done, we can likely proceed with divorcing. I also am pretty low on work. I have the word out that I will take anything that comes along, however. AND, I have to focus on getting taxes done.

I am not asking for anything huge. I'm not sure, either, what the rush is. You have the emotional freedom to do what you need to do and seem pretty happy about your situation (otherwise I don't think you would have posted, so proudly, a picture of the VT house on Facebook). If you still want to talk, that's fine. But not today. I am exhausted.

After I climbed back into bed, I slept, but I woke up an hour later at 9:30 AM. The anxiety once again shot through my body as soon as I snapped into consciousness, back into a life, back into circumstances I didn't ask for. I felt like I was free-falling.

Feeling desperate, I locked my hands together in prayer and I pleaded, "Dear God, I don't know what to do. I cannot stand this constant state of fear and anxiety. Please help me. Please."

I looked up at the ceiling and gave a quick nod of acknowledgement to Whomsoever; and for whatever reason, I felt a bit better.

Slipping out of bed, I went to my desk and called my brother.

"I think I need to find religion, or something along those lines," I said.

As always, he was a great comfort but perfectly pragmatic. "Good idea but talk to your lawyer first."

I promised him I would—after I went back to bed for a nap. I was so tired from the lack of sleep and emotional stress I felt physically sick. But knowing I'd be going out later to meet my friend Sarah gave me a little bit of a lift.

JANUARY 22

A SEPARATION DIET AND A BEVY OF RATS

Since Andrew was going to be calling me in ten minutes to discuss our "future," or lack thereof, I headed into the bathroom to take a hit of Pepto Bismol but found that I was out. So instead I popped a Xanax.

I was pretty sure I was going to start weeping and was also fearful of what he was going to say. Like he'd changed his mind and we had to sell the NY house immediately and he was going to fight me every step of the way, and he was going to take away my health insurance, since he felt he has done his job in supporting me all these years in that regard.

But none of these fears materialized when we talked; in fact, he didn't say anything we hadn't in our emails, and neither one of us expressed any animosity. I was actually happy to hear his voice, but it deepened my sense of loneliness.

I was also quite certain at this point that Chicken Lady was no longer part of his life since he mentioned that he'd lost weight in large part because "when you cook for yourself, you don't create such elaborate meals." (Unlike when we were together and would make a huge pot of pasta and eat the whole thing in one sitting.)

My weight was better, too, mainly because for months after we'd separated I felt so sick to my stomach I could barely eat. So maybe, I thought to myself, I'll write a book, call it *The Separation Diet: Benefiting from Unmitigated Heartache*. It would probably make millions.

"Lori has seen rats," I told Andrew. Unfortunately, they periodically came up from the reservoir to take advantage of the bird food that spilled out from the feeders she had placed around the cottage. My husband and I discussed how to deal with them: no poison, since that would end up harming all the other creatures up the food chain.

"I'll get a safe trap and drop them off at the woods by the mall; they can do a little shopping," I said.

Before we hung up, I told Andrew once again how much I had grown to love him over the years, but it fell on deaf ears.

"It's different, now," he said.

His voice sounded strong and appealing, not at all like it did when I first met him and he was far less poised.

JANUARY 23

GETTING PLOUGHED ON THE FIRST SNOW OF THE YEAR

It was very quiet outside when I rolled out of bed and went into the bathroom. I looked out the window at the blanket of white that now covered the ground. It was lovely, but I knew I was not appreciating the beauty as deeply as I might have if Andrew were here to share it with me. I missed my partner tremendously.

After ingesting my morning vitamins and slugging down my daily packet of Green Vibrance, a super food that supposedly increases energy and stamina (and how I needed that), I toddled off to my computer and fired it up. Still no work had come through, which certainly didn't help my state of mind.

There were lots of emails, however, including one from my therapist in response to the one I had forwarded to her where Andy told me he would spend the rest of his life looking for the passion he felt he never had (someone who desperately wanted him).

KATARINA: *Did you really feel passion for him...and did he bring you to it? Or did you bring something from the spanking to the two of you? Which is how it sounds when you describe it. If so—he's looking to make you "crazy" for him and has come to terms with the fact that it's not going to happen. Very hard, but it may be true. If not, and you were wild for him finally, and still are, then you must try to tell him that.*

At this point, I was afraid that whatever I said wouldn't make a difference—that Andy had done more than just compartmentalize his feelings; that he had completely shut down, shut off his feelings for me. Something told me I was spot on about that.

PART V—THE JOURNEY BACK TO SELF

IN THE FORM OF A FRIEND

A friend of mine once described his own angst brilliantly: It was like you were a sheep and the wool was growing on the inside instead of the outside. And that was how I felt when I bolted awake at 4:00 AM.

And that was a baaaaaahhhhddd feeling, so I took a Xanax, got back in bed and folded my hands together. "George? God, rather, it's me. Again." I paused. "I don't even know what to say at this point, other than I could really use some help here."

I didn't "hear" anything back, but perhaps help came in the form of a friend in California, who called me immediately after I'd sent an email plainly stating how very depressed I was. "It's supposed to get easier," I told her, which I had been saying for months now.

"You have to know that everything really does happen for a reason," she said, speaking my thoughts of last night. "When I went through my darkest place and thought I would die of a broken heart when my last boyfriend dumped me, what I didn't see was that there was something much better up ahead."

"But I really want my marriage. So much of it doesn't make sense."

My friend knew all the sad little details. "I really think he's going through a midlife crisis. Sounds classic," she said.

"Why couldn't he just have gone out and purchased a Porsche? That would have been a hell of a lot less destructive."

"You have to trust that that there is something you both need to learn from this. And it will bring you to where you need—and want—to be." (From your lips, dear friend...)

JANUARY 26

TRUE COURAGE

Over coffee at a local patisserie, my playwright friend, Julie, said to me that if I wanted to convince Andy to come back I needed to approach him as if it were a business situation. Send a bullet-point list, she told me, as it's easier for men to process information that way (without all the emotion).

"And it's not about finding someone who wants to jump his bones," Julie said. "It's about having the courage to grow with another human being, to explore who you are as a person, and that means getting in touch with your emotional self."

"Andrew ran away," I said again.

"He took the easy way out. Surviving in the woods means nothing. I survived cancer. It's not physical survival that makes a person strong. It's their willingness to grow and change. If he had true courage, he would have agreed to go into counseling with you."

I later went down to Flanagan's for dinner. Feeling extraordinarily fragile, I was thankful when the waitress seated me in a large booth away from the people who dined at tables on the other side of the restaurant.

Before my friend Sarah arrived, a man I'd known throughout the years who still suffered from post-traumatic stress from the Vietnam War stopped by to say hello.

He asked how I was doing.

"Oh, you know. Life on planet earth," I said, forcing a smile.

"What's the matter?"

"Nothing. Everything is fine," I said, knowing I was not very adept at hiding my feelings.

His brow furrowed with concern. "What can I do to help? I'm a great fix-it guy. You know, like broken cabinets."

I wanted to ask, How about a broken heart? But I knew if I said anything else, it would set me off, so I told him that everything was really okay. He sensed that he wouldn't get anything else out of me, told me to take care of myself, and wandered over to the bar.

And suddenly I felt angry, since all this grief depleted me of my strength and robbed me of my energy to help, along with the polar bears, other people—people like this man, who I'd spent many hours with in the past, letting him vent about his debilitating experiences during the Vietnam War.

"I did things. Terrible things," he would say.

"It was war. You did what was expected of you. You have a good heart. The best thing you can do for yourself is to let go of the past and give what you can here and now."

(Maybe I should heed my own damn advice.)

Sarah finally arrived and could see the pain in my face.

"What's wrong?"

"I am so tired of feeling this way," I said.

Ned, the disabled man who had the car accident when he was a teenager, suddenly appeared at our booth and asked if he could sit with Sarah and me.

"Of course," I said, extending a hand.

"You okay?" Ned asked.

"Yes. I really am."

"Are you sure it's alright for me to sit here?"

"Ned, you are always welcome. You know that."

My challenges—healing a broken heart—were nothing compared to what Ned has had to deal with: living inside a broken body that would never heal. My heart would heal—eventually.

JANUARY 27

HI YA GOD, ME AGAIN

In addition to love, compassion, and some gentle touch, I seemed to be craving protein, so I boiled two soy dogs, which Andrew used to say tasted like latex paint. But tonight, even at 1:30 AM, they hit the spot.

After tossing back the dogs, I went upstairs and climbed into bed, read a few pages of Marianne Williamson's book *The Gift of Change*, and settled down to what I hoped would be a restful, revitalizing sleep. No such luck.

At 4:30 AM, my eyes flew open. I sat upright and took in a deep breath, trying to quell the anxiety that once again flooded my body. (I was not quite able to see the gift in this dramatic change that had been forced upon me.) Once I'd popped half a Xanax and three Calmes Fortes, I decided to give Williamson's book another shot.

I flipped it open and immediately came across a passage that said that through prayer we could work miracles in our lives. Right now, more than ever I needed God. I didn't need hot sex. I didn't need my ego stroked (or anything else); I needed a simple, fucking miracle—a miracle of the heart. I decided I had no other choice but to give God another chance (my salary and job be damned).

I put the book down, laid my head on my pillow, and clasped my hands in prayer. "Please, I am no longer capable of handling this on my own. Please release me from this fear and anxiety. I don't think I can take much more." I felt the calm I had been craving for months spread throughout my body; the same sense of calm I felt during my encounter with the "haloed" man I met on the train. "And by the way, God," I petitioned, "please help my cat stay healthy. I really need her to hang in with me for a while. Thanks, and have a good week, wherever you happen to be working." I finally fell asleep.

Come the normal waking hours, I heard my phone plink with an incoming text message. It was from Andrew.

ANDREW: *After four days with no water and temps above freezing, I am thinking the problem may be the pump or part of the control assembly, which is ancient. Do you know where I can find the name of the guy who worked on the well? Had to be July or August when Curt and Wanda were here. And I need to get that guy here pronto. Thanks.*

I called my sister, asked her to look in her old check register, since Andrew and I were back in NY when it happened, and Wanda and her husband offered to pay the guy. I got the name and emailed Andy:

ME: *DeLongo Artesian Wells. U can always come back to NY, Andrew. It's your house too. We have plenty of room :) And think of the money we'll save!!!*

HIM: *Thanks!*

He did not take me up on my offer.

(What is the definition of insanity? Doing the same thing over and over again and expecting a different result? Maybe I needed to go back to seeing my therapist once a week.)

MORE LOVE.COM, GOD, PSYCHOTICS
FOR POSITIVE CHANGE

"So, God," I said, upon wakening, "what's up with you and the jobs? I have absolutely no work whatsoever right now. And this restructuring that management is doing...?" I hadn't heard one word back from anyone after I'd expressed interest in taking part in the new writing program.

"Take advantage of this free time," a voice in my head said.

"Focus on your creative work."

"I am!!!!," I screamed back.

I looked around my desk. The bills had started piling up, so I methodically went through each one and mentally calculated the total and compared it with what was in our joint checking account. And it was not a pretty picture. Andy's AMEX bill, which still came to the NY house, was over $5,500. I scanned through the line items, checking for any charges that might be in error, and saw one for match.com. So, just as I thought, Andrew was done with Chicken Lady. But he was obviously still on his "quest." Good luck, I thought, and God bless. It's hell out there in date.com land.

And suddenly dawned on me what my husband was doing. His whole quest to stay alive and survive the VT winters was to prove his selfhood—perhaps his manhood, since my foray into BDSM probably emasculated him on some level. But if it did, I never meant it to.

So, maybe Andy needed to find out who he really was, as he'd said in his email. And maybe last summer I was intuitively picking up on this when I'd ask him, who are you? Maybe this was his own personal quest that had been a long time in the making. Unfortunately, he apparently felt he had to do this on his own—without me.

JANUARY 30

TWO STEPS BACK

Tonight, I met Pran at our favorite bar near Astor Place. It was his birthday, so we did our best to drink and remain upbeat and made a toast to a great year ahead. He brought me up to speed on his trip to Malaysia and asked what's going on with Andrew and me. I filled him in on the latest (and not so greatest).

"I thought for sure you'd be back together by now," Pran said.

"That's what everyone else thought. But nope."

He was, perhaps, glad to hear we had not reunited. Pran also told me that he had turned a page and had moved through and beyond the pain of losing his wife. And I envied that.

My friend quickly circled around to the subject of consummating our relationship when we were seated for dinner at a small, dark restaurant on Third Avenue.

"I want to lick your breasts," Pran said.

All I could do was squeal, but it was not necessarily a squeal of delight. I told him that right now the thought of being naked in front of any man other than Andrew freaked me out.

"I feel like a born-again virgin," I said.

"It's no big deal," Pran remarked.

"To you, maybe," I said, half serious. But for whatever reason—perhaps because I felt obligated to at least consider the possibility of us exchanging bodily fluids—I allowed my friend to engage me in a discussion of how we would do it and where.

"Neutral territory would be best," Pran said.

"Such as?"

"There are these motels in Connecticut that you book for like four hours. They have hot tubs and everything,"

"Good God. Do they have those coin-operated vibrating beds too?"

Pran laughed, but I was not embracing the humor.

"And how do you know about these places?" I asked.

My friend smiled but didn't answer. I was not sure I wanted to know, anyway.

We wrapped up the night by going back to our favorite bar and tossed back a couple of frothy shots of something that tasted like a mango popsicle (courtesy of the manager). Once we settled up, we grabbed a taxi, which dropped me off at Grand Central. On the train ride to Tarrytown, upon observing a man and a woman in the seat next to me who were obviously in love, I suddenly felt that I was ready to open up to someone new, or I was at least getting ready to, but I knew unequivocally that those shoes would be filled by someone other than Pran.

Once at home, I went up to my room after taking my vitamins, and it hit like a sudden flash of lightening: a feeling of such intense rage and anger I thought I'd explode. I grabbed Marianne Williamson's book and flung it across the room with every ounce of strength I could muster, not caring what was in its path (other than my cat). Screaming into the emptiness, I railed against a God that I felt had abandoned me. "I ask for peace and I get more anxiety! I ask to feel whole again, and I feel like I'm coming apart at the fucking seams! I hate you, God. I hate you! Why don't you just fucking let me die?!"

For one brief moment, I flashed on the bottle of Xanax in the bathroom, and wondered if twenty pills would be enough to do me in. But I knew that wasn't the answer. I was stronger than that, or so I told myself. After I'd managed to calm myself down, I curled up on the bed beside my now very-deaf cat and waited for the curtain of sleep to fall—having taken just one Xanax.

JANUARY 31

NO DOPE, JUST COPE

"It's clear I don't feel safe in the world," I said to my therapist. "I had this nightmare where I went downstairs, and all the windows and doors were open. I knew someone or something dangerous had gotten into the house. Then, out of the far corner of the dining room, this 'evil force' grabbed a fistful of my hair and yanked me backwards, pulling me into total darkness."

"Maybe you should see a psycho-pharmacologist who can prescribe the right medication."

"I don't trust the drug companies," I said. "They give you drugs to counter the side effects of the other drugs they want you to take. And there are these ads on TV that tell you to seek treatment immediately, call your doctor, whatever, if you experience any one of a myriad of side effects, which can include death. How in the name of heaven can you call your doctor if you're dead? Forget it. I'll cope."

I also told her that I felt like I truly loathed Andrew, down to my very core, and I hated what he had done to me and to our life, which was quite a shift from how I felt a few days ago.

"I know he's given me a lot, but I also helped him grow," I said. "We helped each other grow. And this is how he repays me? He runs away, because it's now all about his needs?"

But I pushed the vitriol aside and read her the two-page email that I planned to send to Andrew, an appeal to him to redeem what we'd built together.

(Again, what's the definition of insanity?)

I ended it with a sort of plea:

ME: *If you do not feel up to taking risks and have the faith to join me, so be it, but this is my assessment of how I believe a partnership such as we've built should go forward—with a sense of integrity and honesty and openness, and that is the way I wish to continue living my life. I am hoping (sadly, against hope) that this might at least open up a dialogue between us. As always, Deborah*

"So, should I send it to the fucking moron?"

Katarina laughed out loud. Even in this fragile emotional state, I was able to make my therapist laugh.

(I didn't send the email, however.)

FEBRUARY 1

THE FORGOTTEN RATS

This time it was the rats that triggered my wrath. Lori's brother, at her prodding, had cut back the ivy in front of the cottage, which was providing shelter for the rodents, in hopes of discouraging them. I had completely forgotten about them since Lori had been away for the past week. But today she'd asked her brother, who comes to the cottage to take care of her animals, if the problem had been addressed, and so naturally I got a text from him:

HIM: *Lori is freaking out about the rats, and she's coming home tomorrow.*

(Would this shit storm ever blow over?)

ME: *Sorry. I got distracted.*

HIM: *I looked at Home Depot. There are several kinds of traps. I really feel I shouldn't be in the middle of this.*

ME: *No. You should not. It's not your problem. Going to get trap today.*

And I did—a live trap, as I'd discussed with Andrew. Although if I could have tossed aside my compassion for all creatures, I'd rather have shot the fuckers.

"This is the last goddamn thing I should have to deal with," I said aloud, standing in the kitchen, turning the metal cage this way and that. At this point I could hardly get through one day without feeling like I was having a heart attack. I spent another fifteen minutes messing with the contraption, but I could not figure out for the life of me how to set it up.

Flipping it over one more time, I felt my throat constrict and the heat rise up into my face. Simply put, I wigged. I snatched the object nearest to me (a large plastic cup) and slammed it on the floor, thinking in error that it would not do any damage. (Once again, that good old controlled rage.)

"You fucking asshole! I hate your fucking guts, Andrew!"

The cup bounced off the travertine tile, jetted into the dining room, and hit the floor-to-ceiling antique hutch, shattering one of the beveled glass panes.

I ranted and wailed some more, angry at my husband and angry at myself for still being so bloody angry.

"Fuck it. Fuck everything!" I said and stomped upstairs, not caring that shards of glass were now scattered all over the place.

I closed the door to my room to keep Mamie inside and away from the broken glass and forced myself to chill out. I sat down at my desk and, as if I were making a perfunctory grocery list, I scribbled a note to call the glass man tomorrow to see if he could help me get the pane replaced. Or perhaps I'd check with Home Depot first (something for everyone and every need): *Pissed off at your husband and need a two-by-four? At Home Depot, we can help. We also carry a wide range of picks and axes. Pissed off in general? We can find you the perfect tool for releasing that inner rage. Break a mirror? We can't restore your good luck, but we can provide you with a replacement.*

Before going to sleep, I did not read Marianne Williamson, since right now I was hating her guts too and her saccharine approach. (No Marianne, I do not feel like I can love and forgive my husband.) I couldn't stand her unrealistic spiritual approach to "love this" and "love that" because "God is love." And those ludicrous prayers like "Dear God, please bless this union with me and [insert name of philandering, mentally deranged husband]; I release this relationship to God, for God will heal it with love."

I would have preferred to heal it with a shovel from Home Depot—a shovel right smack in the middle of Andrew's thick head.

FEBRUARY 2

MY HUSBAND'S ASPERGERY ASS

I received an email from my sister describing Asperger's syndrome. Andrew definitely had some of the symptoms, and it made me feel badly for him. For maybe ten seconds. But it did not keep the fire from creeping up my spine.

I shot an email back to my sister.

My sister called me right away, and I melted into tears. "I cannot do this anymore," I told her. "I feel like the fucking Lone Ranger. And where the fuck is Tonto? Even the Lone Ranger had a side kick." My sister could not help but laugh, but I did not find much of anything funny at this point. "I want off this planet. I am done. I am going to stop taking care of myself. I just want to get the hell out of here."

"Don't let one person ruin your life."

"Well, one person did."

It then became clear that I'd been giving my husband power over me, my feelings, my sense of self, and yes, my life. That, I thought, had to stop immediately. "Well, at least I have my writing group today," I said to my sister.

"It sounds healing," Wanda said.

"You have no idea."

FEBRUARY 5

LEAP YEARS AHEAD

My cell phone rang at ten-thirty in the morning. I didn't bother going over to pick it up, since I was not in the mood to chat with anyone. But I did check to see who had called. It was my husband. But he didn't leave a message. I didn't call him back and decided that later tonight I'd send him the email I'd read to my therapist. So maybe he'd misdialed; he also had a bunch of DVDs sent to our house in NY versus VT. I had to wonder if he was subliminally reaching out? Or maybe I was subliminally off my rocker and grasping at straws. (That was probably more like it. And twice again, what was the definition of insanity?)

Sadly, Andrew stayed on my mind all day and during dinner at Ted and Eva's house, I read them the email I was thinking of sending to my husband.

"He won't be able to respond on an emotional level," Ted said. "You're leap years ahead of where Andrew needs to go in terms of personal growth."

"Then maybe I really need to let him go," I said. "Once and for all."

(Let go and let George?)

The Big Guy actually seemed to be popping up all over the place as of late, in conversations with other people, such as the one I had the other day with a colleague, in spite of my rants against the Almighty and spiritual teachers like Marianne W. Over lunch, he told me about his very-painful divorce and how a twelve-step program really helped him. "It's all about recognizing that we are powerless over another human and that to get through the tough times, it really does help to have a spiritual foundation. So, instead of swimming upstream, turn it over to God." I took in the information and made a silent promise to let "George" do some of the footwork, stop questioning everything so much, and stop looking for immediate results. As my therapist said, the Universe works in strange ways. (But could it hurry the hell up and do its job?)

FEBRUARY 6

WORST CASE

I woke up with a scratchy throat. I also noticed a red bump on my knuckle and had an immediate attack of paranoia, thinking that it was that flesh-eating bacterium, since I knew my emotional state had wreaked havoc on my immune system. I laid in bed and envisioned the worst-case scenario: I'm stoned out on Xanax, alone in some hospital bed being pumped full of antibiotics by uncaring nurses who tell me in cold monotone voices that I could very well lose my arm.

"Now that's a fine way to greet a stunningly sunny day," I said as I picked up the covers and looked at my cat who was nestled between my legs. (These days, that was about all I wanted down there other than my "battery-powered friend.")

I wandered over to my desk and realized that it was February—a new month, which meant an updated horoscope. Hopefully it would be somewhat positive, encouraging, and not something like "for the first time in the history of the creation, the planets have all gone retrograde, so you might want to hide out in the basement for the next several months, or think about stockpiling that cyanide." And if it was good, I decided I'd make the choice to believe it.

"So there," I remarked to Mamie, who usually followed me around like a dog and was now resting in my opened desk drawer.

I logged on to my usual site, which once again mentioned the significant influence that Saturn was having over my life. *Visits from Saturn are sobering periods, it said, but they help a person grow in maturity and wisdom.* (Never, ever assume you're done with personal growth.) But there was some bright light at the end of the tunnel: Saturn, which was now moving away from my Sun sign, won't be back until 2039.

"Good. I'll probably be dead by then. So, just try and find me, you fucker."

FEBRUARY 8

IS IT SAFE???

We had a slight problem. The pizza dough had developed a ring of whitish liquid around the top.

"It looks like placenta," I said to my tenant, Lori, who was sitting at my kitchen table.

I shot Andrew an email on my cell (subject line: *Question for Mr. Science*) about the mysterious liquid, asking him if he thought the dough was safe.

The emails between us tonight were playful, and I felt connected to my husband, once again—hopeful, even. Until Lori mentioned that she'd checked out Andrews's match.com profile.

"It says he likes walks in the woods," Lori said.

"You're kidding me." I felt totally repulsed.

"Guys always say that, thinking it's what women want to hear."

Andy's page also showed a picture of our house up in Vermont. And it said he was looking for…guess what? Passion.

"Translation: he wants to get laid—a lot," I said. "What woman in her right mind won't see through that? Passion, my ass."

Lori and I had a good laugh about Andrew's pursuit and called it a night.

After my tenant left, it occurred to me that I never would have gotten to know Lori as well had my marriage stayed intact. So, once again, I reminded myself that something good comes out of everything, and in this case, it was a wonderful, rich friendship.

I headed upstairs and for whatever reason—perhaps because of the discussion about Andrew's online profile—I went over to my desk, logged on to my computer, and deleted myself from okcupid. com.

And like I did with spanking and discipline, I slammed the door on e-dating.

FEBRUARY 9

THE ONLY CONSTANT

As the adage goes, the only constant in life is change, and the lightness I was beginning to feel was gone. I was not only finding it harder and harder to be in the house, I was also feeling further away from my husband, psychically. But that was probably because I was now beginning to see him as a sorry, mixed-up soul—and all with a little help from my sister, who had read the email I wanted to send Andrew.

WANDA: *What a beautiful missive. Truly coming from your heart (and mind) without the entanglements of sheer emotion and cutting grief. I hope Andrew reads your note carefully and it compels him to reflect in a more meaningful way on his behavior as a man with self-limiting beliefs and self-centered obsessions. Send it!*

Within minutes, I got a text from my husband asking how the pizza was.

ME: *Lethal.*

ANDREW: *Nice knowing you.*

ME: *You too, babe.*

(Could the subtext have been any clearer?)

At Barnes and Noble that afternoon I ran into the guy who worked behind the counter at the store's café. He was jubilant. Not because it was his day off, but because his life had completely turned around.

"The manager asked me what was wrong with me," he said.

"Because you're so happy?"

"Yes. She says she can't handle the change. I'm usually so morose and despondent and contemptuous. Not anymore." He was, in brief, in love. And like me, he did not like being alone.

So maybe that was why I kept gravitating toward Pran, who I later met at a Greek restaurant, where he once again addressed consummating our relationship. I quickly changed the subject.

"So, can you explain again exactly what a securities lawyer does? Do you like your calamari grilled or lightly fried?"

FEBRUARY 10

LA LA LAND

The flight to LA was smooth, and by 10:00 PM I had arrived at June and Kim's apartment in the Miracle Mile district. The three of us talked until almost midnight—me spinning out the details of my separation, and them the latest about their jobs and where they were in life. It seemed we were all a bit fearful of the future. The world was not an easy place when you didn't have piles of money and people were living longer.

"There's always the pillow-over-the-face trick," I said. "As long as you have willing friends and/or family."

"Yeah, the operative word being 'willing'," June said. "Unfortunately, Dr. Kevorkian is no longer with us."

June went off to bed, since she had to be up early for work, and Kim and I stayed up and discussed our challenges; she also had issues with feeling "safe."

"I've always had to deal with a certain degree of anxiety, but I always felt safe with Andy," I told her. "Being married feels like you have a safety net of sorts—someone who has your back and vice versa."

"Marriage shcmarriage."

"Maybe, but you have your sister."

Kim nodded knowingly. "Sorry, Deborah. Really."

FEBRUARY 11

GETTING BACK

"Your husband is getting back at you. He won," my friend Angie the novelist said over shared seaweed salad at a Thai restaurant in West Hollywood. "He got you back for all those years he felt you didn't love him."

"But I did," I said. "Well, I grew to love him."

My friend, who was in town from Paris on business, ignored my comment. "And that's why he left," she said. "To give you some of the medicine he felt he'd been swallowing all these years."

Next up: a discussion of Andrew's tendency toward codependency. "Maybe that's why he gave me such an amazing amount of freedom," I commented, also mentioning how generous he was—such as the time he used his frequent flyer miles to send me ultra first-class to an island off the coast of Indonesia to stay with my girlfriend at a fancy resort.

"He did all that to make you love him," Angie said.

I took another bite of my rice dish. "I'm tired of talking about my husband, Angie. I know I need to move on. And if he comes back, great. But there will be work to do."

My friend, who had been divorced for over twenty years, said that she wished she'd worked it out with her husband. But it was the late 1980s, and there had been a backlash against the prior generation where husbands and wives would stick together no matter how miserable they were. "My therapist and all my friends were telling me to get out. Leave," Angie said. "His, too. I wish to hell I didn't listen."

I had never heard Angie admit to that. I always thought she was glad she ended the marriage and I said so.

"Well, you see how well it's worked out for me." Angie's words were laced with sarcasm.

My friend, who had been single ever since her divorce, despite a highly developed intellect, a successful writing career, and a stunning face and personality, switched gears. "But, you know, I like being free," she said. "And I like variety." Angie rattled off a list of lovers who lived around the globe, some in exotic places. "I see a few of them every other month or so. That way I avoid all the messy parts of relationships where you see sides of a person that are less than perfect," she said, clearly trying to convince herself, rationalize, that this was the only way to live—and love.

"I don't mind the messy sides. That's part of being intimate with someone; someone you are totally comfortable with. Someone you can pee and poop in front of, are sick in front of, brush your teeth and fart in front of. I really miss that."

"I don't," Angie said emphatically. She looked at me. "Fart?"

"Of course," I said, laughing. "We all do it, don't we?"

FEBRUARY 13

A DAY OF ENLIGHTENMENT AND NOT SO GOOD NEWS

My old friend Erica, who arrived last night from South Africa and was also staying with June and Kim, dragged me to Barnes and Noble to look for a book that she promised would be beneficial. Based on a personality assessment tool, it was called *The Enneagram: Understanding Yourself and Others in Your Life.* The not-so-good news: I was a number four; in other words, a "tragic romantic." Fours often find themselves wanting what they cannot have, finding themselves in relationships where the person can't commit or is unavailable, and longing for something that is always out of reach. Feelings of loss and abandonment also abound. (Bingo.)

"I thought I had broken the pattern of being attracted to emotionally unavailable men when I married Andrew," I told Erica. "I thought I had made a wise choice."

"I guess not," Erica said, with a touch of sympathy.

"More to learn," I suppose. "And maybe that's why I didn't fall head over heels for Andy—because he was 'too available.' Unlike my father. I guess we are pretty much programmed from childhood in who and what we respond to. Perhaps if Andy was more like my

245

father...Oh well, a little late with the revelations."

I read further. Unfortunately, the book also said that for the tragic romantic, progress toward happiness will be slow.

"Crap," I said.

FEBRUARY 14

A HEARTLESS DAY

Ugh.

FEBRUARY 15

DESPERATELY SEEKING WISDOM

The book Erica ordered for me (a more extensive look into the nine personality types—*The Wisdom of the Enneagram*) arrived. I brought it inside and immediately went to the "tools" section at the end, bypassing all other chapters. Among other things, the authors suggested finding a spiritual practice or an activity like yoga. So, I decided to check out the new yoga studio that just opened up in Piermont when I returned.

Later, however, when we switched on the TV and came across a NY Times journalist being interviewed about a recent book he wrote on yoga, I decided I needed to rethink my drink. Although he said yoga had changed his life, helping him to cope with the horrors he witnessed as a foreign war correspondent, he delivered a caveat. "You have to be careful," the journalist said. "In rare cases, certain yoga moves can cause a stroke." He pointed to a plastic prototype of the human spine and a few areas around the neck, which were painted a cautionary red.

I honestly felt like I was part of some cosmic joke and struck yoga from my list of "things to do to keep me sane."

FEBRUARY 16

LEAVING LA LA LAND

My flight was scheduled to depart at 10:10 PM, so I figured I'd leave for the airport around seven to give myself ample time to maneuver through LA traffic.

The apartment was devoid of human life when I left, since June and Kim had not yet gotten home from work, and my levels of anxiety were at an all-time high. I didn't want to go back east, but I didn't want to stay in LA either. I didn't know where I wanted to be—or where I belonged.

STRAIGHT JACKETS AND THE GEORGE WITHIN

The connecting flight from Philadelphia to White Plains was enough to put me in a straightjacket. The turbulence was almost unbearable—especially without a Xanax, which I had vowed to give up. Even the tough-looking guy with the massive arms in the seat across from me looked like he was staring death in the face. But why the pilot did not announce over the speaker that it was "business as usual, just some troublesome air mass" was beyond me. When we landed, however, he came out of the cockpit and apologized for the "bumpy" ride.

"Bumpy?" I said to the man who sits beside me. "More like riding a roller coaster to hell."

When my feet hit the tarmac, the tremendous sense of relief I felt to be on solid ground was quickly replaced by a heavy bout of melancholy, since, for the first time in more than a decade, Andrew would not be here to pick me up. Instead, Lori greeted me outside the terminal.

Throughout the drive back to the other side of the river, Lori chattered gaily, updating me on her job and life in general. Once we got home, I let myself into the house, went upstairs to see my cat and burst into tears. After wiping my face dry, I turned on my small battery-operated radio to fill in the empty space and called my sister, who, as always, was there for me.

"Pull in the light," she said. "You have to work at pulling in the light."

"I am pulling, Wanda. I am pulling with all my might."

My husband called fifteen minutes later, saying he wanted to discuss finances. He told me about a retirement account that his company was liquidating. I would have to sign papers, and we would split the proceeds, he said. He also mentioned that it was unlikely he'd be paying alimony, and I needed to figure out a way to take care of myself going forward. What the fuck? At this age? What was I supposed to do? Go to medical school? Law school? Thank goodness I didn't quit my job when my husband suggested that I focus solely on my creative projects, so I had some savings. I'd said I wouldn't do that and also told him that if one of my creative projects took off, he could quit his job.

But what was he thinking? That he could just toss me aside like an old dish rag? No court of law would let him get away with that, especially since we'd been married for over fourteen years and he'd been the primary bread winner. This cut straight through my heart, but I now realized Andrew was truly only thinking about himself. He was "saving himself."

Strangely, however, my husband and I did talk about the possibility of reuniting, although it was clear that he wanted to date— because he'd never had a chance to sow his oats. He repeated that he'd "always been married." No breaks in between. And again, I reminded him that it was not my fault.

"My therapist encouraged me to date," he said.

"Your therapist?"

(What kind of moronic therapist would do that? Tell him to date instead of seeing if he can work things out with his wife? A wife he says he supposedly speaks so highly of to everyone he meets?)

I was surprised when he told me that, but not when he casually mentioned that he and Trudy had broken up. "She was unstable."

(No shit. Everyone knew it—even the tarot card reader.)

"You know," Andy said, "if there is any chance of us getting back together, we need to be careful in the meantime."

"Are you seeing anyone?" he asked.

"Sort of, but I'm not ready to plunge into bed."

"Anyone I know?"

"Not really." For whatever reason I didn't want to tell him about Pran, who he knew. I also talked about the beautiful life he and I had created together; he agreed that there was so much that was good about it.

"I also now have a much deeper understanding of myself," I said, recognizing that any dissatisfaction I felt, with myself or my lack of success, had nothing to do with Andrew. "In the past I'd always long for things that seemed out of reach," I said, speaking like the Enneagram's true tragic romantic. "I don't want to do that anymore."

"So how do you change that?" he asked.

"By recognizing the pattern and changing your thoughts," I said, knowing that this takes significant effort. But I was working on it. Change your thoughts, change your mind. Change your mind, change your life. I just wished I could change my thoughts about my husband. Today I was not hating him—at all.

FEBRUARY 18

ANXIETY, THREE—BACK TO TEN

I got out of bed feeling a bit more optimistic today (anxiety three on a scale from one to ten). With Andrew and bills on my mind, I sent my husband an email about some checks I was sending out and mentioned that I had thought of asking him to meet me in Boston, since there were some things I wanted to say to him in person. I also told him I was looking into becoming a certified life coach. He fired back a response, its tone markedly different than our conversation of yesterday.

ANDREW: *PLEASE do the coaching thing. You would be awesome at it and you NEED a backup. We have to be honest; our chances of getting back together are slim but I will always care about you regardless. Have a great weekend!*

Anxiety was now back to ten. Naturally, this brought up those tremendous abandonment issues I had with my father, who helped me out with rent throughout my thirties while I pursued an acting career. Then, when he remarried, he cut me off, and I was left with a three-bedroom apartment (my roommates had just moved out), no money for rent, and no job on the horizon. But I survived. And once again something good came out of dire circumstances. I met June and Kim, who became my roommates.

FEBRUARY 19

KNOCK KNOCK

"It sounds like your husband is planning his own retirement," said Kenny the lawyer, who advised me to serve Andrew with divorce papers. "God only knows what kind of judge you'll get in a podunk Vermont town. You need to keep this in New York."

The divorce attorney also informed me that if we did go forward, he'd require a retainer fee of $10,000, and I momentarily wondered if that was the reason he was instilling "the fear of Andrew and redneck judges" in me.

During my session with my therapist I addressed my concerns. "If I do serve my husband, though, the friendship will be over, and the door will be permanently shut." Katarina agreed, and I decided to hold off on securing an attorney.

Later in the day, Andrew sent me an email telling me he fully intended ("over his dead body") to keep the place up in VT and, once again, said that the best thing would be to sell the NY house.

Best thing? For whom? Him? Of course! It was all about Andrew now. On my way to Main Street Café I ran into Willy, the pot-smoking "angel" with the balding crown and long white hair. He reminded me: it all starts in the mind. "Look at me," he said. "In spite of my challenges, I'm centered and at peace."

I could see that he was. His eyes were kind and gentle and stress-free. (But it could have been the marijuana.)

"Lucky you," I said. "I constantly feel like I'm having a heart attack."

"Stop sending those messages to yourself," he said.

I thought of the mantra I used on the plane coming back from Philadelphia when I felt certain we were going to end up in the Hudson River: "I am safe, I am loved, God is with me and within me." And I vowed that I would be vigilant and watch my thoughts.

Tonight, unfortunately, my mind went spinning out of control in a million unwanted directions, and I wasn't able to control them. So I looked to my homeopathic friends to help me sleep, proud that I was still able to avoid the Xanax.

FEBRUARY 21

HIGH ON ANXIETY

Andrew called me at home around noon. "Friggin' Bank of America," he said. "They're useless. They put a moratorium on refinancing for the next two months."

"Refinancing?"

"To save money. On the Vermont house."

Andrew said he was looking into another company, and it dawned on me: he wanted to refinance so he could get my name off the mortgage. The attorney was right. My husband was planning his own retirement. His own future. Sans moi.

My heart started to hammer, and I realized I needed to keep an emotional lid on things and start being my own advocate. I needed to take care of myself, like he was doing. And bloody hell, I would do just that. We got into another discussion about splitting up. And like the typical used car salesman who would not give up, I reminded him how ironic it was that toward the end we'd begun to enjoy our sex life. "That's when you split," I said.

I repeated that I had no desire to be with anyone else.

"I do," Andy said.

I was not shaken. "Remember when I came up in September? When you showed me that little bird house you were working on? I looked at you and I thought, how beautiful this man is."

He paused for a moment. "If we reunited and it failed, I couldn't bear it."

I knew at that point that he was afraid. He was just as afraid of what that failure would do to him on an emotional level as I was of losing him for good.

"There's no reason why it should fail, Andy," I said. "I wouldn't let it." My comment was met with silence. I sighed, wished him a good night, and hung up.

After I got changed, ingested a can of sardines, standing over the sink like the quintessential bachelorette, I drove down to a local club. A couple of Alexis' friends were playing in a band and since it was nearly impossible to get a table, we sidled up to the bar. Alexis was going through her own personal hell, challenged by money issues and a son who seemed to be pulling away from her.

I told her that I'd been becoming more spiritual as the days went by—or trying to. "Sometimes you just can't do things on your own and have to turn your affairs over to, you know, the Big Cheese," I said, looking up toward the ceiling.

"God, you mean," she said.

"Yup."

"Why not? Nothing else has worked," my friend commented.

"Ain't that the damn truth."

FEBRUARY 22

TO GIVE IS TO RECEIVE

After forcing myself to wash the sheets that had been on my bed for well over a month, and replenishing my underwear drawer with laundered panties, I took off for NYC to meet my friend Gaby. When the train pulled into Grand Central and I shuffled out through the exit along with a hundred or more people frantically racing off into the urban night, I spotted a tall, dark-haired man staring at gate 116. The door had a "closed" sign on it. He seemed perplexed and looked quite worried.

"Are you lost?" I asked. He turned toward me, and I immediately sensed he was a gentle, kind soul.

He pointed to the sign and held up a train ticket. "Is right gate?"

The man, who appeared to be in his fifties, spoke with a thick accent. I placed it from somewhere in South America, maybe Spain.

"Let me see," I said, taking his ticket. There was no information on it other than where he was going: Bridgeport, CT. But I knew this could not be the right gate and told him to "come with me."

"Sorry, my English bad," he said as we made our way up the escalator.

"Mine, too," I said.

He smiled. The humor was not lost in translation.

Once on the main level, I led him to the information booth. "Hi," I said to the man behind the glass, shoving the ticket through the opening. "This gentleman needs some help finding his gate. I don't see his train listed on the directory."

The man in the booth looked down at the ticket. "Gate eighteen. It leaves in a few minutes," he said, pointing. I turned to the tall man with the black hair. "We need to hurry."

He dashed after me as I raced east down the terminal, leading the way.

"There it is," I said, stopping suddenly, gesturing.

The man looked at the gate, his face brightening. He put his hand over his heart and bowed to me. "Thank you. Thank you. Thank you."

"My pleasure," I said, as I placed my own hand over my heart. "Safe journey."

As I walked toward the subway that would take me down to 23rd Street, I realized how good, how right it felt to help another human being. So maybe, just maybe, I was truly beginning to heal.

I left Grand Central feeling lighter and silently thanked the man for passing through my life.

FEBRUARY 28

BUDGETS, BIOLOGY, AND BOOKS

I checked my cell phone when I got up and saw that I had missed a text from Andrew. It came in at 11:40 PM the night before.

ANDREW: *Talked to Gwen Sunday at RJ's. She has a new boyfriend, a dentist. Seems very happy. She misses you and has a very high opinion of you. She asked if she could contact you. I gave her your email. Be nice to her. Gwen was never an issue, just a pretty woman, and not as pretty as you; none of them are. I think you know that, or you should.*

This was the second email he had sent about someone missing me, which I found odd, since I never knew either of these women he had mentioned very well. I felt a surge of optimism, which may or may not have been a good thing. In truth, the emotional ping-pong game going on inside me—where one minute I'd feel hopeful and the next I'd be besieged by gloominess—was beginning to wear me out, and Andrew's seeming ambivalence only served to exacerbate my fatigue. So clearly, I had to get philosophical and let things play out the way they were going to. Or I needed to truly find the courage to release my husband from my psyche, my heart, my life, and get on with my own once and for all. Not an easy task—especially since our lives were still entwined, and we had to discuss things like budgeting so we could maintain these two houses without going broke.

"I'll come down to New York so we can work on a financial plan we can both follow," Andrew said later when he phoned.

"That's fine," I said and almost requested that we do it via email, since I knew that seeing him would make me miss him even more.

And like the ever-spinning record, we got into the discussion about his need for intense passion.

"What I hear you say every time is that it goes away," he said.

"It's not what I said, Andrew. It changes. It has to," I said, now dead tired from having to repeat the same thing over and over. "You cannot sustain the intensity you experience at the beginning of a relationship. It would kill you. We are not biologically programmed for that. You know that."

Andy said nothing.

"Couples who are together a long time have to work at it to rekindle passion. And we did," I said, not mentioning the fact that the spark was never there from the beginning.

"It might have worked for you—the spanking."

"You sure as hell weren't complaining, Andrew," I commented, reminding him of my increased sex drive.

My husband sighed. I told him that he really needed to talk to other couples to clear his perspective.

"I have," he said, but I didn't quite believe him, and changed my tack.

"You know, all it might take for me is to read a book, a sexy book."

"I tried that," he said.

He did. On Christmas a few years ago, my husband gave me *Lady Chatterley's Lover* and some other book that was considered ris-

253

qué for its time. Unfortunately, they were far too tame by today's standards to satisfy my needs, so the books ended up on the shelf unread. I probably should have said something. Just like Andrew should have said something before he bolted—I should have made an effort to communicate.

"Andrew..." I said, but stopped myself, since there was no point in beating this already very dead horse that had probably been brought back to life more times than anyone could count. "See you tomorrow."

Later in the day I sent my husband an email. (The poor horse had once again risen from the dead, ready for another beating.)

ME: *No one's fault, but the books weren't the right ones.*

He responded several hours later.

ANDREW: *What does this mean? What books?*

Andrew had already forgotten.

ME: *Vis a vis our earlier conversation.*

Again, I didn't hear back from him.

MARCH 1

HOT SEX, CRAZY PEOPLE

Andrew texted me when he got to the NY house, and I headed home from Main Street Café. The door was unlocked, and I went inside.

"Hey," I heard my husband say from the kitchen.

I put my bags down and went over to him, giving him a big hug.

He held me tightly. "Let's go out to dinner. Let's get out of here," Andrew said, his eyes welling up.

I was in complete agreement that a night out was necessary. Screw the money.

Over dinner at Flanagan's, we conversed pleasantly, and I did my best to stay cheerful. Andrew brought up Trudy and said that he thought she was a multiple personality.

"Some of the hottest sex I've ever had, though" he said. I had to wonder if Andrew wasn't rubbing salt in the open gaping wound called my heart, but I couldn't help but find his prior comment amusing.

I put my hand on Andrew's arm. "Okay, so how many personalities are we talking about?"

"Don't know," he said. "But when we were together, you know, physically, she'd become this other person. She'd say, here comes Mavis, and jump on me like there was no tomorrow. Then on the way home in the car, after we broke up—which was a very emotional scene over dinner—she called up a friend in Europe and started chattering gaily in this other voice. It was a high squeaky voice I didn't recognize. She was acting like there was nothing wrong. That nothing had happened."

My husband said that he got so angry he had to work hard to restrain himself. "I think I scared her."

"Wow," I said, a bit surprised since I had never seen a violent side in Andrew. A few temper tantrums, but that was it. "So, who broke up with whom?"

"She broke up with me. If I were to be perfectly honest, it was my sexual neediness that drove her away."

"Oh, Andy, what have I been trying to tell you all these years?" I said, not in a mean-spirited manner, but with a good bit of frustration.

But I knew I was part of the problem, too. It was our dynamic as a couple; the more he pushed for sex (and, granted, men do equate physical intimacy with being loved), the more I would retreat. My mind quickly drifted back to the time not too long ago when Andrew begged me to kiss him as we lay in bed, which did nothing to enhance my desire. And there was the remark I'd made to our Vermont friends at the bar. "You know, the real reason Andy and I got married was to get me on his health insurance." And even though I'd said it in a joking manner, it must have cut my husband to the bone. Perhaps that was the last straw for him.

I looked over at Andy and was filled with a soul-shattering sadness. I never intended to hurt him. And at that moment, I loved him with all my heart.

MARCH 2

REPAIRING THE DAMAGE (TO THE TREES)

My husband and I went out to the yard to assess the damage done to the trees during the intense snowstorm that came through in October.

"You know, I have the name of a very good tree guy who can take care of it," I said.

"Let me fire up the chain saw."

"You really don't have to do this."

But Andy was insistent, and we spent the next few hours cleaning up the yard, him cutting up the damaged trees while I planted myself at the bottom of the ladder to make sure he was safe while working on the high-hanging limbs.

Once we'd finished, we changed our clothes and went to find a local Starbucks where we planned to discuss how to disperse the funds from Andrew's recently liquidated company retirement plan. We grabbed two seats along the far wall at the coffee store. I felt extremely on edge.

"Shall we get our usual Chai lattes?" my husband asked and handed me a twenty-dollar bill.

"That's all right. I've got my Starbucks card," I said, hoping Andrew would acknowledge my desire for financial "independence." But I realized how ridiculous I was being, how I'd somehow let him make me feel guilty for wanting what was rightfully mine, but I sprung for the drinks anyway.

I brought the lattes back to our table. After we figured out the best liquidation strategy, he proceeded to tell me he needed to set up a separate checking account, which triggered an intense surge of separation anxiety. My heart began pounding. I felt completely out of control—of my life, myself, my emotions, of everything—and I began to weep.

"Andrew, this is so hard for me. I miss you so much," I said, putting a hand up to shield my teary face from the people walking by.

"I'm sorry," he said.

"This is all so stupid," I said, meaning all that had happened between us. "Let's just go and get this over with."

At the bank, after we got the paperwork notarized, Andrew did not mention setting up a separate checking account—perhaps because he didn't want to deal with another emotional meltdown.

Once we were back at the house, after riding back in semi-silence, Andy packed his bag, and I walked him out to his car. But I couldn't help myself and the tears began to flow once again.

"Damn it, Andrew," I said.

He moved in to hug me. "I don't mean to cause you any pain."

"On some level, you must."

Andrew said nothing in return, and I released him. He got into the driver's seat, fired up the engine, and maneuvered the Honda down the narrow driveway.

My hands hanging by my side, my mood darkening, I looked on as his car moved out onto the street and disappeared from my view. I went inside, got dressed, and headed into the city to spend the night with Gaby and Claire.

It turned out to be a pleasant time, as I always delighted in being with good friends, and I returned home feeling a bit more centered—until I checked the messages on my desk phone.

"Deb," Andrew said from somewhere on the road. "I'm really upset. I come down there, pretty up the yard, and give you $150,000. I'm always taking care of everyone else's needs. I feel like you're playing me. This has got to stop. If it doesn't, I'm going to have to consider getting an attorney."

Playing him? How? How could I possibly do that? Did he think I manufactured those tears? Did he not understand how much pain I'd been in for the past six months? And what did he mean, give me $150,000? It was rolled into another retirement account—a different one. It wasn't like he gave me a wad of cash. I wondered if he had really, truly snapped.

I picked up the phone, dialed his cell, and was a bit surprised when he answered, since it was late.

"Andrew, I didn't ask you to work on the trees. Remember? I told you I'd get a tree guy. I don't understand why you're so upset."

"This always happens. I get around you, and I put your needs first," he said and repeated what he'd said months ago. "I've been doing this for thirty years. It's got to stop. It's my turn now."

"Look, Andy, I never put any pressure on you to do anything. You know that. And if I did, it was only with both of us in mind."

I got the sense he "heard me," or rather, I hoped he did, and when we hung up, my husband and I seemed to be back on good terms.

I impulsively logged onto the Internet and keyed in *define codependency*. One of the first links was to Wikipedia. I clicked onto the site and read, fascinated. Codependents, the site said, had a tendency to put another's needs first and in doing so it created a sense that they were needed (loved). The codependent also lacked empathy for the feelings of others, even though they thought they were always tending to other people's needs.

The site also said that sometimes in an attempt to recover from codependency, a person will go from being overly giving to being overly aggressive or excessively narcissistic. And that about nailed Andrew's recent behavior on the head. Even his daughter had said he was not the same person. "Dad's being extremely selfish right now," Courtney had said to me a month or so ago.

I just wished to hell my husband and I could have recognized the issues and dealt with them before our marriage broke apart. I also wished Andrew had been willing to go into therapy with me.

"There is no reason you can't work on yourself and your marriage at the same time," I'd said to him. Obviously, he felt otherwise.

After I kissed my cat goodnight, slid under the covers, and turned out the lights, it hit me. And it hit me hard: I could not convince my husband to come back. Nor would I try. Not anymore. It was truly over.

MARCH 13

A BEAUTIFUL MISSIVE

I received a heartfelt email from Courtney.

COURTNEY: *I just wanted you to know you've been in my thoughts a lot lately; you mean so much to me. Rod and I spent a while talking last night, and we both feel like my father is a much better person with you than without you. We also feel that you will always enrich our family and our lives and challenge us to be better people. I just need you to know how appreciative I am to have you in my life. You are a wonderful and amazing person; I cherish you and continue to hope and pray that Dad begins to realize he is making a terrible mistake. But you also have to understand that what happened has less to do with you than you might think. Dad is just trying to find himself, after all these years.*

And I knew Courtney was right: My husband was on a journey that he probably needed to begin years ago—one that had consequently altered my life path, my own journey.

MARCH 14

DIFFERENT BOOKS—A WHOLE DIFFERENT FEELING

The day felt lighter, and I felt a bit brighter and spent the afternoon cleaning the house and gathering up papers for recycling.

I met my friend Sarah for dinner, during which we talked about art, the crappy job they did on the sidewalks downtown, and the nature of personal reality. "In fleeting moments, I feel I 'get it', and on some cosmic level it all makes sense." I said, adding, "But, mostly not."

"The mystery abounds," my friend remarked.

We also talked about relationships.

"Do you think you want someone in your life?" I asked.

"Sometimes. But I've been alone for thirty years, so I'm used to it," my artist friend said. Sarah looked at me thoughtfully. "You know, Deborah, it's not about Andrew anymore. Just like he's taking care of his needs, you now need to take care of your own. You need to fight for your own happiness."

I knew she was right. I also knew it would be a long, upward climb.

"And you know what? Maybe this simply had to happen."

"Perhaps," I said. "You're not the first person to say that." I thought that maybe I would someday come to realize that things really did happen for a reason and look back on what happened as a gift of sorts; that there really was something better up ahead—and someone with whom I shared a deep physical and soul-level bond.

Feeling sated with food and friendship, I drove myself home and immediately went upstairs to check on my cat who was curled up peacefully on her pillow as usual. I touched her lightly, not wanting to wake her as she'd recently been slowing down and had become a bit shaky on her feet. "Hey," I whispered as my eyes filled up. I knew her time was limited, and my heart would surely break when she passed—just like it broke when my husband left. But I was certain I would find the strength to handle it.

I looked over at the pile of books on the bed where Andrew used to sleep and reflected back on the ones that used to sit on the floor on my side, out of sight from my husband: *Carrie's Story: An Erotic S&M Novel* by Molly Weatherfield; *The Adult Spanking Handbook* by Mistress Gemma Forbes; *It's Supposed to Hurt* by Cassandra Park; *Submission* by Marthe Blau.

A smile formed on my face as I scanned over my current reads: *A New Earth—Awakening to Your Life's Purpose* by Eckhart Tolle; *The Power of Thought* by Florence Scovel Schinn; *Conversations with God (Book 3)* by Neale Donald Walsch; *Buddha's Brain, the practical neuroscience of happiness, love & wisdom* by Rick Handson PhD. It was a whole different collection and focus. But I also had a few books in the "to-read" pile, including one by Candace Bushnell who wrote *Sex and the City*, which told me I was moving back, albeit slowly, to a more balanced state. After all, I had no plans to join a monastery or become a spiritual guru.

I looked over at Mamie who was now up on her feet and looking for some love. I scratched her lightly under her chin and felt a ping of gratitude. "Yes, things have certainly changed," I said quietly to my cat.

EPILOGUE (A NEW BEGINNING)

I had to put Mamie down at the end of March. My tenant and now close friend, Lori, came with me (the assistant assumed we were a lesbian couple). The vet was compassionate but firm and reminded me that although it was hard "to let my beautiful cat go," it was the kindest thing to do. Mamie's leg at that point had become oedemic, and she was having a difficult time walking. Both Lori and I stayed in the room, tears streaming down our faces, while the veterinarian injected my cat with the sedative that would push her gently to the other side. I placed my hand on Mamie's head and as she went to sleep, she reached out with her paw and placed it on my forearm—almost as if she was comforting me.

My friend and former dom, Carl, also continued to IM me, to check in and see how I was doing. Every once in a while, he would tease me with images I once found so enticing: *Just imagine being over a man's knee, a blush of red slowly spreading across your tender white cheeks as you are being spanked for your misdeeds.* I usually told him to knock it off, with a touch of humor, of course, and reminded him that I'd left all that behind (pun intended).

What I hadn't left behind was a sense of hope and ever-growing optimism that everything was going to be more than just okay. Even the grapefruit tree, which I thought was a goner, began sprouting leaves.

(Now <u>that</u> has <u>got</u> to be a sign.)

ACKNOWLEDGMENTS

I gratefully thank everyone who made this book possible, including all the "players." And thanks to the following people for their sage input and editorial expertise (in alphabetical order): Karen Essex, Helene Gardner, Linda Herskovic, Margaret Johnson, Bette Siler, Amanda Walgrove, Susan Vines, and the women in my writing group. (If I forgot anyone, ring me up and I'll buy you dinner.) Additional thanks to Cali Alpert, Steven Beer, Laura Clines, and Susan Konig for their insights. And a big thumbs up to Maya Roman for a wonderful, snappy cover.

ABOUT THE AUTHOR

Deborah Vines (www.deborahvines.net), an award-winning film-maker and playwright, has been involved in theater and film as a writer, actor, director, and producer for several years.

She has written 9 screenplays, with 2 development deals under her belt; 2 TV pilots, one of which is currently being pitched.

Her numerous plays, which include one musical (www.lovethat4letterword.com), have been produced in various venues throughout the US, including in Boston, NYC, and LA.

Vines has also worked as a journalist and recently finished a book comprised of 1 novel and 2 novellas (*3x—Jane, Norton and John*).

Vines holds an MS in counseling psychology and is a member of AFTRA/SAG, ASCAP, the Dramatists Guild, NYWIFT, and the Woodstock Fringe Playwrights Unit NYC.